As an entrepreneur in Hollywood, I help launch creative franchises in a global market year round, collaborating with the most talented directors, producers, and performing artists in show business. For over two decades, Rod has helped me provide strategic thinking and creative solutions across multiple platforms when I need it most. When DreamWorks, Warner Bros., Fox, and Sony call on me, they also benefit from the wisdom, skill set, and unique humor of Rod Robertson.

— Cabot McMullen,
Production Designer/Producer of TV/Film

Rod gave me a sneak preview of this book, and as a serial entrepreneur, I still found many insights and pointers that I refer to in my search for another business. Rod sold me a technology company that I recently exited, and this book would have made my buy-side process much easier to understand. It's a great guide for me and sure should help the novice!

— Allen Tait
Past owner of three businesses

I am in the process of bringing in investment dollars or selling my business, and Rod has been a fantastic coach through my experience. I reference *Winning at Entrepreneurship* all the time so I do not have to pester him and other people in the know.

— Mark Weinegge
Owner of CeComm Data Centers

I am a student at the MBA program for entrepreneurship at Babson College and just met Rod for the first time. I have a company I will be starting upon graduation, and in two hours, Rod walked me through the dos and don'ts of my start-up. His book will be a great how-to guide for my fellow students and me.

— Gisela Macedo

Renee!
When will you write
your memoirs?
Boo Rd

WINNING
at
ENTREPRENEURSHIP

Insider's Tips on Buying, Building, and Selling Your Own Business

Rod Robertson

BOOK PUBLISHERS NETWORK
Changing the World One Book at a Time

Book Publishers Network
P.O. Box 2256
Bothell • WA • 98041
Ph • 425-483-3040
www.bookpublishersnetwork.com

10 9 8 7 6 5 4 3 2 1

Printed in the United States of America

    LCCN   2014948130
    ISBN   978-1-940598-47-5

Editor: Julie Scandora
Cover Designer: Laura Zugzda
Book Designer: Melissa Vail Coffman
Production: Scott Book

THE WORD "ENTREPRENEUR"—one who undertakes, manages, and assumes the risk of a new enterprise—comes from the French, where it literally means "undertaker." The word was borrowed into English in the mid-19th century—perhaps the golden age of the entrepreneur—when the number of new economic niches was exploding and the hand of government was at its lightest in history. The activity of entrepreneurship, of course, is much older, going back to ancient times. As for America, our nation was founded, quite literally, by entrepreneurs.

—*John Steele Gordon*

Table of Contents

Foreword

ROD ROBERTSON CHOSE ME for this foreword because I am a thirty-year veteran of the entrepreneurial world. I have successfully started over thirty businesses (not all made it easy to start) while digesting over 750 business plans and working with hundreds of business owners seeking to find their path to success. I invest my own dollars in each deal so I am fully engaged in this world of buying and owning businesses.

When Rod let me read his book, I instinctively knew it was the right time for such a full-cycle understanding of how to start, grow, and sell a business. Many books have been written about each step in the process, but no author in recent memory has given such an action-packed guide in how to succeed and avoid the many pitfalls that can derail an entrepreneur's fledgling enterprise.

The timing of this book is impeccable, given the gyrations of valuations and evolution of technology in the marketplace. Your success in raising cash, buying a business, and growing it before heading to a successful exit depends upon understanding current market conditions—what caused the most recent triumphs and failures in your sector. The real-life experiences Rod gives you in the case studies and events depicted in this fascinating book are actually unfolding in today's workplace and are perhaps your best tools to succeed.

Rod, in owning multiple firms and being involved in over a dozen undertakings at any one time for the last fifteen years, is at the heart of the action. He invests his own money, raises cash for his and others' transactions, and guides scores of buyers and eventual sellers through the wickets to a successful exit. As a business owner, Rod has also suffered through crash and burns and non-starters. He has earned the right to publish a meaningful learning and teaching guide through his successes and failures. More important, he has a worldly gift for observing, understanding, and conveying to the public how to move forward with their dreams and turn them into reality.

Glenn Hanson
CEO/Founder
Colony Hills Capital

Preface

WE ALL HEAR OF THE MONSTER SUCCESS STORIES of big business blaring from our 24/7 media machines that have engulfed our country. This onslaught fires the engine for any would-be business owner who has a great idea revving up or has the drive to buy a business. Oftentimes, it can also agitate current owners of successful or stalled-out businesses on how to drive their enterprise to their dreamed-of winner's circle.

The motivation is there, but what is their yellow-brick road?

America is a land of three generations. The online, app-driven generation lives in an exploding world where anything is possible and the blocking and tackling business of yore has become passé. The focus of this new generation, whose members immediately need to jump quickly before becoming eclipsed, has led to a pell-mell and frenetic world of go, go, go! Each day, their sector ripples with excitement of untold riches to be had yet deep-seated concerns of being passed by like-minded leaders on the field.

The older generation, where over 20 percent of new businesses are being formed, comprises those over age fifty. These individuals are predominantly not of the new tech generation, fueled by social media mania. They are executives from the blocking-and-tackling world that has been eclipsed by world developments. These potential business owners have a nest egg they can put into play for one last shot at making a financial windfall, or perhaps they have been downsized or become irrelevant by someone else's standard. They bring old-world sensibility to the entrepreneurial ranks.

The middle generation is citizens with a leg in each world. They feel the magnetic pull of the social media/app generation yet also worked within the hip business culture of technology fostered in the eighties and nineties. They are a bi-product of the offshore exodus that has morphed the US economy of small businesses into predominantly service-sector firms and are relegated to working at America's surviving manufacturing entities with "just in time" capabilities.

Although the app generation understands and embraces the newest technologies, the older generations cannot be dismissed in the entrepreneurial world. Far from it. According to Whitney Johnson in "Entrepreneurs Get Better with Age":

> The average age of a successful entrepreneur in high-growth industries such as computers, health care, and aerospace is 40. Twice as many successful entrepreneurs are over 50 as under 25. The vast majority—75 percent—have more than six years of industry experience and half have more than 10 years when they create their startup," says Duke University scholar Vivek Wadhwa, who studied 549 successful technology ventures. Meanwhile, data from the Kauffman Foundation indicates the highest rate of entrepreneurship in America has shifted to the 55-64 age group, with people over 55 almost twice as likely to found successful companies than those between 20 and 34.[1]

All three generations are plunging into business ownership at a prodigious clip. Certainly the behemoth organizations that dominate the headlines are booming and growing rapidly, but most Americas dream of owning their own business. Never has there been a time in America's history where more people want to become entrepreneurs or business owners. In the past, this quest for ownership was mostly the domain of the wealthy or tech driven, but now a myriad of reasons ranging from corporate downsizing and lack of viable new job opportunities to the easy ability to access cash are driving the thundering herd of would-be entrepreneurs.

A report issued by Babson and Baruch Colleges and mentioned in *Forbes* points to an exciting trend in the US. economy:

> The percentage of adults involved in startups in 2012 hit 13%—a record high since Babson began tracking entrepreneurship rates in 1999.

> Better yet, the vast majority of these folks started businesses to pursue opportunity, rather than out of necessity. A whopping 43 percent of Americans believe there are good opportunities for entrepreneurship, up by more than 20 percent since 2011 and the highest level recorded in the history of the study, called the Global Entrepreneurship Monitor U.S. report.[2]

Every year, I have been besieged by literally hundreds of prospective buyers, inventors, and other individuals seeking to start, own, or obtain an equity position in a smaller enterprise. Oftentimes my team views their drive for ownership with deep concern as many exhibit the lack of skill sets or understanding of market dynamics to become successful. To the vast majority of wannabes, we greatly discourage their quest, as most end in disaster. Though we admire their pluck, we see disaster looming for the under-funded and idealistic-driven dreams of owning your own business. Like the newborn turtles scuttling for the sea amid a gauntlet of perils, for these potential entrepreneurs, danger looms with every step.

Winning at Entrepreneurship is a guide to avoid these perils and maximize your ability to realize your dream of owning and eventually selling your business for a personal bonanza. Our business world is now geared to give individuals all the tools needed to realize their dreams. Banks, **angel** groups, and upward through the great industrial feeding chain are thousands of organizations that can assist and partner with entrepreneurs in their drive to own their own business

Eight major experts in the industry have shared their wisdom with me, and now with you; each has written a chapter in this book. All these contributors are in the field of play and have salient advice and information for the novice and experienced players alike.

Learning through the great deeds of others and clinically understanding the downfall of unfortunates can greatly assist entrepreneurs in their quest. This book exposes you to both through real life experiences while outlining thought processes to guide you in obtaining your dreams. But reading will take you only so far. In the end, your direct experience and connecting to the right sources will be keys to entering the winner's circle.

NOTES

[1] Whitney Johnson, "Entrepreneurs Get Better with Age," *Harvard Business Review*, June 27, 2013, http://blogs.hbr.org/2013/06/ entrepreneurs-get-better-with/.

[2] Elaine Pofeldt, "U.S. Entrepreneurship Hits Record High," *Forbes*, May 27, 2013, http://www.forbes.com/sites/elainepofeldt/2013/05/27/u-s-entrepreneurship-hits-record-high/.

Acknowledgments

A HEARTFELT THANKS to my eight contributing scribes—Rebecca Hicks, Glenn Hanson, Russ Robb, Dan Murphy, Marsha Friedman, Nancy Parsons, Bill Mahony, and Alfred Nadoff.

About the Author

ROD ROBERTSON IS THE MANAGING PARTNER of Briggs Capital, a Boston-based mergers-and-acquisitions firm (www.briggscapital.com) that he has managed since 2001. Rod has personally directed over fifty of the firm's transactions in raising cash and leading buy-or-sell-side assignments for the firm's clients. Briggs Capital's deals typically range from one million to thirty million dollars in enterprise value, and Briggs has established itself as a leading transaction firm in New England for entrepreneurs and the small-business market.

While at Briggs, Rod has enjoyed traveling the globe and being involved in multiple transactions as a principal and broker in developing countries. Rod spends considerable time in Panama, where Briggs has an office, performing numerous roles as business owner and intermediary. He is a motivational and guest speaker on a wide range of topics domestically and abroad and is a regular speaker at the Harvard Business School and the Babson MBA program, among other venues.

Before Briggs, Rod owned or was an equity partner in three businesses in the consumer products, technology, and real estate sectors. In all three, Rod led the successful sale of the businesses. Rod's fascinating life style has had him visiting over fifty-five countries, and he is a collector of eclectic military antiques from around the globe. Most recently, Rod has been gallivanting through Romania and Moldova and has led a trade delegation to the Ukraine, sharing America's best practices in business.

Chapter 1

The Truth of It All

THE PAINFUL TRUTH is that the majority of first-time entrepreneurs who take the plunge into business ownership fail early and often. The seeds of their downfall are sown early as the entrepreneur's blind ambition and belief in their personal quest often leaves logic and sound planning in the compost pile. In this day and age, virtually all businesses' strategies are to grow quickly with alliances and other strategic partners. Gone are the days of building a business one brick at a time and taking pride in 5 to 10 percent annual corporate growth.

Over the last two decades, I have tracked and interacted with approximately 315 firms. Of these, approximately 22 percent, or seventy, of the firms reached the minimum baseline of success they had set out for themselves. About thirty-three of these baseline firms have truly built or sold the business of their dreams, and thirteen of these firms would be considered a smashing success. These sobering facts—those thirteen successful ones represent barely 4 percent of those that began— should warn the players in the arena, as well as those ready to leap in, that you must be prepared more than ever for launching correctly and being able to execute quickly. These numbers are reflective of national averages so caveat emptor, or buyer beware!

The following charts emphasize this point, that entrepreneurs have a hard road to travel. And some industries make for an especially challenging route.

Industry	Percent Still Operating After Four Years
Finance Insurance and Real Estate	58 %
Education and Health	56 %
Agriculture	56 %
Services	55 %
Wholesale	54 %
Mining	51 %
Manufacturing	49 %
Construction	47 %
Retail	47 %
Transportation, Communication and Utilities	45 %
Information	37 %

The chart below shows the overall failure rate of businesses, no matter the sector or industry.

Year	Percent Failed
Year 1	25 %
Year 2	36 %
Year 3	44 %
Year 4	50 %
Year 5	55 %
Year 6	60 %
Year 7	63 %
Year 8	66 %
Year 9	69 %
Year 10	71 %

Major Cause	Percentage of Failures	Specific Pitfalls
Incompetence	46 %	Emotional pricing Living too high for the business Nonpayment of taxes No knowledge of pricing Lack of planning No knowledge of financing No experience in record-keeping
Unbalanced Experience or Lack of Managerial Experience	30 %	Poor credit granting practices Expansion too rapid Inadequate borrowing practices
Lack of Experiences in line of goods or services	11 %	Carry inadequate inventory No knowledge of suppliers Wasted advertising budget
Neglect, fraud, disaster	1 %	

LEADING MANAGEMENT MISTAKES

- Going into business for the wrong reasons
- Advice from family and friends
- Being in the wrong place at the wrong time
- Entrepreneur gets worn-out and/or underestimated the time requirements
- Family pressure on time and money commitments Pride
- Lack of market awareness
- The entrepreneur falls in love with the product/business
- Lack of financial responsibility and awareness
- Lack of a clear focus
- Too much money
- Optimistic/Realistic/Pessimistic

BUSINESSES WITH BEST RATE OF SUCCESS AFTER FIFTH YEAR

- Religious Organizations
- Apartment Building Operators
- Vegetable Crop Productions
- Offices & Clinics of Medical Doctors
- Child Day Care Services

BUSINESS WITH WORST RATE OF SUCCESS AFTER FIFTH YEAR

- Plumbing, Heating, Air Conditioning
- Single-family Housing Construction
- Grocery Stores
- Eating Places
- Security Brokers and Dealers
- Local Trucking

Source: http://www.statisticbrain.com/wp-content/uploads/2011/07/business-failure.jpg.

In virtually every sector looms the fear and specter of a competitor taking quantum leaps ahead that will eclipse your own Herculean efforts. Endlessly we hear the lament of a business owner about some far-off company or competitor, an obscure participant on the playing field, who suddenly releases a new product that has dire consequences for the rest of the players!

Time and timing are your two cruel enemies. There is no longer the luxury of stepping back and admiring what you have created. As an owner, what you have built today you must metamorphose drastically month after month. Scalability and foundations for growth will be your hallmarks of success. Unless you have a unique patent or technology that needs not be deployed, the race or "land grab" for market share is always underway in a helter-skelter rush to market prominence.

> Why is the failure rate [of new businesses] so high?
>
> There are too many "unfit" entrepreneurs entering markets for the wrong reasons. They are drawn to entrepreneurship by the perceived image of the entrepreneur—a rich, famous, smart individual who stands out as hero ... I use the term "unfit" here to refer to people who, while [they] may be good at the technical work they do, are NOT good at creating, running, or growing businesses.[1]

Over the last decade, the rapid turnover and creation of new businesses has shifted the focus of small to medium-size business from "build to hold" to "build to sell." The enormous amount of **capital** that can now be deployed by strategic partners, **private equity groups**, angels, and **family offices** to buy what once would have been considered a firm not ready for market has changed the playing field forever. This is all good news for the entrepreneurs who have come out of the chute hard and built their company to be acquired. These professional buyers and investors are not necessarily looking for a perfectly humming company. They are seeking to acquire an organization that is advancing rapidly in its industry and oftentimes has a large geographic or industry footprint. These future buyers of entrepreneurial businesses pride themselves (for right or wrong) in having a deep bullpen that can join or direct the entrepreneur's firm to even more rapid growth. These professional buyers seek to combine it with other synergistic partners to drive the company further and faster in a way a stand-alone entrepreneur never could.

If, however, entrepreneurs seek a lifestyle business or want to buy a job, then their goals and aspirations are different from a "build to sell" campaign. The long-hold owners can run their business in a much looser fashion and take liberties that they will not be called on the carpet for. Being part of a stable industry and supplying a service or product to their community is an honorable and less risky affair; it has lesser returns but more sanity. Long-term owners do not have to heed midnight calls or texts that the world is coming to an end from investors or potential buyers focused on maximum productivity. The risks and rewards shift dramatically for the long-hold entrepreneur—lesser risks in their favor, rewards not so much!

One of the major stumbling blocks we see is people who have horse blinders on and willingly ignore the truth because it undermines their dream. It is amazing how many people plow their life savings, sacrifice the well-being of their families, and risk their physical health in a business endeavor that is doomed from the outset. With horrid fascination, we watch these slow-motion train wrecks unfold. At some time in this disastrous process, they grasp reality. But, then, are they too late to salvage or set their course for salvation?

No matter where you are in the life cycle of your business, you must surround yourself with trusted advisors. There is a difference between advisors and decision makers! Entrepreneurs can call the shots as it is their show, but they should make sure they have wise and learned people weigh in for each key component of their business. It is never too early or too late to have up-to-date pertinent opinions from successful professionals in their area of experience. Don't let the lawyer give the buyer advice on the **balance sheet**, and don't have the accountant weigh in on a growth strategy. Instead, accumulate their opinions at critical junctures, and as the buyer/entrepreneur, make your own informed decisions. Perhaps the buyers/operators should have a Grand Wizard with whom they speak on their overall strategy tying in data and feedback from each of these disciplines. Even a buyer/operator's closest friends and colleagues don't like to work for free. An entrepreneur should find a way to bind them to the firm for the duration, as common goals and joint history give great insights for decision-making.

NOTES

[1] Raymond Adeyemiking, "The failure rate is so high because …," http://adeyemiking.com/post/319250723/the-failure-rate-is-so-high-because.

Chapter 2

Do You Have What It Takes?

W E ARE ALL DREAMERS OR RISK TAKERS or you wouldn't be reading this book. We all think we know our strengths and weaknesses, but do our assessments correspond with reality? Assessing ourselves to see if we have "the right stuff" is becoming a science. There are many psychological testing services that can accurately assess your strengths and weaknesses. These and other tools are just another component to use in self-evaluation as you propel yourself forth in your quest.

Being bold is a prerequisite to success, but we cannot let it carry us away. We must critically assess our capabilities and understand the financial runway; we have to pass each checkpoint on the flight to our destination. Running out of gas—or money—to propel the machine forward is an obvious but essential self-critique to be undertaken. To be caught in the frustrating netherworld of having a great strategy on the drawing board but not being able to implement it is painful beyond words. Thousands of promising plans for start-ups or existing companies' initiatives die on the infertile plains of non-funding. Having the flight plan to success can be as much as a curse as a blessing without growth capital.

Owners and executives often retreat into a world of secrecy and suspicion thinking their brainchild will be stolen or shanghaied. Better to share your initiative with a potential partner who can take it to market quicker through existing channels than to let it languish until it becomes dated and eventually eclipsed by a more open-minded competitor. Speed to market is the key to success.

Do you have the financial resources to undertake this odyssey? Many first-time buyers or start-up entrepreneurs make a fatal judgment out of the chute. They all can calculate the cost of acquisition, but many do not focus on the follow-on cash needed to propel the business forward. Over a third of new or acquired businesses, in our experience, run into cash-flow issues by the end of year one of operations. Buyers usually have the cash to pay at closing the agreed-upon terms, but the road to heighten profitability eludes them.

In contrast to an acquisition, a start-up needs an even longer runway to reach profitability as it has no existing sales. Start-ups' main issues lie with time to market and ability to keep plowing ahead, despite the maddeningly slow pace of generating sales, let alone cash flow. To run a start-up with all its inherent risks, you must have the ability to carry on financially month after month. You must examine your reserves, understand your limitations, avoid signing up for debt you cannot pay back, and learn to use others at no cost to the mother ship!

This may sound cruel, but the best start-up operators are the slyest foxes in the forest. Telling the story, entrancing executives of influence in the sector, and trolling through their connections are absolutely key undertakings in your quest. The experienced players involved in start-ups understand and admire those **founders** that whittle and cajole others to do their bidding for no apparent up-front compensation. Creating an aura of excitement will attract talent and have "influencers" drifting along in the hopes that, if and when the company leaps forward, their services of the past will be rewarded. Many a time have I sat back and laughed with admiration about a founder or team member of a promising company that has me doing their bidding *gratis*.

To grow a business, you must be a storyteller. Learn to turn your dull widget into a fascinating oracle of the industry. If you are new to the business, show fire and enthusiasm that will be welcomed by the established players on the field. Let them find renewed fun in the industry from you by mentoring and showing you the path. These existing players can cut years off your learning curve and provide contacts and venders that you would stumble past in your ignorance. The existing firms in the space are all going through their own life cycle, and who knows how you could fit into their grand plans? You could be a pawn on their board and not even know it. They could be looking for a hard-charging heir to their throne. You could be someone to unload product lines on, or your fledgling organization could become a vehicle for their marketing and sales. Do not try to show off how smart you are but, rather at times, consider using the old "Uncle Buck" or "Mickey the Dunce" syndrome to endear yourself to all.

Making a world-shaking start in a new game is to awaken your potential rivals and put them on guard about your entrée into the arena. Better to let them eye you with wary but benign interest and not try to block you when you've hardly advanced the ball! Business is fierce competition, and until your strategy starts impacting the marketplace, keep your plans and strategies to yourself and your key players.

One of the best courses I ever took in graduate school I thought was a lark and would be an easy A. This course, "Work, Love, & Play," actually turned out to be a fascinating depiction of how we must continually strive to balance our lives. Entrepreneurs and business owners with their helter-skelter lives truly are at risk of falling out of kilter. Maintaining balance makes sense, but as business owners operating in the unregulated and self-driven world of entrepreneurship, we must set boundaries, or off the tracks we go!

Keeping the balance between work, love, and play is a tough task for folks with an unregimented life. For those hard-driving men and women in the driver's seat of their own business, work always has to come first, to the detriment of all else. As an owner, you have no off switch at the end of a day's labor. Our minds keep grinding on, switching through multiple scenarios as the evening hours wear on. For many of us, the later at night, the more ominous the indicators are for doom and disaster. Winston Churchill called these hours "the black dog."

Burning the midnight oil, entrepreneurs work long hours.

> It's hard work being an entrepreneur—they work on average 63 per cent more than other workers ...

> Ed Reeves, co-founder of Penelope, says ... "Being the owner and operator of a micro business means taking on multiple roles and being everything to every customer.

> "Many micro business owners are both time and cash-strapped ..."

> However, 60 per cent [of surveyed entrepreneurs] would prefer more money than more time.[1]

As Jessica Bruder says in "The Psychological Price of Entrepreneurship," "No one said building a company was easy. But it's time to be honest about how brutal it really is—and the price so many founders secretly pay."[2]

Would-be entrepreneurs have to do a self-check to see if they have the fortitude and even keel to navigate choppy times. Having a smooth life on the home front with no static or backlash for your long absences is a must for longevity. Sharing the exhilarating highs of the business should be paramount to a relationship. Too much talk about the business and ill tidings, on the other hand, can rock the boat of your partners or loved ones. Share the good news and mute the bad! Bad news oftentimes is over blown and dissipates, so let time run by before you alarm others. The captain of the ship must be serene and confident at all times, even though you are racked with inner turmoil. Today's fears are tomorrow's forgotten memories. Why share the pain before it becomes reality?

Do you have the primal work ethic to undertake buying and building an enterprise? Outside of an act of God or just blind good fortune, business owners work more hours than any other category of employment. You really have to critique yourself physically for the rigors ahead. We often recommend an actual physical before an acquisition that assists you in evaluating your health. Many people's life energy starts waning at fifty, while others rip well into their mid-sixties. As your own boss, you can come and go as you please, so always find the time for exercise.

Stress is a killer! Entrepreneurs swap stories all the time of crippling health scares or even tragic collapses of business owners. This road less traveled becomes a test of how much pressure one can bring upon oneself and still function. Weight loss, false heart attacks, and other equally frightening incidents can beset an embattled entrepreneur. Most times, these events are in the beginning of business ownership when stress is the highest. Once a business reaches some level of operational equilibrium, it seems our bodies adjust to this new atmosphere, and the signs of pending health disasters recede. What doesn't kill us makes us stronger!

— CASE STUDY —

When I initially purchased a small pet-supply company in New England, there were five smaller distributers my size, three larger regional players, and three nationals. I instinctively understood that I immediately needed to drive out of business or acquire my three like-size competitors and, once I had a bigger regional footprint, had to prep my company to be acquired. It was easier to compete than buy these competitors, so I eventually absorbed two of these companies. But the third small competitor eluded me. The remaining company had a new CEO and was hidden up in Maine. I spoke with him once and understood immediately he was a threat for the long term since he was lying low and gathering momentum, as my firm was. I eventually exited, but this third competitor, a relative newcomer, grew to twenty-five million dollars in sales before merging with another industry player. He is an example of staying out of sight, out of mind until bursting on the stage with a large merger. As an epilogue—or more fitting, his epitaph—he become the CEO of a fifty-million-dollar business that, for reasons covered later in this book, never successfully integrated and eventually crashed and burned.

NOTES

[1] Jack Torrance, "Entrepreneurs work 63% longer than average workers," *Real Business*, August 13, 2013, http://realbusiness.co.uk/article/22838-entrepreneurs-work-63-longer-than-average-workers.

[2] Jessica Bruder, "The Psychological Price of Entrepreneurship," *Inc.*, September 2013, hhttp://www.inc.com/magazine/201309/jessica-bruder/psychological-price-of-entrepreneurship.html).

Chapter 3

Assessing Your Entrepreneurial Capability
By Nancy Parsons

Nancy Parsons is president of Tulsa-based CDR Assessments Group, Inc., which offers breakthrough leadership development and talent management assessments and services for global clients. Nancy provides coaching services for C-suite executives and key leaders, facilitates strategic executive team development and custom authentic leadership workshops, and trains and mentors executive coaches. In 1998, Nancy and co-founder Kimberly Leverage, PhD, developed CDR 3-D, which reveals insights about leaders, character-risk factors for derailment, and drivers/reward needs. The suite is in five languages and is used for coaching, development succession, custom training, teams, staffing decisions, research, diversity, and more. Nancy can be reached at nparsons@CDRAssessmentGroup.com.

Y ou may be surprised to learn the real reason that only about 10 percent of entrepreneurs succeed is because very few people have the hard wiring to succeed. Many people have some of the inherent capabilities needed, but very few have the whole package. Before investing your life savings and your blood, sweat, and tears in a new venture, consider two things: 1) your inherent suitability as an entrepreneur and 2) your team's make-up and balance.

Your entrepreneurial capability cannot be evaluated by considering your educational pedigree, skills, and experience as sufficient data for this all-consuming business leap.

> Whether someone is the "right person" has more to do with character traits and innate capabilities than with specific knowledge, background or skills.
> — Jim Collins, *Good to Great*

In addition, no matter how amazing and scalable your business idea may be, the sad truth is that most terrific ideas become mired into the quicksand of human failure or inherent shortcomings.

MUST HAVES

A would-be entrepreneur's capability is best evaluated with psychometric measures, including a scientifically validated character (personality), risks for derailment, and motivational assessment instruments. It is important to note that personality characteristics are firmly rooted by the time an individual reaches adulthood. We develop these ingrained traits from infancy on up, based on our social/family environment and experiences on top of predispositions at birth. Once one reaches working age or adulthood, these character traits are fairly well set. Short of a mind-altering accident or injury, longevity studies of ten, twenty, and thirty years show that our character traits do not change in any marked way. That is why measuring character traits to determine entrepreneurial-fitness is the first hurdle to identify the "must haves."

The myth espoused by many educators and consultants—that you can be anything you want to if you put your mind to it—is simply not true. We cannot teach fish to fly. So you need to find out what you are inherently well suited to do and then do (or develop) that.

Entrepreneurial leader profile ranges in Figure 3.1 highlight characteristics for success. The stars indicate where in the competency range a successful entrepreneur should be according to CDR Assessment Group's research and profile studies.

Entrepreneurial Leadership Character and Competency Profile Ranges

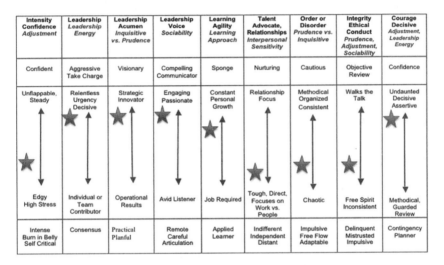

Intensity Confidence Adjustment	Leadership Leadership Energy	Leadership Acumen Inquisitive vs. Prudence	Leadership Voice Sociability	Learning Agility Learning Approach	Talent Advocate, Relationships Interpersonal Sensitivity	Order or Disorder Prudence vs. Inquisitive	Integrity Ethical Conduct Prudence, Adjustment, Sociability	Courage Decisive Adjustment, Leadership Energy
Confident	Aggressive Take Charge	Visionary	Compelling Communicator	Sponge	Nurturing	Cautious	Objective Review	Confidence
Unflappable, Steady	Relentless Urgency Decisive	Strategic Innovator	Engaging Passionate	Constant Personal Growth	Relationship Focus	Methodical Organized Consistent	Walks the Talk	Undaunted Decisive Assertive
Edgy High Stress	Individual or Team Contributor	Operational Results	Avid Listener	Job Required	Tough, Direct, Focuses on Work vs. People	Chaotic	Free Spirit Inconsistent	Methodical, Guarded Review
Intense Burn in Belly Self Critical	Consensus	Practical Planful	Remote Careful Articulation	Applied Learner	Indifferent Independent Distant	Impulsive Free Flow Adaptable	Delinquent Mistrusted Impulsive	Contingency Planner

Figure 3.1. The stars indicate the position a successful entrepreneur should hold for that characteristic. (*Source*: N. E. Parsons, CDR Leader & Entrepreneurial Character Profile Ranges (2002 Rev. 2014), CDR Assessment Group, Inc., Tulsa, OK.)

The most important character strengths for a successful entrepreneur are:

- **Leadership energy:** natural leader, aggressiveness, confidence, achievement, and goal-drive
- **Intensity:** burn in belly
- **Innovative, strategic, and clever**
- **Compelling communicator**: leader voice, initiator
- **Courageous:** bold
- **Tough:** indifferent to others
- **Risk taker**

- **Adaptable:** flexible, resilient
- **Quick study:** resourceful
- **Moderately practical:** logical

Many of these traits are obvious. However, what makes the entrepreneurial success profile so unique is that there are some unusual combinations or trait configurations needed that are not typical among leaders in general.

Clearly, you need to be a person who is leader-like. Being aggressive or pushy, having a sense of urgency, being confident as a decision maker, pushing ideas fervently, and being able to inspire others to act are part of the package. Achievement and goal drive are imperative too.

While having natural confidence as a leader and not regularly second-guessing decisions is important, having an "edge" on what is called the "adjustment" trait is critical. People with lower adjustment tend to have high levels of "burn in the belly" and tend to be self-critical, which provides them with extra intensity to out-perform. They dig deeper and are relentless in pursuit to prove themselves successful. So, achievement and goal drive alone fall short. A strong dose of intensity is required too.

The downside of lower adjustment is that people who are edgy and intense tend to be less stress tolerant. Therefore, they are prone to crack or become emotionally volatile. So, it is a fine line for the entrepreneur to maneuver. This is why having life balance and some productive outlets to relieve stress for the start-up entrepreneur can be pivotal to success. Since you will be on a tightrope in many ways, having a fair degree of life balance, support on the home front, and outlets for stress are needed. Undoubtedly, being innovative, seeing the future, and having the knack for creativity and cleverness are required to succeed. This is why the wannabe entrepreneur is moving forward in the first place— for the excitement of idea, the novelty, and the thrill of the chase. Risk taking is also second nature with the ability to turn on a dime to adapt to changing conditions or competitive forces.

Your leadership voice and talent as a compelling communicator can make or break the deal. This is where scientists, technology experts, and financial types often fall short. Being able to tell a story in a way that is convincing can be a tall order yet is essential for the entrepreneur. Being able to sell the idea and get the support of others—investors, customers, employees, and other stakeholders or contributors are musts. This character trait is called "high sociability," and sub-factors of this trait that equip the entrepreneur well are known as "exhibitionist" and "entertaining." Welcoming opportunities to be in the limelight, along with having the charm and the wittiness factor, will go a long way. If you are slightly lacking in this trait, you can develop some improved skills and techniques. However, if this is a sheer gap for you or sends shivers up your spine, another career path may be in order.

Being able to nurture, support, build, and sustain relationships and help others, on the surface, may seem like a reasonable trait for an entrepreneur. The truth is the highly successful entrepreneurs are not warm and sensitive. They tend to be tough, indifferent to the needs of others, and make difficult decisions on the fly. An example of one such leader with low interpersonal sensitivity advised me that, when it comes to tough people decisions, you just need to "rip them off like a Band-Aid."

Be careful not to confuse warmth with charm. You need a leader voice with charm and charisma-like energy that pulls people towards your message. The positive, persuasive communications skills are like those exhibited by many politicians and trial lawyers. For the entrepreneur, having a deep sense of warmth, empathy, and caring tendencies towards others can easily thwart success.

People that care too much, often give too much. For example, they help others to the extent that it takes away from their own goals and time. Kind people struggle being direct. They hang onto problem employees too long before letting them go. Perhaps most injurious to the wannabe entrepreneurs who have a big heart is that they have difficulty making quick, objective, and sometime harsh people decisions. At times, entrepreneurs need to be pretty ruthless in their quest to succeed. It is far easier if they lack strong feelings or emotions for others that would become distractions or impediments to their goals. So, having a bit of the hard-ass factor (without being a total jerk) is more of an asset than a liability for the entrepreneur—providing you have the ability to communicate in a compelling way.

You must be able to sell your vision and ideas. Frequently, charm is mistaken for caring. Entrepreneurs need the former.

The CDR Leadership Character Assessment is used for leader and employee selection, development, succession, team review, and more. This measures the "must haves" or inherent characteristics essential for success. Figure 3.2 is a graphic display of a candidate that, from this bright-side measure of strengths and acumen, appears to have potential to be a successful entrepreneur. Potential does not equal success, but at least the door is open.

CDR Character Assessment—Entrepreneur Suitability Score Ranges

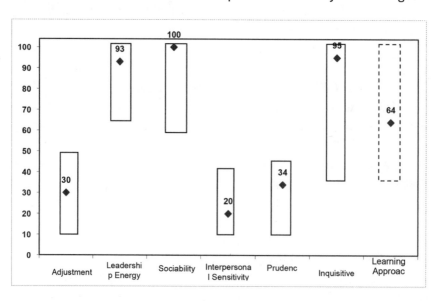

Figure 3.2. This CDR Leadership Character Assessment is for a particular individual. The boxes represent the area within which the ideal candidate's characteristics would fall. The diamonds represent this person's results, all clearly within the boxes and thus, from this standpoint, having the potential of success in entrepreneurship. (*Source*: N. E. Parsons, CDR Leadership Character Assessment— Selection Report (1998, Rev. 2002, 2014), Tulsa, OK: CDR Assessment Group. Inc.)

CDR CHARACTER ASSESSMENT SCALE DEFINITIONS[1]

Adjustment
Calm, self-assured, and steady under pressure versus being self-critical, edgy, and intense performer.

Leadership Energy
Inclined to take charge, be leader-like, be interested in upward career mobility, and be highly competitive versus tendencies to avoid leadership roles, not to direct others, and to be unconcerned with upward mobility as a measure for success.

Sociability
Outgoing, enjoys social interaction, is extraverted, is stimulated by dialoging with others versus having more introversion tendencies such as preferring less social interaction, maintaining a lower profile, keeping to oneself, being quiet and perhaps shy.

Interpersonal Sensitivity
Warm, caring, sensitive towards the needs of others, interpersonally skilled, and perceptive versus being task focused, hard-nosed, and apathetic towards the needs of others.

Prudence
Practical, conscientious, self-controlled, disciplined, steady, reliable, stable, and logical in a steadfast way versus being spontaneous, risk taking, adventurous, potentially creative, adaptable, and inventive.

Inquisitive
Adventurous, clever, original, creative, imaginative, and curious versus being practical, task and process focused, detail oriented, and more down to earth.

Learning Approach

Typically seeking learning for the sake of personal enrichment and having academic interests versus being more interested in practical educational approaches, such as on-the-job training and hands-on learning.

If someone scores slightly outside of the ranges of the solid boxes above, then it is important for other leadership team members to have character profiles that shore up the gaps.

Entrepreneurial quests are not for the light-hearted, and a multifaceted, objective review is essential before moving forward. Fitting into the entrepreneurial character profile is step one. Obviously, if your character traits are clearly outside the ranges above, this would be a deal breaker, and you'd be well advised to pursue a different dream or quest. Keep in mind, from a character-trait standpoint, the above graphic is a narrowly found profile. In fact, this is not too far from a "delinquent profile" so all the more reason to analyze the propensity for success.[2]

There is more to consider too. Your motivation and inherent risk factors for derailment can make or break success as well.

MOTIVATION AND STAYING FOCUSED

Are you intrinsically motivated or driven to succeed as an entrepreneur? Following are ten "drivers and reward" facets. Of these, the first two with two asterisks (**) are key drivers to propel performance and perseverance to achieve the entrepreneurial goals; the next four with a single asterisk (*) are also very important. Lacking these, you may wander off course, lose interest, become more prone to frustration, or give up when things get tough.

CDR DRIVERS AND REWARD FACETS THAT DRIVE ENTREPRENEURS[3]

**Power and Competition

Indicative of a strong interest in goal attainment, pursuit of excellence, achieving status, strategic career planning, and being the best at any activity.

**Business and Finance

Interests in commerce and industry, especially budget and financial performance.

*Scientific Reasoning

Interests in scientific analysis and discovery, fascination with technology, and a lifestyle organized around the pursuit of knowledge concerning how things work.

*Fame and Feedback

Need for recognition and fame, receiving credit for ideas and accomplishments, and being well respected within one's profession.

*Artistic Endeavors

A passion for the arts, strong interests in working in artistic fields, and a lifestyle organized around opportunities for creative self-expression.

*Amusement and Hedonism

Need for fun, personal indulgence, freedom to spend time in ways that are entertaining, and an overall philosophy of enjoying life to the fullest.

Humanitarian Efforts

Interested in helping the less fortunate and promoting social justice; having a lifestyle organized around a commitment to making a positive difference in society.

Companionship and Affiliation

Need for friendship, camaraderie, social interaction; the enjoyment of working closely with others in a team environment.

Moral Platform

Unwavering concern for moral standards, strong interests in spiritual matters, and a lifestyle organized around virtue and traditional values.

Safety and Security

Need for long-term financial and employment stability, insulation from harm, and avoiding or minimizing externally directed change and the unpredictable.

Most important are "power and competition" and "business and finance." Being goal driven, pushing to win, and eagerness to compete can provide the energy to push forward, despite setbacks. Winning is not an option; it is an imperative. Having a good eye on the financials at all times is crucial. If you lack quantitative interest or financial focus, this can undermine your success.

One or more of the following drivers may also be beneficial, depending on the product or service the entrepreneur is launching:

- **Scientific Reasoning** – if your product is highly technical or medically or scientifically oriented.

- **Fame and Feedback** – welcoming the visibility and opportunities to shine in public.

- **Artistic Endeavors** – typically found with highly creative people.

- **Amusement and Hedonism** – having a sense of humor; having fun can impact the communications approach and relaxed presence of an entrepreneur. Also, having a sense of humor or a good belly laugh now and then can be a great help in minimizing stress.

An Entrepreneur's CDR Drivers and Rewards Assessment Graph

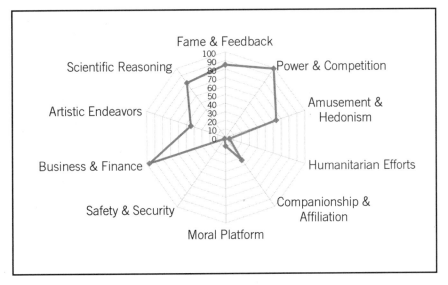

Figure 3.3. (*Source*: K. R. (Brinkmeyer) Leverage and N. E. Parsons, CDR Drivers & Rewards Assessment Report, Tulsa, OK: CDR Assessment Group (1999).)

DON'T HAVES AND DEAL BREAKERS FOR ENTREPRENEURIAL SUCCESS

A high need for safety and security would be a pure deal breaker. Risk taking is essential. High humanitarian efforts likely is not a fit, as this could impinge on one's ability to be tough and direct as needed.

RISK FACTORS THAT CAN DERAIL SUCCESS

Everyone has inherent risk factors, or ineffective coping strategies, that can undermine or sabotage success. These show under stress, conflict, and adversity. Frequently, entrepreneurs' risk factors run amok due to the constant pressure they are under. These, gone unchecked, can throw even the most promising entrepreneurial venture off track. Also, certain risks are more acceptable, or less disruptive, than others. A 2013 Gallup study demonstrated how destructive these inherent risks are. They reported that 450 to 550 billion dollars are wasted annually due to leadership derailment behaviors.

The first five CDR leadership risk factors below in the list following are common traits that can interfere with success for the entrepreneur. While they may seem to go with the territory, some of these can cause the best business plans to crash. The other six risk factors may also contribute to problematic behaviors but are not as common. Of these, the last four high-risk factors may especially make the journey frustrating or impossible, as these traits may tend to inhibit a successful path.

Most entrepreneurs love pushing the limits, testing boundaries, and going outside the field of play regularly (rule breaker). They sell their ideas and push their solutions until well past the time when audiences' eyes have glazed over (upstage). They are often odd, unusual in their thinking, and march to their own beat (eccentric). They may be overly self-confident, arrogant, full of themselves, and dismiss feedback since no one is as smart as they are (egotist). Many are mistrustful of others' work or intentions and simply ask too many questions (cynics.)

INHERENT RISK FACTORS TYPICAL OF AN ENTREPRENEURIAL PROFILE[4]

1. **Rule Breaker:** Ignores rules, tests the limits, does what feels good, risks company resources, does not think through consequences.

2. **Upstager:** Excessively dramatic and histrionic, dominates meetings and airtime, constantly selling a personal vision and viewpoint, demonstrates inability to go with the tide.

3. **Eccentric:** Quite unusual in their thinking and behaving, perhaps whimsical, weird, out of social step or norms, peculiar in some ways.

4. **Egotist:** Self-centered, has sense of entitlement and superiority, takes credit for others' accomplishments, hard-nosed competitor.

5. **Cynic:** Skeptical, mistrustful, pessimistic, always looking for problems, constantly questions decisions, resists innovation.

6. **Hyper-moody:** Unpredictable emotional swings, moodiness, volatility, potentially explosive outbursts, and vacillation of focus or interest.

7. **False Advocate:** Passive-aggressive tendencies; appears outwardly supportive while covertly resisting.

8. **Worrier:** Unwillingness to make decisions due to fear of failure or criticism.

9. **Perfectionist:** Micromanages, clings to details, has high need to control, has compulsive tendencies, sets unreasonably high standards.

10. **Pleaser:** Depends on others for feedback and approval, is eager to please the boss, avoids making decisions alone, won't challenge status quo, refuses to rock the boat.

11. **Detached:** Withdraws, fades away, fails to communicate, avoids confrontation, is aloof, tunes out others.

TEAM BALANCE AND ALIGNMENT

Clearly, fitting perfectly within the ideal entrepreneurial profile is a tough hurdle. Smashing entrepreneurial success, as noted in Chapter 1, is extremely rare too. What is essential for you as the emerging entrepreneur is having the self-awareness of your own propensities for success before making the leap and commitment. Do you understand your character traits, risk factors, and motivational drivers?

As mentioned before, it is important to have team members with the inherent attributes to make up the deficiencies in your traits. Your leadership team, or general management team, needs to be diverse in their personality characteristics on key leadership competencies. So, someone who has a true entrepreneurial profile needs a person with higher prudence on the leadership team to focus on process, implementation, regulatory issues, practical and administrative matters, and the like. Also, having a leadership team member with a bit more interpersonal sensitivity may be helpful to attract and keep top talent as well as tolerate the difficult or intense personality of the entrepreneur.

LEADERSHIP TEAM DIVERSITY[5]

- Homogeneous leadership teams fail more often than those with divergent capabilities.

- Talent balance should be aligned with business strategy and values.

- Talent cloning (often in one's own image or comfort zone) is detrimental to business performance results.

- Talent gaps cause blind spots, competitive disadvantages, and performance weaknesses.

- When leadership teams lack broad-based inherent competencies, staffs frequently suffer from similar gaps.

- Nearly 70 percent of executives have egotist tendencies making them reluctant to agree to objective analysis that might reveal talent vulnerabilities

Be sure to gain a clear understanding of your inherent talents, risks, and motivators before investing your time, energy, and passion into what seems to be a tremendous business venture. Undoubtedly, you will analyze the business, technical, marketing, and financial aspects of opportunity carefully. However, keep in mind you are the most important factor to the business venture—so take time to assess your capability to succeed.

Last, by undergoing this rigorous entrepreneurial assessment of your inherent suitability and the leadership team analysis, you will have procured a scientifically validated evaluation and report that predicts success. Therefore, this up-front **due diligence** can add to the appeal of your deal for the serious investor. Moreover, this thorough review will give you the added confidence and performance and development insights to help you assure your venture is a huge success.

NOTES

[1] K. R. (Brinkmeyer) Leverage and N. E. Parsons, "Definitions Summary," CDR Leadership Character Assessment Report, Tulsa, OK: CDR Assessment Group (1998).

[2] N. E. Parsons, "The Real Enron Risk: Energy Traders," Risk Management Magazine Letters, August & November Issues (2002).

[3] K. R. (Brinkmeyer) Leverage and N. E. Parsons, CDR Drivers & Rewards Assessment Report, Tulsa, OK: CDR Assessment Group (1999).

[4] K. R. (Brinkmeyer) Leverage and N. E. Parsons, CDR Leadership Risk Assessment Report, Tulsa, OK: CDR Assessment Group (1998).

[5] N. E. Parsons, Executive Team Performance Forecast, Tulsa, OK: CDR Assessment Group, Inc. (2009).

Chapter 4

Mergers and Acquisitions

T HE WORLD OF **MERGERS AND ACQUISITIONS** gently mirrors the capital markets and reflects the turbulence they suffer. At the turn of the century when the dot.com boom and bubble were rising and valuations in Internet companies screamed along with them, there was euphoria in the industry. The subsequent popping of the bubble followed by the tragedy of 9/11 brought the buying and selling and/or funding of companies to a screeching halt. The sale of small to medium-size businesses and the IPO mania all came tumbling down, and a quiet period ensued that had virtually every segment of the market realigning itself. There was a great loss in paper value, most all parties concerned got back to basics and declared blocking and tackling was the main path to solid and respectable growth. This quiet period lasted through 2003 to 2004, and then came the advent of the private-equity players.

Up until the rapid growth of **private equity**, companies were sold the old-fashioned way, to competitors or to well-backed investors who wanted to run a business. The rise of third-party-money sources to buy controlling interest in businesses was a dramatic shift away from venture capital firms that had become notorious in their dealing with sellers and/or companies. The private-equity industry quickly changed the landscape as the privately held companies suddenly had buyers that would give them a high strategic valuation and let them still control their company using third-party funds. This allowed entrepreneurial owners who were oftentimes frustrated no way of implementing the grand strategies they had on the drawing board. Traditional sellers' new majority-owners (private-equity partners) could fund these original owners' growth strategies now operating under the umbrella of a larger ownership entity.

Thousands of firms were rapidly sold during the heyday of private equity that ramped right up to the Great Recession in 2008. Sellers could cash out and roll over some of their equity into the new company and charge forth with a larger company's bank account. The entrepreneur suddenly could hire, implement growth strategies, and acquire competitors or synergistic companies that they had been lusting after for years. The early-to-the-marketplace private-equity firms made tremendous acquisitions in prolific numbers. The sellers were happy, and these private-equity buyers had big bankrolls from equity sources (insurance companies, pension funds, etc.) that had been held back on the sidelines. This harvesting continued for years, but the playing field was soon flooded with multitudes of buyers. This naturally drove up the price of the selling companies as family-owned businesses soon understood the new rules and positioned themselves for even more lucrative paydays.

Roll-up: the purchase by an investment group or large company to buy smaller competitors in the same business locally as well as nationally.

As the stock market sky rocketed and public firms were trading shares at all-time highs, a parallel universe was unfolding in the mergers-and-acquisition world for small to medium-size businesses. The private-equity and hedge-fund investors were paying extremely high prices for operating businesses that were not sustainable. Auctions were often undertaken for sellers where over one hundred bidders would be interested and a selling frenzy would ensue. The private-equity firms were amassing portfolios of companies to use to attract other businesses. They also tried to conduct **roll-ups**—buying similar operations in different geographic footprints. These roll-ups were conducted in every conceivable industry, ranging from funeral homes to medical centers. In the beginning, they were called **category killer**s, but as time unfolded, the roll-up syndrome began to show a multitude of issues that bedeviled these new chains of like operations.

Back-end synergies: financial benefits resulting when one company buys another and reduces costs in one or both companies because of redundancy.

During 2006–2008, the private-equity deal level was almost on par with deals done by strategic players, which had traditionally ruled the **M&A** domain. These private-equity firms, however, did not have the **back-end synergies** of being able to cut costs in operations by eliminating duplicate personnel or job functions as **strategic buyers** could. Many strategic deals were done with the intent of post-closing mass firing and elimination of real estate held by the company just bought. This was a competitive edge over the private-equity firms that had no back-end synergies, thus cost cutting. This led to private-equity firms with large war chests to overpay for many firms in the craze that led the peak of the private-equity surge.

Strategic buyer: a company that is usually a large player in an industry seeking to buy smaller companies.

THE GREAT RECESSION WAS THE WORST POST-WORLD WAR II CONTRACTION ON RECORD.

- Real gross domestic product (GDP) began contracting in the third quarter of 2008 and, by early 2009, was falling at an annualized pace not seen since the 1950s.

- Capital investment, which was in decline year-on-year since the final quarter of 2006, matched the 1957–58 post-war record in the first quarter of 2009. The pace of collapse in residential investment picked up speed in the first quarter of 2009, dropping 23.2 percent year-on-year, nearly four percentage points faster than in the previous quarter.

- Domestic demand, in decline for five straight quarters, is still three months shy of the 1974–75 record, but the pace—down 2.6 percent per quarter vs. 1.9 percent in the earlier period—is a record-breaker already.

The onset of the Great Recession led to the catastrophic end for many companies bought with leveraged money. Banks with huge operating loans to companies were suddenly drilling down into their clients' financials and were aghast at the number of their portfolio companies that were **out of covenant**. Literally thousands of firms were forced to take draconian measures to tighten up their financials, which led to cuts in head count, inventories, and the reeling in of **accounts payable**. All this had a domino effect on the marketplace, and the witch-hunt by the banks unfolded. Companies that were profitable were suddenly driven into insolvency, and they became a sinkhole for other firms related to them. This plague spread and engulfed much of the small-to-medium-size business market. If these events did not drive companies to bankruptcy, they certainly pushed a huge multitude of firms back years in their development. Yesteryear's 10 to 20 percent growth was now replaced by operators pleased with just breaking even after having made gut-wrenching cuts. These cost-cutting measures kept the recession running strong. This vicious cycle of cutbacks and conservative business practices, augmented by the banks' backlash, ensured the Great Recession would drag on for years.

Out of covenant: for a company with a loan, breaking the terms of the operating guidelines of the loan.

During the recession that ran from 2008 to 2010 and beyond, companies at first took drastic corrective action and then plowed through their reserves. Business owners and entrepreneurs were determined to ride out the recession, but its dreary month-after-month effects finally led in 2010 and 2011 to a tremendous number of businesses closing and filing for bankruptcy. They became easy prey for industry predators that swooped in and bought them for pennies on the dollar. A new industry took wing. Self-proclaimed **work out** specialist firms and consultants set forth to do triage work on many a company and oftentimes butchered their clients. Fortunes were lost, dreams were crushed, and there was a huge correction afoot. The tide was out, and left on the beach were the flotsam and jetsam of many a fine firm.

Work out: a troubled company working through its issues.

For years and into the recovery period of 2011–2013, the firms that weathered the recession by being in a good industry or by adroit management had their earnings reports depressed. These owners who did not have to sell, hunkered down and began to spin the wheels of commerce once again as the economy recovered and banks began to supply working and operating capital. The majority of these well-positioned companies would not consider selling on depressed earnings and just soldiered on. Many firms, however, that were caught up in the recession had no choice but to sell, and for four years, the marketplace was dominated by large numbers of these troubled sales. By mid to late 2012, however, the resiliency of the American small-business ownership once again came to the forefront.

A new era has unfolded with scarred and savvy business owners who have truly become captains of industry. The recession and aftermath has cleansed much of the market of firms that were riding artificially high during the private-equity boom years. Firms with sloppy business habits and strung-out **accounts receivable/accounts payable** and other sins against the machine have mostly been eradicated or sold off. The year 2013 saw prices rise once again to near pre-recession highs. But the firms getting these excellent valuations deserve them. In 2013, there was much less deal activity, and the number of firms sold though less, still had many competing buyers ferociously bidding for fewer and fewer quality deals.

And what kinds of businesses are selling? Geneva Business Services in Irvine, California, set forth the following different types of buyers.

Group	Less than $3 million	$3–$10 million	$10+ million
Individuals	44%	26%	4%
Public companies	28%	21%	17%
Private companies	11%	14%	14%
Investment groups	17%	29%	47%
Foreign companies	-	10%	18%
Total	100%	100%	100%

According to data from "The State of Small Business" report, "55% of all US businesses have sales volume under $500,000 and 74% the sales volume of less than $1 million." In terms of employees, the Small Business Administration estimates the breakdown of companies as follows:

Category	Number of employees	Percent of businesses
Very small	1–19	89%
Small	20–99	9%
Medium	100–499	1%
Large	500 or more	1%

To go one step further, the SBA estimates that the small-business market is broken down into four common types of companies as follows:

Retail	41%
Services	34%
Distribution	16%
Manufacturing	9%

But no type or size of business is immune to the forces of a recession. Sound business practices matter in good times and bad. During 2013-2014, a higher percentage of deals failed due diligence than ever before. The buyers have learned through trial and error that intense scrutiny on deals of all sizes is necessary. Due-diligence costs have risen dramatically as teams of specialists swarm companies to ensure what the seller has set forth is in fact true. Many sellers are unpleasantly surprised to find out the dirty underbelly of their operations that they have lived with for years does not pass muster. The teams of specialists that take the company through due diligence range from the usual suspects of accountants and lawyers and now have grown to include many other disciplines. Psychologists interviewing senior staff, analysts calculating financial ratios, and specialists performing quick tests in conjunction with grueling exercises on future strategic plans are additional hurdles a seller oftentimes has to work through.

The years 2014 and beyond seem to be poised for a continuation of many buyers competing for well-managed organizations. The competition is fierce for any reasonably profitable firm that shows earnings over one million dollars. Many strategic companies that are buyers in their sectors have excellent reserves to compete with the private-equity players.

It is truly a seller's market but beware of due diligence.

Chapter 5

Start, Buy, or Franchise?

PICK YOUR POISON!
Consider these questions before you make the leap into business ownership. Then we'll discuss, in general here and in more detail in later chapters, their implications to a successful venture.

- How much cash do you have?
- Do you have access to cash from family and friends?
- Do you have good credit and a good financial track record?
- What does your bio look like?
- Are you networked in this sector?
- Can you carry yourself and/or your family financially for a year?
- Is your skill set in this arena?
- Who comprises your network of advisors?
- Do you have banking relationships?
- Are you **judgment proof**?
- Are you willing to sign personally with a bank?
- Is your spouse or significant other behind you?
- How are you presenting yourself to the arena?
- Are you schooled in mergers and acquisitions?

- For how long do you want to do this?
- Do you have the physical stamina and well-being to deal with the stress?
- Have you assessed your strengths and weaknesses as an operator?

Judgment proof: in regard to an individual's personal assets, protected and sheltered from creditors.

OPTION A: START YOUR OWN BUSINESS

To start a business, you must have expertise in that industry. To try to parachute into a new world with a new concept will most certainly lead to a painful and inglorious end. You most likely will be plucked liked the proverbial chicken by your new "friends" in the industry if you don't have ground-breaking technology or have a location, distribution, or strategic partnership angle to pursue. If you are low on funds and do not have access to cash, then bootstrapping a start-up may be the only way to go if you are determined to become an entrepreneur. The path will be long and painful, but keep an eye peeled for any possible play to make a **joint venture**, sell through existing channels, or piggyback on more mature organizations to gather momentum. (See Chapter 8, "Start-ups.")

Joint venture: two companies working together to achieve goals.

OPTION B: BUY AN EXISTING ENTERPRISE

To buy an existing business, you should have financial resources in excess of $250,000 and the capability to lay in additional funds equal to approximately 50 percent of your down payment amount for **working capital** (after the close) before you start. You should also have the ability to go without a salary for at least six months; this should make you a reasonably qualified candidate to buy an operating business. This three-headed hydra of cash down, cash to carry, and no salary is a true litmus test. Running out of cash after purchase is the most overlooked stumbling block to building a successful business. Very few businesses allow the new owner to step into a smoothly running machine and pull down a $125,000 per annum salary to start. (See Chapter 9, "Buying an Existing Business.")

Working capital: money available to run a business on a daily basis.

OPTION C: PURCHASING A FRANCHISE

Often overlooked (for good reason!) is the option to purchase a **franchise**. There are literally hundreds of fascinating options to consider. However, franchising is an industry full of pitfalls and endless fees, as you are tethered to the franchisor and dependent upon a corporation that is supplying you with knowledge, know-how, and a road map to success. Considering the risk factor and money needed, it is a compromise solution between a start-up and buying an enterprise as outlined above. As the franchise's "proof of concept" has been supposedly laid out for you and your path to success defined by prior **franchisee** successes, many of the vagaries of expansion and its inherent risk have been allayed. You have a step-by-step process to follow and a cadre of experienced and successful **franchisors** who will steer you to victory.

Franchise: a contract between a company and a franchisee to operate a business under the company's name and often guidance for a fee; for example, McDonald's.

Franchisee: buyer of a franchise.

Franchisor: a company that sells franchises of its business.

But why, then, do 75 percent of franchisees end in dissatisfaction and dismay, as well as financial ruin? Running with the thundering herd of franchisees has great comfort, especially for the first-time buyer, but your upside is also usually limited. Your exit strategy and "cashing out" are often confined by the very people that sold you your business or are other franchisees. In the end, most buyers of franchises are disappointed at the net results of a sale of their enterprise, but they had much less risk to endure during their ownership cycle.

However, you may very well secure a spot in that 25 percent of franchisees that succeed with a solid game plan laid out by others. See Chapter 12, "Buying a Franchise," to increase your odds if you feel this is the route for you.

Chapter 6

Raising Cash

UNLESS YOU ARE IN THE ULTRA-MINORITY of the very wealthy, you will have to wrestle with how much you can allocate to this adventure. Again, funds needed are not just the cash upfront but also the ability to fund growth and carry yourself to profitability. Often poised is the question, "How much risk do I take? Do I bet the ranch and go down with the ship if the company tanks?" What is your threshold for loss and will it endanger the well-being of the family unit? Do you put in enough that if you lose your investment you will endanger the home front? You and your advisors must dispassionately look at this acquisition and find your level of commitment. If this needed level of commitment goes beyond what you are capable of putting up or, better yet, willing to put up yourself, a whole new and (mostly unfortunate) world must be explored of partnering up.

Understanding your risk threshold comes from evaluating your personal Balance Sheet. Where does your significant other play into this? He or she really should be on board for this roller-coaster ride. You should explain to this person the risks/rewards and how you are going to be absent many a day and night in this all-consuming passion to own a business. Coming home from grueling long days and facing a confused and angry spouse who does not understand the trial by fire you're going through is a recipe for disaster. Studies show that the average entrepreneur oftentimes sacrifices personal relationships and even good health, especially during the launch cycle of a new business.

STEWARDSHIP OF OTHER PEOPLE'S MONEY

The responsibility of being the steward of other people's investments and their almost blind trust in you are very serious responsibilities. Your conduct is held to high moral and legal standards as well. It is a mixed blessing to have partners/investors. Many sole proprietors without outside monies have the luxury of running their business like a frat house. A friend just told me that he bought a Rolls Royce and charged it off to the business, and he is not in the limo industry! I have heard legions of stories of cash under the table, home improvement charges run through the company, and multitudes of other questionable expenditures, all undertaken to beat the taxman. These owners are taking a *BIG RISK* and, in most every instance, have the capital to pay taxes but have decided to try to throw the slider by the government. They usually do not realize the double and triple jeopardy they are playing. If a miffed employee plays whistle-blower or ownership activities throw a wrinkle in their financials that leads to an IRS audit inquiry, the unraveling of their misdeeds can be catastrophic. Not only are they called on the carpet for their one-time sin, but the IRS auditors also will then have the ability to look back year over year for other suspicious activities. Besides the obvious costs and trepidation, IRS deep dives lead to paralysis and then a public censoring that will tarnish the business for years. Any such transgressions could lead to investor lawsuits as well.

Below are a number of ways to run afoul of the IRS.

1. Not having good record keeping from the beginning. It is essential to the financial well-being of your company that you start good bookkeeping from the very beginning and build a sound practice from there.

2. Make sure to separate personal financials from your business financials. Co-mingling funds could lead to a personal audit as well. You may "lend" money to

your business, but it must be recorded and eventually paid back.

3. One must always set aside cash to pay for estimated personal income taxes. Cash flow is always tight up front, but one must be disciplined to set aside monies. Once a new owner falls behind and cash flow is restricted, this can lead to poor decision making at tax time.

4. Make sure not to take a convenient short cut by paying employees as "independent contractors." Although keeping employees under thirty hours or outside of the company avoids health insurance costs and a multitude of other "tag along" issues, the IRS is becoming a stickler on giving workers more protection. They can look at back records and make an owner pay severe retro costs, so beware of this possible trap.

5. Do not ignore IRS calls or inquires. They will not go away. They will circle back, and eventually the owner will have to confront these issues. In recent years, stories of IRS employees browbeating citizens has actually made for a more friendly IRS. Avoiding the IRS is TAX EVASION.

6. When you own a business, speak with your accountant regularly, especially in the beginning of ownership.

7. Keep your business-related receipts, and take the time up front to log everything accordingly. Credit-card receipts without a record of who was entertained are not enough. If the IRS sees sloppy record keeping this year, they may start looking back several years …

There is no need to be afraid of the IRS, but self-employed people *do* have to pay attention to IRS regulations that affect their business. The incredible freedom of owning your own business comes with some additional responsibilities.[1]

There is much operational good associated with taking on investors. Many operators have a tendency to slough off on operational procedures and slip into an operating mode that would be unacceptable to an outside entity. Most investors invest in companies where they have some industry-related experience or have been aware of the company's performance for some time. This level of knowledge changes the landscape, and most sound operators will tighten up their procedures and reporting with other partners on board. Investors should request or be provided with periodic financials that show the course of the company and highlight management's efforts on their behalf. This minimal oversight is extremely beneficial to ownership— no more Rolls-Royces!

"Smart money" that actually wants to assist the company is the best type of investor. This class of investor, usually with industry connections and expertise, will assist in driving revenues and have the owners running a tight ship. With industry experience, the investor can make recommendations on operations, as well as contacts and introductions, that will enhance the returns on their investment.

But what about the pain-in-the-ass, "know-it-all investors? This breed can be a scourge, especially when they *think* they know a better path and are ready to tell the owner/operator ad nauseam how to pilot the ship. Their clucking and hissing can be the proverbial nails on the chalkboard. Bringing in these "masters of the universe" could lead to a serpent in the nest. If the business goes sidewise and these unemployed know-it-alls believe they can do a better job or contribute on a full-time basis, watch your back for their unwanted intervention.

— CASE STUDY —

We had a client, Rich, an officer and a gentleman, who founded a business and grew it to over thirty million dollars in revenues while making it very profitable. Along the way, he took in two hundred thousand dollars from seemingly professional investors. After a good run, however, the company was hammered in the recession and was tottering on insolvency. Rich, like so many clear-thinking executives in his position, decided to go through a quick sale to a strategic player. He had the safety and well-being of his employees in the forefront of his thoughts and realized he could use the strategic horsepower of a major industry player to bring his products to market. We, as intermediaries, were moving briskly to a close with Rich's company to an industry player when the "investors" reared their ugly heads and tried to step in and take over the company while disrupting the sale by every means possible. This included calling the bank that was holding the loan and other shareholders and even threatened us with a lawsuit if we continued with the selling process. They were after a hostile takeover, which was eventually quelled. These were sophisticated investors who simply were looking for a job and attacked the company like bull sharks. Rich held them off and sold the company to an industry leader where the company flourished once again. Post-sale, Rich stayed on as CEO and ramped up sales quickly, and all ended well.

Always understand the motives of your investors, as many can be angling for more than just a return on investment.

A FULL INVESTMENT CYCLE

This chart sets forth a classic example of an individual starting a company that is doing well and needs growth capital. It depicts the sums of cash going into the business ("Funds Invested") by each group and the approximate valuation of the company after each investment. The "Founder's %" column shows the diluting effect to the founder as more cash flows in through investors.

Sample Investment Cycle

Round	Funds Invested	Valuation (post investment)	Founder's %
Founder	$100,000	$200,000	100%
Family and Friends	$250,000	$1,000,000	75%
Angel Group	$750,000	$3,000,000	65%
B Round	$3,000,000	$8,000,000	50%
C Round	$7,000,000	$26,000,000	40%

The sequence below of a sample transaction of forty million dollars shows the estimated cash or "waterfall" of cash that will trickle down to the final tally for the original founder.

Founder's Pay-out

$40,000,000	Sale of operation to strategic buyer
-$5,000,000	(estimated debt pay off)
-$13,000,000	(estimated investor pay off with accumulated interest)
- $7,000,000	(taxes)
$15,000,000	Net cash from sale
x 40%	Founder's stock position –see chart above
$6,000,000	Net to owner

FOUNDERS CONTRIBUTION: ($0–$100,000)

What can you afford to ante up? You certainly do not want to be known as the "mouse that roars." No matter what path you are going to take—sole owner, partner, franchisee—you have to have skin in the game to be taken seriously. Financial players and backers will understand if you're a person of modest means. I often find myself quoting Winston Churchill, "There goes a modest man with much to be modest about," when I see a founder not putting in any cash. If the investors feel you are putting in half of your available cash and that contribution is only, say, 5 percent of the equity needed for the acquisition, they know you are risking your cash reserves. They want you to feel the pain!

Sweat equity: work and effort by an owner that results in an increase in value of his or her company; also the work by an employee that eventually gets stock in firm.

Contributing **sweat equity** is fine, but to maintain a reasonable stake in an enterprise, one must have equity (cash) in play. When one is cranking up a start-up and actually has created value in the enterprise, then the upcoming **dilution** and whittling away of a founder's stock position only becomes an inevitable and painful process. One recurring and always painful theme is when a founder has developed a spreadsheet for world-conquering growth and is drinking the company Kool-Aid by the gallon. Their grandiose growth strategies can reach megalomania proportions. If the founder has a great product and position in a marketplace, the wolves are patient and will sit on their haunches until the time to swoop in is right.

Dilution: the reduction of the value of a company's stock when new investor money comes into that company.

FAMILY AND FRIENDS ($100,000–$250,000)

This certainly is an investment option many would like to avoid! Entrepreneurs often don't have any choice. When you take the money from family and friends, you are on the clock 24/7. You will be dragging yourself home, and there are your in-laws or your sister sitting on the couch, wound up with fresh ideas while you are ready to do a face plant in exhaustion. Their money once in the hopper is most often immediately spent on operations, as it was needed desperately in the first place. Now that they are on board, they own a piece of you.

Although family and friends will be omnipresent, the great point of family and friends is they will not hold you to strict operational procedures or oversee you day to day. They will let their money ride, as they know they are invested early and have other motives besides just seeking a cash-on-cash return. They supposedly are looking for the big return, and thus their money should be considered "patient money." As they are in early and constantly are getting diluted and ignored through the business's life cycle, they are a painful pay-off to be addressed at the end when the business is sold. Most times, they have been overly diluted (at least in their minds), and the founder is having to keep harmony at the home front or with friends and has to compensate them more from his equity than is required on the balance sheet. If the business is not sold and is running break even just paying the bills, some novice investors may eventually get impatient and ask to be cashed out. This is usually an issue unless you can give them a pay-off and financial haircut that benefits the company. This pay-off is often done through cash from the company's line of credit.

The sums taken in from family and friends are usually in increments no lower than twenty-five thousand dollars and preferable in blocks of fifty thousand dollars. Some operators like to say the units are of one hundred thousand dollars, but they will "split" a unit if they can get two individuals ready to take fifty thousand dollars each. It is a bit of a sales tool to split a unit.

ANGEL FUNDING ($250,000–$1,000,000)

For the first time, you will be stepping into the world of professional investors. These are usually experienced players working in teams that will expect you to have a professional approach and know your business backwards and forwards. Typically the angels are far more interested in tech and software-related enterprises that need expertise in scaling. They are not interested in meat-and-potato operations growing at 10 percent per annum. They want the juggernaut, the land grab, the scaling machine that will give them a tenfold return. Their preference is not for a start-up but, rather, a company that has "proof in concept" and has a blue-chip client that has bought into the company's services or products. This "beta" client of the company hopefully has bought repeatedly of its own volition and because it is locked into a first-time contract.

> Virtually all research references state that Angels should get 5X to 20X return. Most seem to say that 10X is realistic and so that should probably be considered a reasonable "best practice" number.

On the one hand, everyone would like a 10-bagger
(10X return on the investment (ROI)) plus, realized in
three-to-five years. Many Angels have also argued for a
30 percent ROI, presumably over a shorter period.

A 30 percent per annum ROI over three years is only
a 2.2X return, while 30 percent ROI over five years is
a bit less than 4X. Conversely, if the Angels demand a
10X return over only three years that is a staggering 115
percent annualized ROI. Over five years that's almost
60 percent.[2]

Angel groups abound, and they are usually retired (not by age),
well-heeled, former operators trying to stay in the game and invest
in sectors where they can bring their industry expertise to the firm
to enhance operations. They usually pride themselves on being
mentors and usually seek an active over-sight affiliation with the firm.
Oftentimes, they bring in strategic thinking and have deep networks
that, if harnessed correctly, could rapidly propel the company
forward. They are seeking an organization that they understand how
to grow rapidly.

Angels are all about rapid growth and time to market. They have
virtually no interest in long technology gestation periods. They will
ride the company for as long as the company is increasing in value.
If the company plateaus out and sees no large expansion upside, they
will seek an exit for their investment or, if locked in, try to manoeuver
the company into a sale. The angels need to have their chips back in
their hands for another investment opportunity that will give them
the big 10X return.

The company shopping for angel money should be wary of
the kindly big brother that, once on board, becomes more involved
and dictatorial. The angels usually seek a board seat and will review
financials and strategies to great extents. A good angel or angel group
can be the key to success for a promising firm. Their wisdom, money,
connections to bigger money, and group think-tank mentality are
great tools for the entrepreneur.

Before you introduce yourself to these groups, undertake a rigorous dress rehearsal with your current team of advisors. Also do your homework on them. Many of these angels or angel groups can be notorious tire kickers who are just keeping themselves busy and not investing very often. They often throw out term sheets that, if carefully analyzed, can be seen as the actions of a pirate! Ask them what deals they have done in the sector and ask for references as well. Do not take their credentials at face value but really drill down to understand their accomplishments. Oftentimes, this due diligence can lead to new relationships with industry players that will continually expand your network.

TEN TIPS FOR FINDING AND WORKING WITH ANGEL INVESTORS
By David Gass

1. **Network, network, network.** Build your network and you'll build your net worth. You don't have to know an angel investor to get a meeting with one; you just need someone in your network that can connect you to an angel investor.

2. **Have a Business Plan.** Once an angel investor says they are interested in learning more they will want a business plan. The business plan should have all key areas mapped out such as a clear explanation of the product/service, the size of the market, the target demographic, return on investment for the investor, exit strategy, financials, pro forma, and organizational structure of the company.

3. **Investors invest in people not the idea.** Don't pretend to be someone you're not in order to solicit an investor. Investors want to work with people they like, they trust, and they believe can grow the business. If you pretend to be someone you're not, the investor will find out over time and the deal will likely blow up.

4. **Have your elevator pitch down.** You never know when you will have the opportunity to get an investor

interested in your deal. You could run into an investor who wants to hear about your deal at a cocktail party, walking down the street, by email, over the phone, in a meeting or just about any way you didn't think would have been the traditional introduction. So be prepared to present a killer elevator pitch that clearly states your offer, your business, and what makes you and your company unique.

5. **Put together a one–two page summary.** In addition to the elevator pitch you need to have a one to two page executive summary on your business, similar to the elevator pitch, but on paper. This is something you can hand to an investor if they want to learn more without boring them with a 30-page business plan.

6. **Know your numbers.** Angel investors don't want to invest in a business when the owner can't articulate what the numbers in the business plan mean. The fastest way to lose confidence in an investor is when you can't explain the numbers.

7. **Learn basic presentation skills.** Investors want to have confidence in their investment. You are their investment. If you have trouble speaking in front of people, you need to learn the skill. You don't need to be the next Tony Robbins, but you do need to be able to provide a clear and interesting presentation that will attract the interest of those listening.

8. **Know your strengths.** Investors know that you aren't going to be an expert at all aspects of running a business. They want to know the truth about what strengths you have and more importantly what you believe are your weaknesses. Then you need to explain how you are going to overcome those weaknesses by outsourcing, hiring experts, or another way.

9. **Have a team.** A team is important for investors to see. They need to know you understand a business isn't built with just one person. You don't have to have

specific individuals in place right away and they don't have to be employees. They can be mentors, board of advisors, board of directors, managers or independent contractors. At minimum have an organizational chart based on a time line for growing the business and what team members you will add over time.

10. **Maintain Focus.** The last thing investors want is to invest in a business only to have the entrepreneur get sidetracked with other ideas. They also want to see focus when you are presenting your deal to them. Don't have too many projects, product lines or ideas. Maintain focus on what you are offering and investors will find clarity in your offer. Clarity = Power.

These tips can be very helpful but if no action is taken to implement them, you'll remain in the same position you are today—little to no chance of getting funded by an Angel. So take the steps to put yourself in a position to get funded:

- Step #1 – Develop your elevator pitch and one page presentation.

- Step #2 – Write out your business plan.

- Step #3 – Join networking groups and attend conferences where investors are likely to be.[3]

B ROUND ($1,000,000–$3,000,000)

This amount of investment in an operating company is usually made only when the company has the platform ready for expansion and the roll-out of new products and services that require additional working capital. The baton is passed from family and friends or angel investors to the next-up round of funding. This raising of equity oftentimes falls into the venture capital arena. These formal financial institutions, besides infusing cash, also bring value-added subject expertise. They operate in a zone where they often have complementary investments, and they can create joint operating synergies. This could range from using existing sales forces to deploy another company's products to creating licensing and marketing joint ventures.

Convertible debenture: a loan issued by a company that can be turned into stock at a given point in time; usually has a lower interest rate than otherwise because of the convertibility factor.

For a traditional operating company (non tech/software), this type of investment is more rare as business owners are loath to give up the equity in the firm to outsiders who will be seeking to recoup their investment in a three- to five-year window. Owners who want to hold their businesses indefinitely have a much more difficult time getting investors, as there is no exit. In these situations, the ownership may want to take on a **convertible debenture**, which is a loan against the company that can be converted into stock by the holder of the loan and, thus, has a lower interest rate than otherwise. Because the group lending the money has the right at certain junctures to turn the loan/note into equity, they obviously do this only if the company looks promising. Conversely, the owner is not always pleased to have the debt suddenly become equity, especially when it looks as if the company is about to make positive growth or increase in value. But this conversion also takes the debt off the balance sheet and converts it into stock that makes the company healthier with less debt. This conversion oftentimes allows the company to get traditional bank financing to continue growth that was previously withheld.

Note: a loan from a bank or private individual.

This round of financing often propels a company onto the playing field of industry giants that now can see this firm with its recent growth and enhanced offerings as a welcome player to the sector.

C ROUND ($5,000,000–$10,000,000)

This round of funding is often seen as the last step before a company is acquired and gives the firm enough cash to implement the strategies that were created and started in earlier rounds of funding. Many times, this round of funding combined with earlier investors has the founder losing majority interest in the company and thus operating control. This change of control is usually implemented at the board level where, by this time, the board should have five members, which could conceivably be the founder, a friend or family investor, an angel, a representative of the B Round, and one from the C Round. The professional investors whose interests are all aligned now would have three of the five seats so they could steer the company to a sale or other event over the objections of the original founder.

STRATEGIC INVESTMENT

Virtually all exits or sales of a growing or mature company are made to a larger industry player from the same sector. There are often a multitude of dialogues between a larger player and the smaller company (the entrepreneurs) about joint synergies, but the discussions most often evolve into an outright sale of the smaller company. It usually makes no sense for the smaller company to be partially owned by a bigger industry player as that would inhibit the growth of the smaller target business. Operational constraints put on a subsidiary company recently bought could hamstring the small firm's value in the long term as well.

EBITDA: earnings before interest, taxes, depreciation, and amortization; most-used method of assessing a company's profitability.

The vast majority of sales of companies with values over twenty million dollars (which is approximately the minimum size a company would be if it went through the full growth cycle of funding outlined above) are made to strategic buyers. Very rarely does an individual or entrepreneurial buyer have the cash and/or the sector experience to buy such a large organization. The price or **multiples** of **EBITDA** (earnings before interest, taxes, depreciation, and amortization) to buy bigger companies is much higher and oftentimes do not make financial sense to the individual buyer. The high price these larger professionally run firms demand make it almost essential that a buyer have the ability to merge the two companies and save operating expenses.

Multiple: a number used to multiply against revenues, profits, or EBITDA of a company to find its valuation. (See next chapter, "Valuation: What Is It Really Worth?" for more information and examples of multiples.)

Strategic sales are also preferred buyers as they are predominantly cash buyers or, at the very least, pay out over 80 percent in cash and the balance in shares of stock, or **earn outs**, over time. Post Great Recession, many strategic buyers have practiced much stricter financial controls and have fattened their war chests. This allows them to pay big premiums for smaller firms that on paper make no sense.

The strategic buyer is most times the
preferred exit vehicle for entrepreneurs.

Earn out: part of the purchase price of a company, paid over time, that a seller must earn based upon the specified post-sale performance of the company.

THE MYTH OF GOING PUBLIC

When I hear a small business owner chattering about going IPO (initial public offering), I immediately understand this owner is not in tune with the marketplace. You have as much chance of seeing a white elephant on Main Street as a ground-zero ramp-up of a firm that drives to a successful IPO. If this IPO mirage were an actual possibility, the firm would already be surrounded by high-end handlers and most likely not be a play for the readers of this book. A firm with this much potential would have to have an *unprecedented* value proposition.

An IPO involves a huge time commitment that can potentially distract business owners from other strategic priorities ...

The Small Business Administration (SBA) says the fees and expenses of going public can reach into the six or seven figures. U.S. investment banks managed to charge a 7 percent spread on IPOs in the past decade, about 3 percentage points higher than their European counterparts, according to researchers at Oxford University ...

It is little wonder that fewer than 1,000 businesses a year are successful at IPOs, according to the SBA. Emerging companies have instead turned to other strategies to cash out investors, such as trying to get acquired.[4]

In the world of small public companies, it costs well over two hundred thousand dollars to stay public. It also takes approximately 30 percent of the top company officer's time to deal with the issues of being a public company and staying a public company. Getting delisted or going "private" is a serious consideration for most underperforming small businesses that are publically traded on any exchange.

NOTES

[1] Veronica Robbins, "10 Ways Small Business Owners Get in Trouble with the IRS," *HubPages*, April 2008, http://veronicarobbins.hubpages.com/hub/IRS-trouble.

[2] "Expect Return on Investment," *Indiana Angel Network*, http://www.indianaangelnetwork.com/expected-return-on-investment.aspx

[3] David Gass, "Ten Tips for Finding and Working with Angel Investors," *Fast Company*, June 27, 2011, http://www.fastcompany.com/1760160/ten-tips-finding-and-working-angel-investors.

[4] "The Ins and Outs of IPOs," *Entrepreneur*, http://www.entrepreneur.com/article/52826.

Chapter 7

Valuation:
What Is It Really Worth?

W E ARE ALWAYS SURPRISED by how little business owners understand about the value of their enterprise. The vast majority, or approximately 70 percent, of business owners' net worth is captured within their operating business. Over time and wishing for the best, owners begin to believe their firm is one of a kind and should not be valued like other firms of its ilk. Friends, associates, and industry colleagues all assure the owner that he or she is sitting on a gold mine. This feedback, almost by osmosis, begins to set value expectations for the owner that are not in context with the marketplace.

In a first meeting with owners as we learn more about the business, the owners subconsciously are pitching us the value of their enterprise. We always listen respectfully, and the eight-hundred-pound gorilla in the room keeps putting on weight as the conversation rolls towards the dreaded question, "What is my business worth?"

In short, the inevitable and regrettable answer is, "Not as much as you think." We often avoid this explosive question and answer because if a quick snapshot of worth is given and not well received, the conversation of selling most likely will be terminated. Even getting a seller this far into a conversation is one in a hundred of sales approaches to business owners. There is no reason to have the mission aborted before you can explain professionally what has to be done to give a reasonable opinion of value.

Net-net: final after-tax money that a seller receives from the sale of company after all costs are paid.

It is a delicate balance to find the right time in discussions with a potential seller to broach this key subject. As the methodologies for valuation are eventually discussed, we, as intermediaries and investors, must begin to discuss not only the overall sales price associated with the sale of their business but also what is the net-net to the seller after all expenses including taxes are paid off. This number is almost always met with dismay, and the owners will bark out, "Well, for that price, I am better off continuing to run the business than selling and getting that @#%&^%!!" And oftentimes this assessment is true, and on and on they go. But as in *Moby Dick*, the harpoon is lodged in the whale's back, and the Nantucket sleigh ride begins! For someday for a variety of reasons—ill health, no successor, a divorce, or a myriad of other reasons—the business will be put on the block.

Goodwill: intangible assets of a company (for example, a brand name, customer list, patents, etc.)

There are four traditional ways a small to mid-size business is evaluated. In seeking a valuation, we try to use at least two and hopefully three of these methodologies and have them all come to the same valuation, give or take 10 percent swing in value.

- Records of comparable sales
- Discounted cash-flow model
- Multiples of revenue/earnings (EBITDA)
- Asset value plus **goodwill**

COMPARABLE SALES

This is really the best barometer for judging business worth. In many industries, like-sales make it relatively easy to compare the value of companies if there are many similar businesses in the same field. This would, in particular, be true for Main Street America as retail, competitive sales organizations, service companies, distributers, and small manufacturing firms litter small-town America's landscape. These companies, especially on a franchise basis, have multitudes of similar companies that have been going through their life cycle and have been sold. It is oftentimes difficult to find out the actual terms of the sale (especially from the seller), but with detective work and persistence, a matrix can usually be assembled to bracket in a sales value. Many evaluators gravitate to Internet research and to sales of "like" but large public companies. Though this information is easier to find, it is most times irrelevant to compare a public entity with a small privately held company.

DISCOUNTED CASH-FLOW MODEL (DCF)

This is a method used by many to determine the present value of a business by rolling out forward-looking projections and discounting them back to a present value. The discounted cash-flow methodology most often favors the seller in gaining a higher valuation. The seller can take the often lackluster, current performance numbers and forecast three to five years in the future, which many times shows (not surprisingly) a sudden performance jump in the business. Many assumptions are tied to this usually heightened valuation, which is mostly an academic exercise in growth. Most DCF exercises do not show downward or non-significant growth. As a tool to buy or evaluate a small business, most experts will concede that DCF is not a true indicator of value. The fortunes of a small business can swing dramatically with an infusion of cash, the loss or gain of a big client, or the departure of a key executive thus heightening or cratering a valuation. This methodology is obviously liked by accountants, CPAs, and CFOs as they enjoy a spreadsheets and the manipulation of numbers. Although it has its drawbacks, DCF is one of the two most used methodologies as it does not require outside data but only the creative mind of the business owner.

MULTIPLE OF REVENUES/EARNINGS

These are two methodologies that can be intertwined in smaller business evaluations. Multiples of revenues methodology is often used when evaluating a small business, oftentimes in the software, technology, or even service sector. Many evaluators in seeking a quick handle on a valuation immediately try to pinpoint what industry or sector a company is in. The evaluators then try to quickly plug a valuation number in that virtually ignores the company's balance sheet and/or performance.

Defining what sector the company is in is as important as the company's performance. As an example, an SaaS (software as a service) company is pegged between 2X and 3X revenue for a company under ten million dollars in sales. Thus a company doing $3M in sales that is struggling but with sound technology could be valued at $7.5M ($3M sales x 2.5), despite having a break-even or negative cash flow. If a firm is showing steady growth at $3M and has upward mobility, it could be valued at $9M, or 3X revenue. Then, of course, the discussion leads to how much cash down and how much has to be kept in the deal.

Multiples of revenues for sales valuations are used in evaluating service businesses or Main Street America businesses as well. Law firms, accounting practices, insurance agencies, as well as a host of other traditional service organizations, are evaluated with the multiples of revenue models. As an example, the firms listed above could be said to be valued at 1X revenue. Thus a CPA firm doing $3M in revenue would be perceived to have a value of $3M ($3M x 1). Looking at traditional retail operations, they all have a revenue multiple attached to them. Dry cleaners, food markets, check-cashing outlets, frame stores, etc. have a prescribed value. But to owners of such businesses, these preset notions of valuation are often vigorously protested for a wide range of reasons and circumstances. For a quick snapshot, however, this methodology does have a purpose—you have to start somewhere!

EBIT: earnings before interest and taxes; an indication of a company's financial performance, or cash-flow bottom line.

Multiples of EBITDA (earnings before interest, taxes, depreciation, and amortization) valuation is the most widely methodology. As a cornerstone of the method for valuing mergers and acquisitions and seen universally as a true measuring tool, EBITDA multiplies are used on virtually any company that has revenues and earnings. But as a stand-alone tool, it is not a true indicator of value if the firm in question is doing under one million dollars in revenues. The key part of the term really is **EBIT** (earnings before interest, taxes), which is a good definition of cash flow, net profit, or earnings of the company. Depreciation and amortization (the DA of EBITDA) are measuring tools that add to a company's bottom line or value on paper but are not truly cash flow numbers. Depreciation is used to add back dollars to the bottom-line value of a company that has a serious amount of equipment, trucks, etc. that have been depreciated over time. Amortization is used as an **add-back** also but does not truly assist in reaching smaller firms' true enterprise value. Non-cash additions of depreciation and amortization in an EBITDA calculation can overvalue a business.

---

add-back: expenses added back to the bottom line of a company's financial statement or EBITDA; usually one-time expenses, such as owners' compensation.

BUSINESS REFERENCE GUIDE

For over 20 years, BRG [Business Reference Guide] has been the essential guide to pricing businesses, providing business transaction professionals with up-to-date rules of thumb and pricing information for 700+ types of businesses.

Most pricing entries contain:
- Rules of Thumb based on both sales and earnings (SDE)
- Pricing Tips from Industry Experts
- Benchmark information that provides comparison data
- Industry Resources such as Associations and Publications with Web sites

- General Information providing industry data, surveys, and comments
- Fascinating facts about many different businesses and industries[1]

EBITDA valuation is the constant matrix initially used to ascribe a value to a company. An EBITDA multiple can range from 3 to 10. The size of the company also greatly impacts the multiple. The larger the firm, the higher the multiple as the increased bottom line and scale of operation increase the value. The smaller a company, the lower the EBITDA multiple usually is. A firm, for instance, with a $1M EBITDA could have a 4X valuation, and a similar company with a $5M EBITDA could have a multiple of 6. The increased size can make the same type of company worth virtually 30–50 percent more. This can makes sense, as the larger firm will have a bigger industry footprint and larger platform to grow quickly from. It usually would have a bigger presence in the marketplace, have the capability to grow faster and obtain growth capital, and have other sought-after attributes.

In summary, a company's EBITDA dollar value times its industry EBITDA multiple gives the company's valuation.

Vertical: short for "vertical market"; a specific industry or sector.

Each separate **vertical**, or industry, has an EBITDA multiple. Within these industries, there are submarkets and sectors that have even a more refined EBITDA multiple. Most discussions involve the multiple for the company. Here is a snapshot of industry multiples for companies with $2–5M in EBITDA.

Food manufacturing	4.5X–5-6X
Commodity manufacturing	3.5X–5X
Niche manufacturing	5.5X–5.6X
Defense manufacturing	5X
Distribution (hard goods)	4X–5X
Distribution (soft goods)	4.5X–6X
Technology	6X–8X
Software	8X–10X
Service sector	3.5X–4.5X

Companies with EBITDA of $5M-10M would have multiples 20 to 40 percent higher than those values listed above.

In evaluating companies with revenues of $3M-$30M and EBITDA of $1M-$5M that do not have large book-value lists of equipment, a buyer/seller or evaluator should really look at EBIT as a true indictor of value. EBIT is close to true cash flow and allows interested parties to see what cash flow is or is not there for operations and bank lending.

ASSET VALUE PLUS GOODWILL

This is a pragmatic methodology that industry players often use to valuate small businesses that do not fall into other valuation buckets. Many firms that do not have strong revenues or have negligible or even negative cash flows still have great value but an EBITDA multiplier cannot be applied to it. We often use this easy-to-understand asset value plus goodwill formula because it allows all parties to comprehend what sometimes can be a complicated task if other methodologies do not work. It is important to give all parties a common denominator to work from for general valuation discussions. More in-depth dialogues can be pursued on a myriad of topics, but this goodwill model is an excellent barometer. Below is an example.

Company with $10M Revenue and Break-even Cash Flow

Assets	
Plant & Equipment	$500,000
Accounts Receivable	$300,000
Inventory	$500,000
Total Assets	$1,300,000
Less	
Accounts Payable	($200,000)
Bank Loan	($400,000)
Total Liabilities	($600,000)
Net Asset Value	$700,000
PLUS Goodwill	$300,000
Total Sales Price	$1,000,000

This model allows you to compare assets to liabilities (which oftentimes break even) and then take a guestimate at what all parties would believe the intangibles of goodwill are. These intangibles could range from reputation to industry knowledge of key executives to patents and customer lists. In many valuations, if a company is not showing great profits and its assets equal liabilities but has solid reasons for its intangibles, then goodwill is a number that will allow the seller to reap some financial reward for his or her efforts of ownership. This is also true when a company is faltering and has a negative drag but its value in the marketplace is such that a non-financial operating value must be applied to complete the valuation. Obviously the goodwill number can be manipulated to meet each party' needs and can be greatly debated. But if everyone concerned wants to make a deal happen, pricing goodwill should be used to close out a valuation exercise.

Many times in seeking to achieve a valuation, a combination of these methodologies can be used to get a cross-reference. As an example, a company that has a 2X revenue model on $3M in sales would have a valuation of $6M. If that same company has a $1M EBITDA and an industry multiplier of 6X, then the company will also have a valuation of $6M using the EBITDA model. These two valuations align. This process of cross-indexing methods can lead to valuating on a company within 5 to 10 percent with the different methods. Oftentimes evaluators will insist on getting duplicate findings to ensure their findings.

The chart below is one we often use with company owners and advisors to demonstrate the four methodologies used in evaluating a business. The four ways to find valuation hopefully intersect plus or minus 10 percent in their determinations.

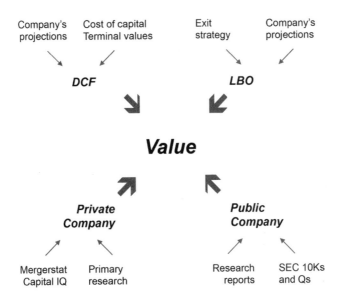

Most companies have traditionally used four matrixes or methodologies to determine the **enterprise value** of an operating business. Often the valuation methodology selected is one that puts the company in the best light to receive the highest valuation. The purpose of valuations is to give the shareholders a pragmatic valuation of a company's worth that will allow interested parties to truly understand the company's equity in the marketplace today. Too many valuations are a theoretical exercise unrelated to current market conditions. Many valuations are based on forward-looking numbers. However, we believe true market value is what a buyer is willing to pay a seller at a specific point in time.

Enterprise value or EV: the full value of a company, including all claims against it; often seen as a more accurate evaluation than market capitalization.

— CASE STUDY —

The CEO of a promising technology firm had a roster of employees to hire. He developed forward-looking pro formas that showed the company's worth at $100M and rapidly escalating from there. He wanted to bring on key employees with "combat pay" salaries but the chance to make millions with the hoped-for rise in stock value. At that time, we believed the company had a value of $3M and tried to help him understand reality.

He remained firm in his stratospheric valuation. Although he was a fantastic storyteller, he couldn't get veteran tech employees to join the firm, even at a $30M valuation (when he reduced from $100M) versus its current market valuation of $3M. As one key potential hire after another walked away, the owner was left to his own devices in the end, and the company terminated operations after one year. He was genuinely puzzled and then became very upset that no one understood his forecast. If he had listened and valued the company at, say, $5M and taken it from there, he would have landed key employees with a generous stock option plan and begun his rollout. His ego and vanity kept him from being successful. If he had given the key hires a percentage of the company instead of shares worth a Confederate dollar, he would have been fine. They all could have ridden the fortunes of the company up to a real nice pay day.

Don't drink an entrepreneur's Kool-Aid!

NOTES

[1] "Business Reference Guide," *Business Brokerage Press*, http://businessbrokeragepress.com/.

Chapter 8

Start-ups ... A Process
By Glenn Hanson

Glenn Hanson is one of the country's most respected and prolific entrepreneurs. Over the course of his career, he has founded, funded, and participated successfully in over thirty businesses. Glenn has started and chaired angel and investment groups that have reviewed over 750 businesses. He personally invests in every deal he asks others to and has a large stable of investors. Glenn most recently entered the real estate arena and, with no major prior experience, has raised over $350M and deployed it successfully in acquiring real estate across the country. Glenn understands the heartbeat of technology and start-up businesses. Glenn can be reached at GHanson@ColonyHillsCapital.com.

B E GOOD WITH FEELING ALONE ... At the end of the day, the decisions made rest with you.

To combat this, you may consider an advisory board. If you do, remember the decisions still rest with you. While the board can be helpful in many ways, they do not know what you know about the real-time life of the start-up. Things change fast, and your instincts will be honed to what needs to happen. You get the answers many nights while staring at the ceiling in bed. Do not hesitate to sleep on major decisions. Some distance creates clarity.

What the board of directors brings:

- Focus back to the plan.
- Somewhat independent viewpoint.
- Good advice for unique challenges that come up.
- Network, which could very well be the best part for the start up.
- Financial advice and access to capital.
- Help in making a final decision when there is a dispute if you have a partnership.

Avoid a partnership unless you keep control. It is simply too hard to agree on all decisions. My brother and I were in business together, and the way we handled this situation of control is as follows. One of us had 51 percent and the other 49 percent, but either one of us could sell the business. That worked for us, and we kept a healthy relationship for many good years.

VACATIONS

Take them. You will be running 24/7 to the extent your body will allow. Time away once a quarter will bring light to your process of leadership. Employee problems are the most challenging. Spending time away will help you see a little clearer from their perspective. If issues are severe, then you will likely find solutions or even come to the decision that you must make a lifestyle change.

EMPLOYEES

Employee problems are just part of the process. Don't take them too seriously. Provide the challenge, paycheck, and incentives that meet both your and your employees' needs. If one is not working out, move on to someone who will. If ones are not meeting your expectations, it is not that they are bad people; this just may not be the right fit for them—or you. Dismiss them with respect and keep them as an ally if possible. Later and at a different time in your process, they may be just right.

WHO MAKES IT

The ones that live it make a go of their business. I can almost guarantee you will not come close to your plan, so don't sweat it. Be tenacious and resolute that you will be successful. Never let doubt sway you for an instant. Get over it. Keep pushing the rock up the hill. You must find new ways, new resources, new customers, new talent, new everything every day. Even though you may not be able to afford the latest technology or rent, etc., keep looking, but never compare yourself to anyone. The reason you are in business for yourself is that you are unique. Run with that. To compare will be disheartening and not lead to anything good. For instance, if your administrative costs are high compared to your competition, there could be a good reason why. It could be as simple as you get the fact that you do not need to be the truck driver, custodian, sweeper, bookkeeper, etc. The point is you may have discovered that you and you alone are a resource unlike any other. You need time to think, plan, make sales, make contacts, and learn, always reaching out. So, if you follow the competition, you may give up the help you have and fall backwards. This is one of many examples of cutting your own path.

HOW TO MAKE IT

Luck ... Yes, that's right, you stay with it until you get lucky. That comes in many forms. For instance:

- New customers you did not cultivate.
- Financing you did not seek.
- Technology combinations you figure out because you are in the game.
- Rent reductions as you are in the right place at the right time.

This luck comes at those in the game every day. The key is to be looking for the luck. If you are not bogged down in work that you can hire out, you will more likely see it or ... make it happen for you.

Do not ever think that things will not work out. The universe is here to help you, and the world is your resource.

THE HIGH ROAD

Yes, take the high road always. It will not seem fair at times, but it will get you to a successful exit, perhaps as much as your own effort. What is fascinating about this is that you will be consistent whilst in a problem. Your motives will be respected, even if they are not agreed with. Your employees will mirror you, so as you grow, you will have built a foundation of trust, and that trust will bode well as you groom your staff for major decision-making efforts.

Enjoy the process ... Yes, it's a process that never ends.

If you think that you will get it going and then be able to back off, forget that. It will be many years before that happens, if ever. And frankly, you don't want it to stop. The game is invigorating, almost like a financial drug. You will become even more driven as you make each small gain towards a worthy goal.

BALANCE

Maintaining balance is the hardest part of the start-up process. Everything is in crisis. Think about it. For example, you have an inventory system that needs access to the Internet. Your Wi-Fi goes down, and you need to make payroll, meet with a customer, get home to your kid's soccer game, or whatever. You are the only one at this early stage that knows the password and how to reset the little gremlin. What do you do? You squeeze more in and do it all.

Here is the problem. We begin to do it all poorly and become frustrated with the process. We begin to think the process is flawed, not realizing that we have spread ourselves too thin. The lack of balance clouds our judgment even more, and we get caught in a hamster wheel simply not going anywhere. Balancing all segments prevents that.

How do you keep everything in balance? Deliberate action. While it's realistically not possible to do it all the time, this deliberate action that works for you will re-plumb the string. One example might be to keep a list of your key attributes in all segments of your life and simply look at those once a week. The power of subliminal messaging should not be overlooked.

LONGER-TERM BROAD GOALS

I like this part. Do this. Take a piece of lined paper and start at the top. Place your age on the left. Then, sequentially list the years ahead, one on each line. Got it? Those lines are the rest of your working life. Not much is it? So, you need to make it count every day. And "make it count" means not only work ... but also work, balance, live, and live well.

Take the sheet and, to the right of the years, put your very broad goals, like this:

30 Start my business
31
32
33 Finish financial courses
34
35
36 Have a child
Etc.

That's it. Now put it in your desk drawer for the rest of your life. Look at it only occasionally. Change it if you like (my bet is you won't) watching how you make it all happen. And, it will not seem like work.

This is not a promise to yourself or a master plan. It is being honest about what you want and being willing to do what it takes to get there. And you will.

OTHER LEADERS YOU ADMIRE

Read about them … not to compare, remember? But to learn how you might grow and apply tactics to your business. Improve on what they do. The ones you admire will give you confidence that you can do it too. I guarantee you none of them had it easy. They, like you, have worked hard, paid the price, and gotten a little luck. Brains are helpful, but I have seen many people, a lot smarter than I am, completely fail. There is an art to this, a rhythm, an insight, and significant focus. You need to find your way, and you do that by *doing*. Get dirty and drive the process. The leaders you read about are doing that, like you, every day.

THE SINGLE-MOST IMPORTANT ITEM TO FOCUS ON

Know what it is?

It is sales, sales, sales.

Sales, revenue, customers, whatever name you give, it's the source of money coming in everyday that you can use to grease the wheels of your own fortune. Overlook this and you are done. I don't mean done and resting. I mean done and dead. Out of business. The quicker you get revenue that covers your costs, the safer and more relaxed you will be, and you will not need to sell part of your company to raise capital. Just do this. Focus on sales. Make sure your employees know this too—that sales is the mission. Live it, speak it, do it. Enough said. Any more and you will miss the point. Most start-ups do. And what happens to most startups?

BANKING AND THE START-UP COMPANY

Oh … this one. I happen to have problems with all banks. Must be me. Whether I have money or not, they simply stink at this stage. If I have money, they require that I put nearly the same amount they would loan me in the bank as collateral, which means you don't have access to your cash. When I don't have money, the bank won't help when I need it. Avoid banks. Run from them. They are not your friend. It is all about risk mitigation, and you are a start-up. You are an ultra-high risk (and someday you will be an ultra-high net worth). They will not ever understand your needs at this stage. They will contribute to your failure. This is true for all banks, credit unions, and brokerage houses, regulated or unregulated. You will get screwed. If you would spend the same brainpower and time building your business that you would spend trying to get a banker to help, you would likely be more successful. Again, in case you did not get it the first time, YOU ARE A START UP ... THE BANKS ARE NOT YOUR FRIEND!

There is a time the banks will help, but not yet. You need revenue and profits first.

LEASING COMPANIES

Different from a bank. Use these folks to get your equipment. They don't care what business you are in. Nor do they need to see your financials. They are lending against the equipment. It may seem expensive, but it's not. Just do it. It is a tax-deductible expense. You can even sell the write-off to someone else to get reduced payments. You are better off paying the cost necessary to have the right equipment and the latest technology for the job.

Remember, there are hidden facets inside the leasing documents that will position the leasing company to continue receiving monthly payments even after the lease term expires. It will be up to you to let them know that you want to exercise your option to buy the machine/equipment for one dollar. Every month that you pay past the term of the lease is all profit for them. They enhance their returns significantly. The leasing company is not obligated to let you know either. It's a great business model, but don't you fall for it!

GROWTH

Do you want growth or just to make a lot of money? I have done both, and making money is more fun. While the ego likes the growth, the business will love the profit. So, ask yourself ... "How do I maximize profit?"

FINANCING

How do you do it?

Buy an existing company with cash flow and get the seller to take back paper. Figure out what motivates him/her to do this, and then be generous and get started.

Find a company that has something you can convert to cash, or create a vehicle to leverage a feature that a more conservative owner would not leverage—like a trust, inventory, equipment, payables, receivables. Be creative. This is why you do not want to be bogged down with minutia. Your job is to think creatively with confidence and get it done. You are not going to fail, so don't let that influence your success.

BREAK-EVEN ANALYSIS

This is probably the only business plan you need. It is the single-most powerful tool for the non-financial entrepreneur.

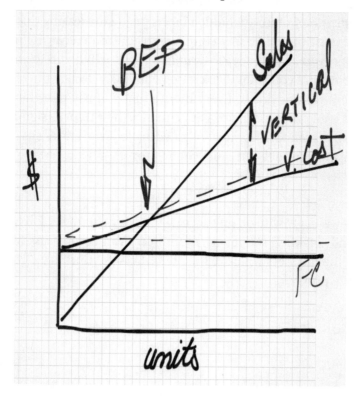

There is more than one way to make a company better. This chart can enlighten you, although some of you may not want to see the value. Indulge me for a few paragraphs and let's see if I can convert you.

Here is how you read the chart. The left, or Y, axis is measured in dollars, and the horizontal X axis is units or things. This depends on your business. Don't try to figure that out just yet.

The line labeled "Fixed Cost" is the total costs that are constant (such as rent), regardless of the number of units on the X axis.

Fixed cost: expense of a business that is constant and independent of the number of products or services produced by the company; for example, rent.

The line labeled "Variable Cost" is everything that varies with the amount of units. So, if you have no units you have no **variable cost**.

The line labeled "Sales" is your revenue, what you get out the door, so to speak. This line starts at the horizontal "Fixed Cost" (FC) line because that is what it took to make the first sale.

The magic of "Vertical," the positive gap between variable costs and sales, is to the right of the point labeled "BEP" (Break-even Point). All the work that you do to that point is consuming cash. You do not get to have any for the entity or you until you reach and maintain scaling/growing your sales, which is past that break-even point. This represents where the operational and your very own money will come from. You do not have to understand all the other accounting terms to get this point. And, your employees can get it too!

Variable cost: an expense that fluctuates according to the level of output in a business, such as labor or materials.

Here is how it works ... Let's say that you are operating at break-even and can't seem to break into that Vertical. This tool helps you visualize options. One might be to increase your **fixed cost** to ensure you have the right resources further ensuring you can make the Vertical happen and happen in a big way. What might that be? Let us pick adding salaries. You see, adding the right cost will ensure you will get to the end point here. Look, I am not a proponent of adding expense to be comfortable, but I can assure you, not adding the right expense at critical times will destroy your opportunity. All opportunity is time-sensitive. Miss the window, and the Vertical gain is lost forever on that one opportunity.

Now, let's get back to that fixed-cost increase we mentioned above. You can see above the solid FC line is the dotted line representing the new Fixed Cost line. This new FC shows that a small movement gives you plenty of money to work with, yet it pales in movement relative to the Vertical, given that you really get there. Also, once you are on the right side—and I mean literally and figuratively—of the break-even point, you will find very good sailing. The wind will be at your back pushing your sails with gentle momentum.

Let's go vertical! When I was skiing in Vail this year, each lift ticket was embedded with an RFID chip. These allow the operator to keep track of our movement on the mountain. At the end of the day, the mountain management sends each lift-ticket holder an email to tell how much vertical the person skied that day. At first, I thought it was a silly idea but then quickly realized it gave me benchmarks, which quickly turned into goals. Not only did it add to the fun; it also caused me to voluntarily push myself just a little harder than I would have without knowing that measure. It turns out that I skied twenty-seven thousand feet of vertical in four days. To me, that sounded like a lot. I felt proud and happy that I accomplished so much and, as important, excited to try it again someday.

With a break-even chart, you can "go vertical" in your business. The magic line is the vertical distance between variable cost and sales just past and to the right of your break-even point.

Drive that line longer and not only will you have made some real money; you will also experience a sensation similar to what I did while being measured for my vertical on the mountain. You see, it is a sport to run a company, and we want to excel. But against what do we excel? For me, it is against myself. How good is my team? How do I measure up? Break-even analysis will give you another tool to measure against.

TEAM

Who is it? What do you want? All members of your team will be a challenge and require care and feeding. This is the second biggest opportunity to succeed. (Do you remember the first? "'Selas" is the answer backwards. Be sure you know this forwards and backwards by now.)

Pick people you never thought you would or could attract. More than not, they want to get out of their boring day job. If you present with integrity, meaning, purpose, and care, they will listen, and if nothing else is honored, you asked and become a resource later. Perhaps, they will give you qualified and familiar referrals. Again, you need to act on this in a deliberate fashion. Don't be bashful. When I wanted to form a board for my small tool shop, I approached the former vice chairman of Allied Signal. He did not say yes, but he did ask me what I wanted. That question alone helped me right then and there. It forced me to frame my desires. He then asked me to send it to him in writing, which later led to his request for me to fly out to Detroit to talk to him. That led to a yes! The cool thing is that his presence on my board gave me a yes for every other person asked. He was an icon. To this day, I cannot figure out what was in it for him. He became a good friend and really helped my company. What's the point? Ask and you may get. And there is value in "face time," that is, time in front of others, up close and in person.

It is an honor and a privilege to join a legitimate start-up. The jobs will be the best experience of everyone's life if done right.

Here is what you don't want:

- The guy that knows he knows it all.
- The guy with small balls.
- The naysayer.
- The conservative pencil counter.
- The one who keeps telling your team you are crazy (and there are those that will do that).

What's left?

Simple ... the superstars. And they are not obvious, nor necessarily experienced.

They're the people who won't steal from you, get jealous of your success, intimidate you, or cheat on you. They are driven to succeed on their own merit. They seek self-improvement and education. They will be constantly pushing you, the company, and most of all, themselves. They will rise to every challenge with ease and grace and work late because they love what the mission is all about. They will feel appreciated because they really are—so make sure you appreciate them. They are the ones who will stand up to you, knowing they will not get fired. They will also not take offense when they do stand up and lose to your wishes because they know they were, and will be, heard. Finally, they are the ones you will recognize that you do not want to lose, and you are probably not compensating them accordingly. You will unknowingly take advantage of them and their unique skills. When that realization strikes you, it is best to adjust their compensation, and do it yesterday! That is the superstar. Nothing more.

What do you do with a superstar? You make sure you do not burn this person out. You show your appreciation every single day, and you teach him or her to bring on more superstars.

Any organization, no matter how big, has only a handful of superstars. Cultivate them and love them for what they are, what they bring, and what they do and contribute. You will not do it alone, nor do you have to.

INCENTIVES

Make incentives big enough, and they will work. They will never be completely fair or always appreciated. But they work. Structure them so people can really change their lives with the payouts. Do not pay out at the risk of the company's cash flow, but accrue them with the intention and commitment to pay them. Come up with a financial ratio that works for your company, and share it with your staff showing a clear trigger point for payout. Share the wealth, and you won't ever feel so all alone. In the darkest days, you will be glad these tools have been established. You will see you can develop trust when you don't need to call on it. Let them see you are not hiding anything here, and be happy to pay it out and do it often.

LEADERSHIP AND ITS FORMS

Who is the leader? Why do we follow the leader?

In the case of a start-up, you are the leader. You set the vision, pace, structure, culture, and you create and maintain the confidence when the world outside is not pretty and is even more ugly inside. It is an incredible challenge and is accomplished most easily by running a transparent organization with your superstar team. I actual like when I scare them away. Now I can get to the next team member who has what it takes. Honestly, it's a crapshoot early on. Use your instincts and forget the fancy predictive indices, Myers Briggs, etc. There is not a measure for a superstar. You will miss the best of the best with personality testing tools.

We follow leaders because we honestly drink the Kool-Aid and we feel the love and our instincts tell us that one plus one equals three, where we are one of the "ones." We feel part of a greater good together. That's it.

PEOPLE AND PERSONALITY TYPES

The Prick

These guys are everywhere and are disguised. You will find them most in unregulated arenas and especially in the financial world. They are the 4 percent of the population that are sociopaths and, by their very natural ability, have no remorse or accountability and attract a team of similar yet less fortunate followers. You can spot them, but you will refuse to believe it's true because they possess what you may need. Can you work with them and survive? Nope! Once you recognize their true nature, move on. Take your hit, whatever it is, and erase it from your memory so it does not plague you for more than one second. You will be easy prey for this type of character. You are vulnerable right now as you are getting off the ground.

The Wolf

He seems like the sheep ... the character that is smooth, apparently successful. And, the kind of person you do not think you have to check out too much. You can just tell that he or she is OK. Right? Not so fast.

Take your time and do some investigation and get references and ask his reference to give you a reference. The story will be there. Find it. You do not want this person close to your lambs.

The Friend

Here is the person we all want to work with. But it will not work that way, so forget it. Don't get too close. Stay professionally distant. You will be making very hard decisions. If anyone becomes what you call a friend at this point, you will not make the right moves, and neither will he or she. All that said, as you gain ground, win some battles, and take hold of your finances, then you can let them in. But they will likely never be friends. That's OK. You will be partners, so to speak, and that is better for your business.

Your Spouse

Are you living under the shadow of a spouse, or are you driven to succeed on your own? It makes little difference really. Once you step onto the start-up journey, it is you who is going to succeed. And succeed you shall. If you are lucky enough to have a spouse, he or she will serve you well. Remember your spouse is in your corner and will be the one that takes the success you create and live happily ever after. You will likely be dead and gone. But my bet is you would not succeed without this person. Those that are married meander the path of business relationships better. There is something in the air that creates trust if someone has a family. Silly actually, but it is just a fact. Use it to your advantage. Remember to respect your spouse in the process of opportunity and success.

If things fall apart in the relationship, remember that it was a team effort. I promise you that your spouse will have a strong influence on your success. Respect that and don't waver in good or bad times. And for God's sake, if you break apart, make sure you compensate him or her accordingly. I see too many break-ups that end where a spouse is left with little. It's a team while you are in the fight. Take care of that. Just the way it should be. You will recover. In fact, you will recover big. The former spouse, on the other hand, did not develop your skills while supporting you. Karma is working here.

FEAR

Is it your own fear or that of your acquaintances? Who has more? My bet is that you get more conservative feedback from people close to you than you would give yourself. So, who is this life about? You or them? What if you fail? Oh my gosh …

Look, we all have fear if we are rational human beings. I remember when I was learning how to fly a fighter aircraft, and we were in simulated dog fights with infrared fake weapons. I came nose to nose while I was in a vertical climb with my opponent who just happened to be coming straight down for a kill. I said to the instructor, "That scared the s^&% out of me." He replied, "That is a healthy reaction." You see, there is always something that can scare us. This start-up idea is no different. The key is our reaction to the fear. Are we going to get hit and die, or are we going to respect the fact it is a healthy reaction and do what it takes to succeed? It is our choice. My Buddhist studies have taught me that desire causes suffering. So, if we desire to succeed, we will suffer when we fail. Just the way it is! Fear will be the by-product and serves no value. So, fear is not something we can or should shun. Respect it as healthy, but let it be our fear and not a fear imposed by others. At the end of the day, we will be just fine. Not to worry. And inside failure is another opportunity. Let's figure out what that is.

EMOTION VS. PASSION

This is a good one. When an entrepreneur has passion, he or she feels it; with emotion, you see it. Know the difference. With passion, we are relentless in our pursuit of making our goals. We are resilient and ever confident that we will make it. Failure along the way will not deter us and is seen as a cost of success. Passion drives innovation, overcomes obstacles, and simply gets the job done. People with passion are not thinking about what they get as much as what is going to achieve the goals; they know that their reward is waiting. The process is the reward. What do you think Steve Jobs had?

WHAT'S IN IT FOR YOU?

Believe it or not, it's not just about money. It is also about freedom. And, I don't mean retirement. You will have the ability to make the rules, work your plan, drive the bus, or if you like, be the passenger (yet still be responsible). Ebb and flow, in and out of what works at each stage of your life, that is, what works for you. You will always have the knot in your belly, but as you learn to live with that sensation, you will have freedom to do many things otherwise not doable.

Again, it is not just the money. It is also about making a difference to the lives of those you work with, philanthropic ventures, expanding your network, etc.

SUCCESS

There are books about the success syndrome. It really exists. I have more than once felt that my success was greater than what was fair. While we are struggling in our new venture, we are constantly justifying to those we know oh so well why we do what we do. All of a sudden, things change. We get some free cash, buy a new car, take trips, and stay at better hotels ... We note that our cohorts are not able to keep up. Well, forget your thoughts about backing off or justifying your success. Remember, you took and are still taking all the risk. Enjoy it! Just try not to flaunt it. (Keep in mind, too, it does not take much for something to change and you to have your head handed to you.) Your friends will remain friends, and you will associate with new friends that have a different perspective. It is part of the process.

Success gives us freedom and also some challenges. This is just another learning process that is part of the fun. Challenges that arrive are driven primarily by your own reaction and behavior as you become successful. The best part is this is mostly in your control, unlike so many other facets on the path to get here.

What is success? Stephen Covey, author of *The Seven Habits of Highly Effective People*, taught the best lesson I have learned. Here it is ... you are successful when, at your own wake, the people who visit you say what you wanted them to think of you.

THE RELATIONSHIP GAP

The art of cultivating relationships is the most important thing that one can learn in the world of sales. It doesn't matter how many excellent leads are acquired if one fails actually to close the sale. I have seen many fine sales executives start out with the best of intentions when working with potential investors and clients. They use many notable and popular sales and marketing techniques for presenting their cases, but the goal is not reached. Why, then, do so many deals fall through in the end?

The secret lies in creating a strategic long-term plan designed to cultivate a synergistic relationship. Timing is essential, and if unfolded carefully and properly, an effective plan will gain momentum by advancing the relationship towards closure. No matter how well the plan is played out, however, it is impossible to achieve the desired outcome without reaching what I call "the relationship gap." The gap is a point in time when circumstances are actively aligned so that closure can occur. Crossing over into the gap requires courage, perseverance, and timing so that a mutually beneficial agreement is achieved. Elaborating on the three gap factors:

- **Courage:** Simply the initiative to get started. Stop with the excuses and begin.

- **Perseverance:** This is the part we most often fail at. We think reaching the gap is over for a multitude of reasons ... and it really never is. The question needs to be asked: "Is it worth the time and money to get to the gap?" If the answer at that moment is yes, then stay the course you started.

- **Timing:** This is the magic. You really have to pay attention to this one. So, watch, really listen, and be willing to wait. When the time is right, the sale is so easy. A lot of work goes into getting there.

People who have not been sales professionals will never grasp how hard this is and how much risk there is in making a mistake in this process. It is like fine wine. So, never justify to anyone why you do what you do to get to the gap. Just do it.

WHAT MAKES A GOOD IDEA?

I cofounded an angel investment group and was the initial chairman for the first four years. This was a ton of work, but it gave me tools I needed to grow. One of the positive results was that I was the one screening new deals. In the last ten years, I have screened over 750 deals. Each one taught me a little more and always a different perspective on how to approach an opportunity. As I distilled the ones that I would recommend for investment, I discovered the following list of filters.

- Recession proof
- Scalable (means you can make your company really big)
- Can't go to China
- Wildly profitable
- Fragmented market

Where does your business idea stack up to this list?

ONE LAST THOUGHT

When I was flying helicopters, we had to land the helicopter, which has no wheels, on a raised platform on wheels, called a "dolly." This allowed the helicopter to be towed into the hanger. A helicopter is inherently unstable, and given certain wind conditions, air density, and loading of fuel and passengers, it can be a bit squirrelly to manage. Each time I returned from a flight, knowing the time had come for that perfect performance, I had to get myself in a mindset to win, be successful, no matter what. In addition to that mindset of significant determination, I needed to understand that safety was first, as there would likely be no recovery from a failure, from landing only partially on this little platform. There is a lesson learned with this experience: With the right caution and determination while being in control, I could land that massive machine of moving parts gently on the dolly every time. I bring this up because you require this same concentration once you embark on the role as CEO of your own company.

There is no better game on earth! Enjoy the process!

Chapter 9

Buying an Existing Business

The right price is not necessarily all cash for the seller. Listen closely to the sellers and solve the riddle of what they are seeking for themselves and their employees.

THE FUTURE SUCCESS of an acquired entity is often determined by the initial terms of the deal. In the long and often frustrating hunt to find a business to own and operate, the entrepreneur will often make huge mistakes in overpaying or succumbing to the seller's unrealistic demands. Sellers most often have the upper hand in negotiations as there are usually many parties competing to acquire the company of a committed seller. Real or imaginary competitive buyers, if adroitly positioned by a cunning seller, can reap big benefits for the seller at the buyer's expense. In critical moments, when key negotiations are being played out, a newly acquired company's future can be made or broken, dependent upon the initial terms. An overzealous buyer, with a swipe of a pen or a quick decision under stress, can commit his future company to dig out of debt for years to come.

— CASE STUDY —

A friend of mine was acquiring a pub, and the seller was holding firm on the interest rate on a seller's note at 12 percent instead of 6 percent. The note was for $1.2M over five years, and the differential was $300,000 in interest payments over time. Once it was translated to the buyer that this was equivalent to selling 1,200 draft beers a month for five years at no profit did the buyer come to his senses and really focus on this exorbitant interest rate.

It is key for a buyer not to be railroaded into a deal based on time constraints forced upon him by the seller! The buyer should have his deal team ready to give him pragmatic advice during clutch negotiation sessions. The consequences of a higher interest rate on a seller's note, taking on questionable accounts receivables, and agreeing to shorter paybacks on seller's notes all can have dire consequences that must be modeled out quickly to see if, post-closing, the new company can afford and carry such burdens. No matter the size of the company or the industry, when a large change has been made in the deal structure, a new financial model must be run before agreeing to new terms that could adversely affect the business going forward. This is especially true if you have investors on board. Post-acquisition, most companies do not live up to their pro formas and projected income statements. Many investor-backed deals start off well but turn sour as goals are not met, and financial performance suffers as the new management team learns the hard realities of the new company. Investors are usually more sophisticated than operators and have put in place **full ratchets**, **clawbacks**, and other such mechanisms that protect their position at the expense of the primary operator and/or owner. Many new owners find, after the dust clears and the reality of the new company is upon them, that they will have to work ceaselessly just to pay the debt on notes and other consequences of poor deal negotiations when they become operating realities. They now have hamstrung the new owner's dreams of eventually selling and getting the nest egg, for his or her efforts have a very low prospect of materializing.

Full ratchet: an anti-dilution clause for stock where, if the company issues an option, the investor keeps the same percentage ownership as in the initial investment.

Understanding where to draw the line on an acquisition and walking away are the keys to success and physical well-being.

FINDING THE SLEEPER BUSINESS

Many buyers are on the hunt for a business that is neglected and dormant, that is ready to spring forth with a new strategy and influx of growth capital or management know-how. Most every buyer wants to buy the diamond in the rough. Buyers salivate when they encounter an octogenarian who has run a business into the ground or a company not metamorphosing with the new sales and marketing strategies needed for online expansion.

Clawback: investors' right, specified in a contract, to have monies returned for poor performance.

It takes a different approach to win over these wise-owl sellers and gain their respect and trust. To become the anointed buyer, it takes patience and the ability to LISTEN! After presenting your credentials, it is really time for the buyer to sit back and listen for hours and during multiple sessions of war stories by the seller as he or she gives you the historic backdrop on how the business evolved. The buyer must be ready to ohh and ahhh over the epic saga of how the business grew for decades and its trials and tribulations. What seems like an incredibly boring business can actually become a fascinating study as you learn of the life cycle of the company. The classic widget company can soon be painted by a good storyteller into an engine of commerce that the seller has heroically led against all odds to its current market position. I have often murmured platitudes and stroked the seller of many a boring company, but it is essential to understand the story and salute the seller for his or her Herculean efforts.

Many prospective buyers plunge into their first meeting and want to dig into the numbers right away. This almost seems like a generational issue, as older buyers instinctively understand that they must listen while the new generation of go-go entrepreneurs just wants to get to the numbers. The new-generation buyers miss the boat and are doomed with the seller before they know it when they just set up their computer and start quizzing the seller about the income statement and balance sheet. The first meeting is to listen and learn and be modest about your accomplishments as a buyer. Braggarts and blowhards do not do well with hard-working sellers. After many a first introductory meeting, the good listening buyer often receives excellent reviews from the potential seller, compared to the fellow doing handstands.

FIVE TOP OBJECTIONS AND CONCERNS IN A SALE

Whether a sleeper or not, a business you have your eye on must be evaluated for its readiness to sell, which means gauging if the seller really wants to sell—and if you have the means to buy it. Common sense, yes, but sometimes focus on the prize obscures basic considerations you need to keep in mind.

1. **Is the seller a committed seller?**

   Investigate the history of the seller to see if the company has been on and off the market and understand why. Understand and satisfy yourself about why the seller is selling. Perhaps there is a fundamental change in the industry you are not aware of.

2. **Does the seller have the stamina and know-how to go through the process?**

   Naïve sellers oftentimes fade on a deal just when the buyer is kicking into gear. If the sellers are worn out and just creatures of their business without any fundamental understanding of transactions, beware that they may pull out of the deal in confusion or misplaced umbrage.

3. **"I can wait a few more years to sell."**

Many sellers think they are going to live forever. In these fast-changing times, non-adaption to new trends and technology can leave a business crippled or on the rocks before ownership realizes it. Most older sellers are reluctant to adapt, and it is the buyer's job to gently make them aware that they may lose the value of their major asset if they keep postponing a sale.

4. **"I will wait until next year when my numbers are better."**

Unfortunately, the buyer will most likely be long gone. Many sellers pick an unrealistic sales value with poor logic for their "magic" number. They realize they are asking too much but believe, perhaps by next year or even the year after, that they will be hitting their transaction number. This rarely happens when subjective numbers are selected by the seller as the goals. The buyer must structure a deal on paper that shows future earnings of the company hitting the seller's dream number. In structuring a transaction in such a fashion, the company, if it hits its benchmarks, will also allow the seller to reach his.

5. **Does the buyer have enough cash post-closing for working capital?**

Many buyers compile enough money to meet the amount needed and agreed upon by both parties. However, a constant disastrous theme occurs with transition of ownership. Vender rebellions, customer uprisings, bank tightening, and employee issues all can rapidly occur with the buyer in a precarious financial condition. These perfect storms can cripple and set back new ownership and lead to a crises with the company within the industry.

BUYING AT THE RIGHT PRICE

Being able to walk away from a purchase gives the buyer excellent positioning. This ability must be projected to the seller at all costs, even if it is a mirage. To buy at the right price, the buyer must become intimate with the seller. This means the buyer has to differentiate himself from the other candidates and win the trust of the seller as this can translate into better terms. The top bidder for a business many times is not the winning ticket. In acquisitions of small to medium-size businesses where the business is family owned, wringing every last dollar out of a buyer pales in comparison to a number of the following considerations.

- **Sharing the seller's vision.** The seller can be a multi-generational family enterprise. Great pride in the company is the rule and not the exception. A buyer must understand this mantra of family excellence and promise to carry the banner forward.

- **Be aware of sacred cows.** Sellers will almost always have loyal employees who have seen them through thick and thin. Spend endless time with the seller agonizing over these folks and their contribution to the company. Most sellers will have a guilt complex about rewarding them for their efforts (but rarely do) and will look at the new owner to take care of these employees. Laying out how a buyer will do this and even setting up an equity pool for key employees going forward can assuage the seller's qualms about cashing out and leaving these loyal followers to the mercy of new ownership.

- **Family members.** Inheriting family members who are less than productive employees is oftentimes a problem. As most acquisitions have an ongoing financial relationship between seller and buyer, these inherited team members can range from being disruptive to becoming spies for the old regime. Paying them less and having them work more under new ownership as they are stripped of the emperor's clothes around the office leads to their departing fairly quickly after the sale. There is also a trickle-down effect from the main beneficiary of a sale that sees lesser family members receiving a smaller financial windfall from the transaction that compromises their need to stay employed.

- **Seller's role post-sale.** Learning the ropes from the seller is a must. There are so many nuances in an operation of privately held companies that any sane buyer will want to keep the founder on (even if his or her behavior is disruptive) for an extended period of time. Many operators want to stay on, as running the company is the only professional job they have held. By offering the seller a one-year contract (even if it's an eventual no-show position), you will give the seller comfort that he or she will not be kicked to the curb.

  Some situations call for the buyer to release the owner soon after the sale. For instance, "competitors buying a firm in their specific industry usually have the lowest requirement for the seller to remain with the firm."[1]

- **Seller's early exit.** If during negotiations you feel the seller actually wants to move on as quickly as possible post-closing, please encourage this train of thought. Perhaps some other buyer is trying to chain the seller to the mast and this is not very appealing. The emotional trauma of a sale can exhaust a seller. Still, giving the seller an ongoing consulting contract, which allows him or her to be called upon and paid but not anchored to the firm any longer, can be extremely attractive. As an example, the consulting contract can start out for three months at full salary but graduate down by 25 percent per three-month increments until after a year the seller is officially retired.

- **Seller does the fun job.** When a seller is on the fence about whom to sell to, a deciding factor can be allowing the seller to stay on as the business "ambassador." Many times the seller is reluctant to leave the stage. Make an offer where the owner can stay on and keep in touch with the major vender and customer relationships developed over the years.

- **Seller keeps the toys.** Many business owners run their business like a frat house. They truly enjoy the perks of travel, credit cards, cars, health insurance, and other benefits. Create a package for the seller that shows you are thoughtful about his or her lifestyle and let the seller know, if appropriate, he or she can sustain it for due consideration.

- **The numbers don't add up.** Be ready to hear the confessions of a seller about how the numbers are not the real numbers. Many sellers will have to confide in you at some time in the process that the company is actually worth more than the financials show due to the seller taking liberties with write-offs. By being understanding and flexible, you can win the deal by paying the seller for the real value of the company and not what is necessarily shown on the books.

CLASSIC VALUATIONS VERSUS REALITY

It is a good practice to understand fundamentally the value of a business in the classical sense of cash flow models, multiples of EBITDA, and other methodologies. But the true indicator of worth is what it is it worth to you, the buyer. You may want or need to pay more because:

- you know how to ramp this company up from domain experience,
- you understand the future dynamics of the sector,
- traditional employment is a non-starter or impossible to obtain, or
- the timing is right in regards to cash on hand and other issues.

Buyers get hung up on buying at the correct multiple of EBITDA, be it 4X for a commodity distributer or 6X for a niche manufacturer. In smaller transactions with EBITDA-run rates under $2M, it may be perceived by you and others that you are overpaying, but one new key account post-closing can transform the numbers quickly in your favor. Many times we encourage buyers who have a growth angle or sound strategy to project forward one year and tell us what their EBITDA will be. We then ask them to take this number and factor back to the trailing EBITDA of the year prior to acquisition. The once-formidable and high EBITDA number at acquisition time has suddenly been watered down significantly, and the risk value of the deal is lessened considerably. Even if one discounts the future-year projections and financial returns by 50 percent, the acquisition numbers seem less formidable.

PRAGMATIC MARKET VALUATIONS

Of all methodologies used to evaluate a business and to share your rationale with the seller as a closing tool, recent like-sales are the best and most irrefutable tool. There is no real arguing sales value if a similar-size company that recently sold in the same sector with similar performance matrixes can be found. It is very difficult to find deal information on small sales that are privately held. But the sleuth resides in us all, and you should try to crack the mystery by any means possible. Speaking to venders, other competitors, certain employees, as well as industry gossips, all can have very beneficial findings. By asking throughout the sector, you will make friends and learn more about all the players related to the business.

Non-disclosure agreement or NDA: a contract stipulating confidentiality of shared information.

The detective, however, must keep the reason for his mission cloaked in secrecy for a number of reasons. The primary would be that the seller you are pursuing would most likely not want the industry to know the company is for sale, and I am sure you would have a **non-disclosure agreement** in place by the time you are snooping. As Winston Churchill said, "In wartime, the truth is so precious that she should always be attended by a bodyguard of lies." Perhaps we do not go to this extreme, but business is warfare!

KEEP IT SIMPLE!

When structuring your offer via a term sheet or a **letter of intent**, keep the offer as simple as possible. Many potential buyers like to deliver a document with every possible nuance covered. They do this oftentimes because they are a product of a business school or have been advised by overzealous advisors who want to show their worth. Best bet is to keep it simple. Most likely you are dealing with a seller who does not have great experience in dealing with offers, and their advisors will be more than willing to step in and begin to muck up the process before you have to. Clarity and simplicity are easiest to get accord on. There is a time and place for details and deep dives into a score of issues, but the main job of the offer is to entice the seller to go with your deal versus others. You will stop the harmonious flow in the relationship if you keep bringing up deal points that irritate the seller. Once a deal is under agreement, then you may proceed to get into the secondary issues. You want to get the seller to sign off on your offer that will entail making the seller inform all other suitors that the company is off the market. This period of exclusivity greatly decreases the seller's leverage on upcoming negotiations as you get into the dreaded details of the deal. After the letter of intent or the term sheet has been signed, this is the high-water market for the seller until the deal is closed.

Well-known author and friend Russ Robb (author of *Buying Your Own Business*) feels it is somewhat confusing when you're presented with the financials of a company with thirty-plus line items. Russ believes for a quick analysis, condensing several years of historical results over three year projections as follows:

Balance Sheet

Current assets	Current liabilities
Net plant and equipment	Long-term debt
Other assets	Equity
Total assets	Total liabilities/stockholder equity

Income Statement

	2015	2016	2017
Sales			
Gross profit			
Selling, general, and administrative expenses			
EBIT or EBITDA			

UNDERSTANDING YOUR PREY

Truly understanding sellers and what makes them tick are keys to becoming the preferred buyer. A buyer must become a chameleon, an individual that instinctively understands what is important to the seller. The primary driving force is cash, of course, but the majority of sale terms in companies under $25M in sales and $3M in EBITDA have at least three components in their valuation. Anywhere from 15 to 35 percent of the total agreed-upon enterprise value can be taken over time using a number of financial vehicles (see Chapter 10, "The Four Ways to Pay for a Business"). This means trust and creative thinking must be used to bring the seller a certain level of comfort so he or she will see the balance of his or her sales pay out. You must find out what the seller's hot buttons are—family, charities, sports, travel, whatever. Keep steering the conversation around to these hot points and drill into them. Become a subject-matter expert and let the seller know these pet interests are surprisingly your interests too! If they are not your interests, become fascinated by them and, over time, gently learn to be interested in them. Share the experience with the seller and promote synergies and harmony. If appropriate, somehow make these interests part of the deal in a marginal way. Make the seller's charity the company's charity. Buy those season tickets and join societies or interest groups that show the seller you are listening and are willing to learn and enjoy what he or she has over the years.

OFFER AND DELIVERY

To be one of a blizzard of offers does not bode well for any buyer but the one offering the most. If you are jostling with a crowd of buyers, you most likely will be outbid in the process. There always seems to be one buyer in the crowd that sets forth such a high price that the rest of the pack is puzzled by how that person can ever make it work. Most times, he or she can't! If the seller is driven by high price, then only the high bidder wins. There are many repercussions, but mainly the specter of the re-trade looms.

"A **re-trade** is the practice of renegotiating the purchase price of a business by the buyer after initially agreeing to purchase at a higher price. Typically this occurs after the buyer gets the business under contract and during the period that it is performing due diligence."[2] Due diligence is a reasonable investigation of a proposed investment deal and of the principals offering it before the transaction is finalized to check out an investment's worthiness. Usually the investor's advisors, attorney, and accountant perform this.

Re-trade: after a company is under agreement to be sold, a renegotiation of the sales price initiated by the buyer in his or her favor.

During due diligence, the high-priced bidder often begins to find fault with many of the seller's principles of value and begins to hack away at the sales price lowering it with one set of facts after another. The seller is now in a bind as he or she has blown off the other interested parties and is in an exclusive period for due diligence. Most buyers are more sophisticated than sellers, and when they buy, they often set up formulas in which a portion of the total enterprise value is at risk if they don't hit performance matrixes. It is estimated that up to 30 percent of all deals are eventually re-traded down in the buyer's favor.

We recommend submitting a simple offer that will allow the buyer to get the letter of intent (LOI) signed. Once the business is off the market, then it is time to bring out the more in-depth and testy issues that can be worked through usually with the seller's advisors. We believe it is best if you submit the offer in person so you can gauge the seller's reaction and explain any confusing terms of the deal face to face. Many deals are lost because of fundamental misunderstandings that arise when a seller is left with his oftentimes inept advisors to interpret what the LOI means.

OMG! IT'S MINE!

Much to your amazement, the seller selects or agrees to sell you the business after a period of tense back and forth negotiations. The buyer should immediately begin to work furiously with the seller to delve into the dangerous part of due diligence.

Before the Great Recession of 2008–2010, due diligence was not a huge concern. This process now, however, is arduous and full of peril for both sides. The percentage of deals that have cratered during due diligence has risen from approximately 15 percent prior to the recession to approximately double that rate post-recession. This is particularly true with professional investors ranging from hedge-fund to private-equity firms to individuals sponsored by investor monies.

Do not fall into the trap of allowing your professional advisors (lawyers, accountants, consultants) push you aside and dive in. As a business person, you must monitor all their activities and learn as you go. Giving these advisors carte blanche to do battle with the seller's advisors will lead to huge bills and tensions between camps that could develop into a flash point. Often, sellers are not experienced players in due diligence and have advisors step up in their stead. The buyer should always stay in contact with the seller to reassure him or her that the tension and misunderstandings of the respective handlers is not necessarily the views of the buyer. It is important to keep the personal relationship much as presidents of countries keep the hotline available for reassuring discussions above the fray.

Before your advisors make contact with the seller's team, it is very important to review the rules of engagement you want them to follow. Your people can go off on tangents and rack up large, unnecessary bills as they tango away with their counterparts. Have a hit list, chart, and/or guidelines drawn up with all the steps needed to get to a close. Adhere to your list and rein in your advisors. Due to much more "cover your ass" documents required by banks and lenders, as well as professional advisors, the time for getting a business under LOI to a close has grown as much as 25-30 percent. The costs have similarly grown as well.

— CASE STUDY —

We recently completed a transaction for a consumer-products company to a large national financial institution. The sales size was in the $20M range on sales of $50M. Both parties were ethical and sound thinking groups, and the sale was done relatively easily. One interesting insight was the buyer spent over $400,000 on due diligence while the seller spent $100,000 for total transaction costs. The buyer's legal, accounting, and due diligence team was running amuck on this opportunity as the buyer wanted to make sure all was buttoned up. Was spending that much with the advisors necessary? Would it be for you?

CLOSING IT OUT

As the deal progresses to the home stretch of due diligence and heads to a close, a perilous time is upon the deal. Nerves are frayed, the seller is exasperated, the goodwill you have generated has evaporated, and the dreaded deal fatigue sets in. The seller is often battling with his advisors, while the buyer is dealing with banks and other complications of impending ownership. Again, do not leave the helm to your advisors! Step in and keep the personal touch and beware of the seller's sensitivities. Most sellers get a case of seller's remorse somewhere during the process. This is especially true when they do their homework and fully realize what the "net-net" is to them after the dust settles. This number almost universally is a grave disappointment, and only the finish line in sight keeps them going forward. The buyers must show their mettle and why they are about to become the new skipper of the ship!

POST-CLOSING DEPRESSION AND THE NEW REALITY

Many sellers are like the dog chasing the bus—they don't know what to do when they attain their goal. They run up to a closing, and the many tense and disquieting events surrounding the final countdown to close leave all parties spent and exhausted. Buying a business is an emotional undertaking that few people understand unless they have been through it themselves. The mindset of legalese, putting schedules together, etc. now must be converted quickly to the announcement of the new commanding officer.

There is no following in the footsteps of your predecessor, so don't try! You have to carve out your own reputation. The seller's employees, venders, and customers are all poised for change, but the best course of action is to surprise them and follow the mantra, "steady as she goes!" In the beginning, if the company is running all right, it is best to observe and learn. Oftentimes, it is best to learn every job for a week.

— CASE STUDY —

When I bought my pet-food company, I started off loading bags in the warehouse, then worked at the docks, and then drove the trucks. It was essential for me to understand my new business from the ground up. Afterwards, I worked in customer service, next taking orders for products, and then finally in accounting. After this whirlwind tour of three weeks, I was able to sit at my desk and have a vague understanding of the mechanics of the business. Once I understood enough of the business from my internal tour of duty, I hit the road for two weeks and visited customers. I learned what was good and bad at the company and promised to bring reform to certain issues that were of universal concern.

Never speak ill of the seller! No matter what the employees say in currying favor with the new boss, ties, good or bad, go back for years, and channels to the seller on how you're conducting yourself are everywhere. This blowback could be very important, especially if the buyer and seller are on an earn out or other payment terms over time.

> *Don't kick over the anthill! Don't make radical*
> *changes until you understand the basic operating*
> *premises of the business.*

— CASE STUDY —

When I sold my pet-food company, the new owner jumped in, immediately changed pricing, and declared there was a new sheriff in town. As he demonstrated superior skills in creating new pricing for the company's one thousand customers and dismantled manufacturers' traditional pricing, serious protest reared up. I received numerous calls that all was not well at the beehive and was asked to step back in to coach the new owner. That I was glad to do, especially since I was getting paid 1 percent of gross sales for the next sixty months. The new owner soon had the handle on the company and led it to a rapid rise in sales, as well as made cuts in operating overhead that I had refused to do. The company become much more profitable and went on to become a true cornerstone of the pet-food industry in the region. His management moves were all correct but a little quick on the trigger!

Assert your role through a series of new initiatives at the thirty-day mark. The first month of orientation and familiarity should show your team, venders, and customers that you are an able listener and sensible person. As the buyer going through this process, you should be developing the changes that they want to implement. These can be a wide range of subjects ranging through all operational issues of the business. A new set of eyes can easily see antiquated operational systems, poor communication skills, inadequate logistics, and a whole host of issues that hamper the performance of the company.

Wisdom says promotions, demotions, and sometime firings undertaken immediately send a clear message to all that the new owner is stepping up. In regards to firings, at the time of closing in an **asset sale**, all employees have to be let go and then rehired. If there is a disruptive employee that the seller did not want to deal with and decided to pass the buck to the new buyer, *do not hire these individuals back after the close.* Be bold and do not give this troublemaker the backdrop and legal support that all employees have. Act decisively on the seller's advice if there are employees that should not be rehired.

Asset sale: the sale of a company's assets and not liabilities; a most widely used sales methodology.

Especially in the early months, there is good reason to be depressed and spooked! Taking command is a lonely and difficult job if you are taking over a large company or a restaurant. You no longer can shut off the business at the end of the day and roll into your personal life. Company issues will dog you 24/7 as you wrestle with one issue after another. You will never be the same, and there will be times where the buyer wistfully thinks about the good old days of working for someone else. Weight loss, false heart attacks, stress attacks of all kinds, and a host of other physical health issues may rear their ugly head, but the new operator must adjust or cash out. Finding a new threshold for unrelenting work and pressures not experienced before leads to a new equilibrium in new owners. Finding this balance is imperative, and understanding what stress is doing to you can allow you to develop your own sense of when you have to throttle back.

ALMOST TANKING POST-CLOSING

Many firms go through tremendous upheaval from day one of new ownership. As mentioned before, it is a golden rule for new ownership to have enough working capital that will ensure the company does not stall out for lack of operating cash. Having enough cash to buy the business and none in reserve is setting the buyer up for catastrophic issues right out of the chute. *New ownership should have at least the*

equivalent of 20 percent of their down-payment monies in reserve.
Woe to new ownership that is not ready for the turbulence that is
coming their way. The multitude of other issues that could quickly
arise includes:

- Lack of cash reserve
- Not understanding your cash flow on a day-to-day basis
- Not in control of your receivables, as they could balloon rapidly
- Not understanding the terms of your payables
- Accounts payable/accounts receivable revolt
- Cognoscente of new bank covenants
- Unhappy key employees
- Unawareness of special deals the former owner has with key customers
- Inability to detect non-profitable offerings and/or refusal to terminate them
- Inability to detect inherited operational procedures that should be terminated.

New operators/owners tend to gravitate toward their strengths
and let these issues fester and grow. Instead, having experienced
advisors and quickly understanding when trouble is at hand during
this vulnerable period is key to longevity.

NOTES

[1] "Business Broker: How Long Will a Seller Have to Stay with the Firm
after Selling?" *Whitehurst Mergers & Acquisitions*, June 7, 2011, http://
whitehurst-ma.com/business-broker-how-long-will-a-seller-have-to-
stay-with-the-firm-after-selling/.

[2] AIC Venture, http://www.aicventures.com/partnering-with-aic/we-
never-retrade/.

Chapter 10

The Four Ways to Pay for a Business

S ELLERS IDEALLY WANT TO BE PAID in cash. They hear horror stories of sellers never getting paid with the buyers' methods for reaching the asking price. There is truth to these concerns as the many ways to receive "consideration" leave the seller at risk. Conversely, buyers have opportunities not to pay the full asking price if they are crafty enough to have a deal with many contingencies.

On transactions with value over $20M, you are mostly dealing with professional buyers with professional money behind them. These deals are usually 80 to 90 percent cash with some sort of holdback that has the remaining 10 to 15 percent paid out over twelve to eighteen months as the **reps and warranties** wear out. Reps and warranties for the sale of a company are assurances, usually in the form of cash held back by the buyer for a specified time, that what the seller represented in the paperwork is actually true.

Reps and warranties: guarantees and representations a seller makes to the buyer about his or her company.

In smaller deals, under $20M, the buyers most times are not capable of paying all cash or even 90 percent cash. The buyer has to come up with a combination of ways to pay for the company if the company performs up to expectation. Buyers will often use cash flow from the company to pay the seller over time and often up to five years from closing. This money-over-time syndrome is usually not good for the seller as there are often numerous checks and balances used to ensure future performance of the company. The buyer needs these pay-out options because coming up with the full asking price can be out of most buyers' ability to pay. These payouts, or earn outs, also tether the seller to the company for years to ensure key clients stay on board and provide experience from the old regime to the novice buyer.

The most commonly used forms of consideration paid to sellers in deals under $20M are as follows.

1. **Cash:** The seller seeks to wring every possible dollar out of the buyer. Buyers must also save cash for operating the business so they try to put down at closing as little as possible. The usual matrix is that the seller receives approximately 60 to 70 percent of the sales price in cash at closing. The buyer usually borrows half of this amount from a bank. A bank will loan approximately 75 percent on good accounts receivables and 50 percent on inventory. Other assets, such as trucks, cars, racks, furniture, office equipment, as well as machinery, are difficult to get a loan on.

Sub debt: short for subordinated debt, a loan between the buyer and the seller to pay a certain amount of money over a certain length of time in regular installments.

---

2. **Sub Debt:** This is a loan between the buyer and the seller to pay a certain amount of money over a certain amount of time in regular installments. This is the next best thing for the seller besides being paid in cash. The payments are not predicated on operational

performance but are paid monthly, quarterly, or semi-annually. These seller notes (or mortgage) range from three to five years with the seller trying to get them paid as quickly as possible and the buyer dragging them out.

A seller note typically represents 10 to 20 percent of the overall enterprise value of the company and is about four to eight points over the prime rate. The seller wants the buyer to sign the note or bank loan personally, and the buyer wants the seller note to be secured by the company only. This can often become a true deal point or deal killer as the seller note is behind the senior debt position and is unsecured. If the new buyer decides not to pay for whatever reason and the buyer does not sign personally, the seller's only recourse is to foreclose on the seller note. This foreclosure may have a domino effect and most likely will force the company to miss all payments and could lead to a filing of Chapter 7 or 11.

Senior debt: borrowed money that has first priority among a company's debts in being paid in the case of bankruptcy or liquidation; a traditional bank loan is usually in the first position.

---

3. **Earn Out:** The most dreaded term for a seller, the earn out is a vehicle that has the seller being paid upon the performance of the company over time. There are no guarantees or recourse upon default, and this is a payment schedule that has the seller truly putting his or her money where his or her mouth is. There are three types of earn outs typically used, one that favors the buyer (net earn out), one that favors the seller (gross earn out), and one that is middle ground (net profits).

   • **Net Earn Out** that favors the buyer is a percentage of profits of the bottom line of the company, be it EBIT or net profit. The seller is rightly concerned that the buyer can inflate operating expenses and **SG&A** (selling, general, and administrative expenses) that could wipe out the bottom line that should be shared with the seller. This inflation can be for legitimate reasons but can be a point of serious contention. The range of net earn out profit sharing can fall between 15 and 25 percent to the seller on a deal.

SG&A: selling, general, and administrative costs; a line item on a company's income statement for the expenses of running a business.

- **Gross Earn Out** favors the seller. It is a percentage of gross sales. This is easy to track and hard for the buyer to manipulate. Even if the business is down 10 to 20 percent, the seller still gets paid like clockwork. The usual percentage paid to the seller can be between 1 and 5 percent on gross sales, depending on the size of the company.

- **Net Profits** for an earn out is considered middle ground. It is a certain percentage of net profits after cost of goods sold or other fixed pricing above variable SG&A. The seller is protected from manipulation of operating expenses by the new buyer but is not getting paid off the top line. The range of net profits in an earn out can be 8 to 12 percent on deals less than $20M.

All forms of earn out range from three to five years. In all earn outs, the payments can exceed or be below valuation expectations of the company's worth at close.

4. **Rollover Stock** As more and more professional money is used in buying privately held companies, the buyer oftentimes wants to keep the seller in place and

motivated as there may not be an heir apparent to the throne. The buyer (if an operator) still may want to ensure the seller has skin in the game. If the deal is mostly cash, the buyer may insist or negotiate for the seller to keep a certain percentage of the ownership. This" rollover stock" can range from 10 percent to 25 percent of the overall value of the company. This also helps the buyer, as he or she does not have to pay for all the company up front and is not further burdened by sub debt payments or earn outs. If the seller truly believes in the company and the strategy of the new buyer, the seller should be pleased to keep a piece of the company. Sellers usually achieve their financial goals by receiving the majority money at close so they can roll the dice with new ownership for the second bite of the apple.

The chart below shows the payout of a deal for a $10M sale over time to a seller.

Year		1	2	3	4	5	
	Financing Portion			--Payments (in 000s)--			Total
Cash	50%	$5,000				$5,000	
Sub Debt	10%	$200	$200	$200	$200	$200	$1,000
Earn Out	25%	$300	$400	$500	$600	$700	$2,500
Roll Over	15%					$1,500	$1,500
Total	100%	$5,500	$600	$700	$800	$2,400	$10,000

In an earn out, if the company exceeds expectations and makes more, or falls below expectations and produces less, the final numbers paid to the seller are adjusted up or down, accordingly. A seller still bullish on his or her company's future may very well want to take an earn out to risk making more, rather than a fixed lower price.

Chapter 11

What If the Seller Has Cooked the Books?

I N MANY SMALL BUSINESSES, the seller runs the place like a frat house. We all know the stories of spouses and family members at no show jobs, cars, vacations, with every possible expense racked up on the credit cards. For some unfathomable reason, entrepreneurs of all generations feel it is their right to "screw the tax man." Most owners of traditional businesses are in their fifties and sixties. For decades and at great risk, these hard-working folks have done everything they can to cut their net income and minimize their taxes. Yet if you asked them if they were a tax cheat (which can be a felony), they would be indignant and say they are model citizens. Over the years, I have been amazed when a potential seller is giving me a tour of the plant and there are company employees who are building anything from boats to cars to an endless variety of other non-business–related luxury items. I have heard about owners building their homes and running the invoices through their business and getting the writes-offs. Owners can and do deduct workers' salaries, cost of goods, etc. that will cut into their company's profits and lead to less to pay the tax man.

— CASE STUDY —

I distinctly remember a seller infuriated because he could not get a buyer to pay fair market for his fifteen-chain retail business. He had a big problem, which he seemed unable to see. He was pocketing $300,000 a year in cash out of the registers. In a moment of exasperation, he took me to the company safe, flung the door open, and showed me supposedly $500,000 in cash. It looked like a scene in TV show of a drug kingpin. He said that was where he kept the company cash at the end of the week, but I believe he was letting me know otherwise. In this instance, by taking $300,000 out of cash flow year after year, he was affecting the bottom line by this same number. The business was being evaluated at 5X EBITDA. If you do the simple math and multiply 5 times $300,000, you get $1,500,000—the amount by which he devalued his business at the point of sale by grabbing money out of the till.

It is shocking to me that owners will indicate such pilfering to me, a stranger, meeting them for the first or second time. I always run for the door, as this is bad news for seller, buyer, and all the advisors. If the numbers are off the books, how can the buyer present to banks and investors the true financials and get financing? These same bad books that a buyer is presenting to banks to get financing will net the buyer a lower number as well. Many of these sellers, in cheating year over year, siphon off so much money that they could never true up the books. Oftentimes, the operators/owners rationalize to themselves that this is a one-time situation and they will pay it back to the company. But with no one to correct their behavior, this conduct becomes a habit. If substantial sums are taken under the table for years, the operator can't pay the money back, and this leads to falsifying documents to the banks and investors—a criminal activity.

Horror stories abound of owners making these criminal adjustments with their loyal employees who actually do the maneuvering. Now the employees have the ability to blackmail the owner and can find many reasons to steal themselves, as they know they have the goods on the owner. But if an audit comes down, a bank loan is called, or a bank covenant broken, then an investigation ensues. The employees invariably throw the owner under the bus, and we all can read about it in the news. Once the employees are aware of such legal issues with the IRS and banks, they have incredible leverage over the owner, and they can drop the proverbial dime and make a sizable payday as a whistle blower.

In virtually all privately held or family-owned businesses, there are certain amounts of liberties taken. These benefits usually end, however, when there is professional money involved. Investors understand how to pull apart the financials and often uncover questionable spending habits of management and employees.

ADD-BACK

The term "add-back" is a key one for buying or selling a privately held business. It encompasses and accounts for the owner's spending that can be *added back* to the EBITDA calculation and favors the seller. Many smaller businesses' bottom line can have add-backs that comprise 10-30 percent of the cash flow. If you multiply these add-backs by the multiple for an enterprise valuation (3X-6X), you will see how important these calculations are to most any transaction. Add-backs are also a very sensitive subject and are not usually broached until the end of negotiations or when a certain level of confidence has been built between seller and buyer. Add-backs are often viewed as abuses of ownership and possible tax fraud. It is extremely important for the seller to have a strong confidentiality agreement in place for these potentially damaging disclosures.

Add-backs that are routinely accepted are:

- Purchase of cars and "toys"
- Costs of maintaining cars and "toys"
- Personal meals and entertainment
- Personal travel expenses
- Family members' employment
- Life and health insurance on certain individuals
- Key-man insurance
- Excess salaries paid to key management figures

- Excess bonuses paid to all employees
- Fees for societies, country clubs, or other organizations
- Dividends paid to shareholders
- Petty cash or slush funds
- Expenses for secondary offices or residences
- Any non-conforming expenditure for new owner's income statement

As a business owner, it is best to keep your add-backs to a minimum. They are difficult to explain, often illegal, and do not show the true performance of the company. If a seller truly wants to sell the business, even if it is ten years out, he or she should differentiate business expenses from personal expenses. The tax savings of running it through the business simply are not worth the problems that could arise at any time with sudden disclosures or discovery. For a buyer, big add-backs that are not business related should be a strong warning signal that the books may be cooked!

However, for the more aggressive buyers, there can be a great opportunity in finding a seller that has not been playing by the rules. These sellers will most likely scare off the more mainstream buyers and have fewer prospects to sell to. They also will have to realize that buyers cannot finance the acquisition to the high threshold the seller wants because one can't cook the books forever. For the bold buyer, this paradox can lead to more of an earn out than the seller wants, but the conflicted seller may have to embrace a long-term payout to try to recoup the true value of the enterprise.

Always remember, the taxman gets you one way or another. If you do get away with it, you never know who could drop a dime on you or when a downturn can expose irregularities.

Chapter 12

Buying a Franchise
By Alfred Naddoff

Alfred Naddoff is one the country's top consultants and participants on many levels in the franchising marketplace. Over the last decade, he has been involved in opening up more than two thousand retail franchises nationwide. He was a senior manager and principal with successful franchisors, such as Boston Chicken, Einstein Bagels, Dunkin' Brands, as well as a host of other franchises in the health/beauty and restaurant sector. He has consulted with hundreds of franchisors and franchisees and been instrumental in their success. Alfred has dedicated this section in memory of his father, Alfred N. Naddoff, who was a fantastic life mentor and wonderful father. Alfred can be reached at AlfredGeorge@comcast.net. He currently runs a nationwide consulting practice in the franchise industry.

THE SIMPLE TRUTH about buying a franchise is it's very similar to buying a house. You will have a long relationship with great passion, some rewarding and some not. The more equity you put

into your home, the more it will give back … much like a franchise
business. You can do tons of due diligence and research, or you can fool
yourself and fall into the trap of a poorly run franchise organization
like a poorly built house. It can look great on the outside and even
solid upon closer inspection. However, be sure you turn over as many
rocks as it takes to get the answers to make you truly comfortable. In
the end, it is more of an emotional decision than most of us realize,
even with solid business facts. At least, the emotion will be less
intrusive as long as we follow a process in evaluating the franchise.

ASK YOURSELF THESE QUESTIONS.

- What do you enjoy doing?
- What are your strengths and weaknesses?
- Do you enjoy start-ups, long hours, being in control
  of your future?
- Does the franchisor value family, integrity, hard work?
- Is the franchisor aligned with your values?
- Is the market overly saturated?
- Does the franchise offer territory exclusivity?
- How do they manage the marketing funds?
- Do they run company stores?
- Are they profitable at the store level? Corporate level?

Following are some of the components that make a successful
franchisee.

The franchisee should be someone with a good balance
of risk taking and processes. Being too entrepreneurial and
constantly reinventing the rules is a recipe for failure in the franchise
industry. Why pay a royalty fee or a consulting fee if you decide not to
listen to any of the company's expertise?

There are thousands of opportunities available. You want to be
careful that you do not buy yourself a job and work ridiculous hours
for only $35K-$50K a year.

You always like to see franchise companies that run company
stores. That way, they understand what the operational complexities
are. It is a ten-year agreement, if not longer in most cases, much like
a marriage! After thorough due diligence, you will step back with

yourself or partner(s) and do a gut check to validate your instincts and decide to move forward or not.

The Federal Trade Commission (FTC) has done a great job of regulating the franchise industry in the past thirty years or so, mainly because many franchisors were scam artists giving the industry a bad name. They would sell the sizzle, collect a one-time fee, and then leave the franchisee high and dry moving from city to city. The Franchise Disclosure Document, or FDD, is much like a security or prospectus with a specific format that must be followed for approval by the FTC. In fact, in addition to federal requirements, states have many registration issues that require even more scrutiny. This is all done in the interest of protecting the franchisee, thankfully. The FDD's table of contents will spell out litigation (Item 3), business experience (Item 2), and the one we all like to see, earning capability, or earnings claims (Item 19). Make sure you carefully read the footnotes in each section, as oftentimes they reveal critical details.

Speak with franchisees. Be prepared with questions: Why did you decide to go into business for yourself? What about the franchise do you like, not like? What was the total investment? How is the advertising? Do they support you? Would you do it again? Rent? Bottom-line profit after all fees? Territory protection? Other franchisees' backgrounds, success? Etc.

The beauty of franchising is you can turn over as many rocks as possible until completely satisfied and then some. When buying an existing business, it is often tough to get real numbers, regardless of your due diligence.

Franchising is a proven method of doing business when done properly. Four things really matter to make a franchise successful. You want a good concept, good management, capital, and finally execution or implementation. People can talk about great ideas, but if they cannot execute, they are pontificators. There are millions of people, educated derelicts, who have incredible ideas but can't implement. A successful franchisor has all four cornerstones.

You can expect to pay anywhere from $100K to in excess of $2M to start a franchise (excluding land in most cases). Be careful to ask for total investment or "turnkey" cost. This is disclosed in Item 7 of the FDD. Turnkey investment (soup to nuts) includes franchise fee, fixtures, furniture, equipment, POS systems, grand opening advertising, opening inventory, and working capital. Do not neglect working capital, which is the money the franchisee will need for the first three to six months or longer to survive. How are you financing your franchise? Does the franchisor have financing or bank relationships, and can they introduce you? Call several franchisees that have failed and find out why.

Some of the stronger franchise organizations in the past ten years or so are Panera Bread, Dunkin' Brands, Einstein Bros. Bagels, Planet Fitness, Elizabeth Grady Skin Care Salons, Hampton Hotels, and Great Clips. For a complete list, go to entrepreneur.com. I prefer the food and health/beauty industry because we all have to eat and we all want to stay young. The focus on healthy foods and the fast emergence of organics and farm to table, or sustainability, is almost mainstream as many strong leaders and brands have helped make us more conscious of what we put in our systems. The cost is also quickly coming down to make it available to more of us.

Selling your franchise, if you choose, can be tricky. The franchisor usually has first right of refusal. If they pass and you are doing well and the franchisor and sector you are in is strong, the return can be great. Hopefully, you've made back your initial investment and had several years of strong profits and now are in a position to make your next move. Many franchisees start with one unit and decide two or three will allow them to make a great living.

Remember eight out of ten businesses fail in the first twelve months, but in franchising with a proven model and strong company, the odds of success are significantly higher. Think of the age-old baseball analogy. If you start your own business without a franchise system, you have to get to first base, second base, third, and home. With a good franchise, you are starting on third base or at least second. It is up to you to get home, but if you are already on second or third base, you are halfway or more home.

In the end, you want to work with a brand and people you enjoy. Take time to understand their culture. Visit stores, talk to owners, and look at the competition. Make sure they offer protection around your store. Oftentimes, the existing franchisee will tell you his or her biggest competitor is the franchisee from the same concept across the street. Also, you may need more than one location over time to make the kind of living you want—upwards of $150K–$200K a year.

Being self-employed with the benefit of a support system is oftentimes the best way to be in business for yourself, but not by yourself.

VISIT THESE WEBSITES FOR MORE INFORMATION.

www.Franchise.org
www.Entreprenuer.com
www.FranchiseResearch.org
www.SBA.org

Good luck!

Chapter 13

Buying into a Partnership

W HEN AN INDIVIDUAL is seeking to be granted or buy into a partnership, there are many rules of thumb to follow. In both instances, the new partner most likely will not be the boss and decision maker. He or she will be joining an established organization with set boundaries and operating procedures, as well as structured compensation for all employees. The new partner will have to curb his or her independent style and be in sync with the company mantra and operating theme.

CASH IN THE GAME

Many service businesses are valued at .5X-1X revenues, for an average of .75X. Say an insurance company is doing $5M in sales and has $1M in profits for partner distribution. Using EDITDA, the company could be worth 4X EBITDA, or $4M. Using the revenue multiple, the company would be worth .75 times revenues, or $3.75M. These two methods of valuation would cross over at a value between $3.75M and $4M.

In this example, there are two existing partners, and you were going to be the third. When selling shares in a partnership, the overall enterprise value is reduced up to 25 percent simply because it is hard to sell a minority share in any operating business and get full enterprise value.

To continue with this example, say the enterprise value after the 25 percent reduction is $3M. Hypothetically, the new partner would need to put in $1M to be a third partner (one-third of the total $3M value). Very few prospective partners buying into a partnership have $1M in cash to contribute. To seek parity with the existing two partners, the candidate should at least put in the equivalent of one year's salary (in this example, $250,000) and then have his or her distributions for the next three years funneled back to the other partners as an earn out. At the time when the other partners receive a full $750,000 of future distributions from the partner candidate, then the new partner can finally become fully vested as an equal partner in the business. This $750,000, combined with the $250,000 down payment, makes a $1M, or one-third of the $3M valuation.

SWEAT EQUITY

If an individual has no cash to contribute up front to the partnership, then he or she must labor under the sweat-equity program. With no skin in the game there will be a long period of time (up to five years and beyond) before the person can possibly obtain partnership status.

THE CLIFF

In most partnership scenarios, there is in place a vesting schedule of three to five years, depending upon contribution. At any time, the existing partners can void the deal, unless the candidate installs a **cliff** in the partnership/employment agreement. A cliff is a set time, usually one year from the time of employment, where the new partner is in a trial period. Typically at the one-year mark, the candidate for partnership becomes vested if he or she passes muster. That is to say, if the vesting schedule is for five years and the individual has completed one year, or 20 percent of the vesting time, he or she now owns 20 percent of the agreed-upon shares in the company. Going forward for years two through five, the new partner will own shares on a pro rata basis. In this same example, if the candidate is there for three full years, then the candidate will be vested with 60 percent of his or her shares in the company on a five-year vesting schedule. The key period for both parties is the first year as both sides work to align their interests and make sure each party is holding up its side of the bargain. The time before the cliff is met is often a nerve-wracking period for the candidate, as well as for the partners. Once the trial period is over, if the partners accept the candidate into the ownership structure, they do so irrevocably. So, up to the last minute of the trial period, the pressure is on for both sides.

Cliff: a set time, usually one year from the time of employment, where the new partner who is vested is in a trial period; if the person leaves the company during this time, he or she does not take any of his or her earned equity.

In a manufacturing or retail (non-service) business where there are assets, such as receivables, payables, inventory, **WIP** (work in process), machinery, and plant, buying into a partnership is a much more complex issue. Many of the timing and percentage ownership issues outlined above are relevant, but there is more to be considered. In a service business, many of the roles are the same. In a retail, distribution, or manufacturing entity, most senior roles have a stand-alone job function. All are not pulling at the same oar but, rather, have their different jobs that are critical to the well-being of the mother ship.

WIP: work in process; materials and products not yet finished; excludes raw materials not yet in the production process and products already finished.

A major differential in organizations is that non-service companies usually have bank debt for which the owners have personally signed on the dotted line. One of the curses of being a business owner is that you have to sign personally with the banks. This is complicated when you are not a majority-owner and someone else is making decisions that could affect recourse or banks coming after your personal assets. If a partnership candidate is willing to step up and sign for liabilities and bank notes, then this puts the individual in a greatly enhanced position with ownership, and this gesture could be viewed as equity in the deal instead of cash.

— CASE STUDY —

I had this experience in my early thirties when I was VP of a real estate development company and had no cash. I was ambitious, and the ownership gave me the opportunity to become a partner in a number of self-storage buildings in downtown Boston in areas notorious for hazardous waste. In fact, the building did have hazardous waste on site, but I jumped on the grenade and signed with the banks personally. I earned the respect of ownership by my commitment, and happily these investments turned out to have great financial cash flows for decades after we refinanced and removed me from the bank notes. This risk on my part led to my becoming a partner at the firm and paved the way for my participation as an owner on other deals.

Chapter 14

Buying a Business with No Money

WE HAVE ALL BEEN FASCINATED by the stories of someone somehow wrangling control of a business with no money in. The opportunity and ability needed to do this are exceeded only by the long shot this would be. But in this day and age, there is a way to become an owner without putting money in, but in the end, the money partner most always rules supreme. In a quest to buy a company with no cash, a potential buyer has four options—sponsorless buyer (SB), management buyout (MBO), Employee Stock Ownership Plan (ESOP), or internal sale.

SPONSORLESS BUYER (SB)

A term actually used in the marketplace today, a sponsorless buyer (SB) denotes an individual that has no cash to buy a company but has targeted a company that he or she can envision running on behalf of investors. This individual usually has a skill set and experience related to the industry and targeted company and has run a like-size organization. In a general search effort, an individual is encouraged by investors or investment funds to locate a business that he or she would be willing to buy if the person had the cash. The sponsorless buyer will then approach a specific company or a multitude of players on behalf of the backers. Without a financial/operating partner, the potential seller would most likely not engage in a confidential discussion with a penniless suitor.

Sponsorless buyer or SB: an individual who has little or no money to buy a company and recruits cash partners that pay him or her and possibly provide employment when he or she finds a company that they buy.

The first step is for the SB to develop a meaningful dossier and business strategy of why certain companies should be of interest to the investment group. These targeted investment groups may very well have invested in or own other companies in the sector or in the next vertical over. This would make this a strategic acquisition, or perhaps it even could be a stand-alone **platform deal**. The SB then would get an agreement from the investment group outlining the terms of their arrangement if in fact the SB introduces a suitable target company to the investment group. Then all parties must work to bring the acquisition to a close. The SB then could play two roles—one as an executive in the firm or the other as just collecting a stock or compensation package for the introduction and facilitating the transaction. In most instances, the SB seeks to play a role in the organization and assumes an executive role. Beside the obligatory employment package, the SB now will be granted an equity stake in the business in the form of stock. This stock package could range from 5 to 10 percent of the company, depending upon the size. The bigger the firm, the less amount of stock while conversely the smaller the firm, the bigger the stock position granted. The stock also will be positioned behind the investment dollars in a second position. Upon a sale of the company in the future, the investment dollars are paid out first (oftentimes with a high cumulative interest rate) before the SB gets paid out afterwards. This obviously is a more exposed position for the SB, if the company does not perform well, the traditional bank gets paid first, investors second with their interest, then the SB last along with other non-cash stock awards. Many times, the SB can find that his or her stock is worthless if the company has not grown substantially or has not paid off its senior debt.

Platform deal: a company bought to become the centerpiece of investment to which other companies can be added.

The best way for an SB to get a big stock position and other perks is to find the target company and tie it up with a letter of intent granting exclusivity. The LOI agreement will be with the SB only, and the target company will allow the SB to go shopping for a financial partner. The LOI will not allow the investment group to go directly to the seller and circumvent the SB. They are forced to work with the SB, and then a much better compensation package can be negotiated by the SB with their financial backer. The investment groups are usually pleased that the company has been found, groomed for sale, and even the initial terms negotiated by the SB. This work done by the SB has tremendous value, and the investment group must pay the SB substantially more for his or her efforts. The compensation package to the SB that successfully locates and ties up a target company that can be shopped to different investment groups can include a number of the following.

- Executive role in the company
- Finder's fee ranging between $100,000 and $250,000
- Stock package up to 10 percent (behind cash in)
- Executive compensation package including additional stock

MANAGEMENT BUYOUT (MBO)

As owners contemplate selling their business, they are many times torn in turning over their company to strangers who have no relationship with the employees. The conflicted seller may want to reward loyal managers with the chance to buy the company. An owner, confronted with other transaction-related issues, such as taxes, family succession, concerns about earn outs, etc., may look to sell the company to its managers. Chosen management with ownership approval may be allowed to approach the owner's banks, investors, or related parties to say they have the blessing of ownership to try to finance a sale with no money down. This means the seller is willing to take their sales compensation over time. It can be structured as sub debt (installment payments over three to five years) combined with a possible earn out. The seller would turn over the reins to the new owners and could give stock in an installment sale in return for profits from the company under new management. This can work out well for both parties as the owner still can take back his company if the new management team mismanages it. If things go poorly, the new owners or management group can revert back to becoming employees. If all goes well, many times the new owners will refinance the business and/or bring on new investors that can accelerate the buyout of the seller.

Management buyout or MBO: an acquisition where a company's managers buy the assets and operations of the company from its owners.

EMPLOYEE STOCK OWNERSHIP PLAN (ESOP)

This process allows all employees, from the front office to the loading dock, to become owners. This course of action can be financed by banks and ESOP-related lending institutions. This seems like an ideal opportunity to inspire the company to greater heights of productivity. However, it has fallen from popularity over the last decade. It is a boon to the seller who gets paid a majority of the company's worth up front, but the myriad of regulations and controls needed by the lending institution often hinder the firm post-closing. Over the last five years, the ratio of ESOP-owned companies being sold to non-ESOP entities versus new ESOPs being set up is approximately three to one.

ESOP- employee stock ownership plan; a method of employee-ownership where employees of a firm buy shares in the company they work for.

INTERNAL SALE

In smaller firms, there have been many sales between long-time owners and dutiful and loyal employees. Often, the seller has allowed one key employee to run the business in his or her stead. This internal sale can avoid the trauma associated with an outside sales process and all its uncertainties. The anointed one, in many instances, has no cash so the transfer of the business becomes a cashless transaction. It is a pay-off by the new owner and former manager over time. The pay-off, once again, can be from profits, new investors brought in, or a refinance with a new or existing bank. The seller gets to safeguard the sale by having clauses in the sale contract that allow the seller to regain control of the company if there is a default.

— CASE STUDY —

There was a tough and blustery business owner called "Battlin' Bill," a legend (at least in his own mind) eighty-five-year-old owner of a potentially explosive technology company that many buyers lusted after. In his paranoia and deepening dementia, the world was out to steal his technology. He ran the company like a feudal lord and was a tyrant with all concerned. With the right strategic partner, this dormant but promising technology could make for a new wrinkle in its sector, but it was clear to all that "Battlin' Bill" was going to his grave with it. Strategic buyers and the investment bankers had given up on his rants, and the company was doomed to the dustbin of unrealized expansion plans. But there was a thoughtful, smart young employee that saw the opportunity of being the last man standing. He drafted along and outlasted everyone. He eventually become Bill's confidant and rode out Bill's tantrums and other issues and in the end became the heir apparent by default. With no money in and a succession plan worked through with an exhausted family, this trusted employee with his unflappable nature made himself such a key component to the outside world that he stepped into ownership almost by default. No money down and we salute you—the last man standing!

Chapter 15

Buying a Job or Lifestyle Business

MOST AMERICANS, at one time or another, have dreamed about running their own business. With the proliferation of the Internet, stay-at-home parents, and ability to work from home, the work world has splintered, and the ability to become an entrepreneur is within the reach of many. In addition, many employers are trying to keep employees' work hours below thirty a week to avoid paying them benefits and recognizing them as employees. This is a painful cut-off for many Americans, but it can also be the catalyst to start your own business and not be tied to one company. Having one company pay you for thirty hours a week or less may give you enough cash flow for basic bills, or being a contract employee may allow you to spread your wings and make a go of becoming a true entrepreneur. This is the cashless way to ramp up your own business for many would-be business owners.

The new fiscal tightness that has many companies in America watching their head count closely while shedding employees of all ages and genders is a harsh reality for traditional workers. Many older and even middle-age employees with family are a big burden for companies that would prefer a dedicated work force of twenty-something's they can buggy whip six days a week. For those employees that feel as if they are constantly on the bubble at work or feel they do not have longevity at the firm, there are now viable options to consider. Dedicated employees that have accumulated a nest egg or feel trapped in a mind-numbing repetitive job function can prepare for a life after corporate America and not settle for years of servitude to the big machine.

The overall American employment market has seen a sustained high unemployment rate, but we all know there is a hidden underbelly of non-working people who have technically left the employment ranks. The federal government, in seeking to bolster the employment numbers, has systematically eliminated a whole generation of older workers who have not been able to find work for a long stretch of time. These same skilled employees now are refusing to take jobs that will not allow them to meet their financial obligations. These folks in their forties, fifties, and sixties are at their pinnacle of knowledge and have tremendous skills sets to deploy. Members of this spun-off generation are extremely motivated and are at the apex of their need for income. They are under tremendous pressure to be income producers yet have been flushed off the playing field. Former employees of this lost generation have a great opportunity by default to realize their dreams of owning and operating their own business. Those with a nest egg and family and friends who can back them can make a splash in the autumn of their career.

Buying a job (where the owner has specific functions and less freedom to come and go in the business and where the salary is needed) is a great option for those who want to make a mark on life before the hourglass runs out. Buying a business where you are your own boss, set your own hours, and ratchet the company performance up or down depending upon your wishes is a great luxury. Usually, these businesses are small in size and have ten or fewer employees. Many times, these can be franchise deals or Main Street America mom-and-pop operations.

This chart below shows that people of all ages, but especially the younger groups, are interested in buying businesses.

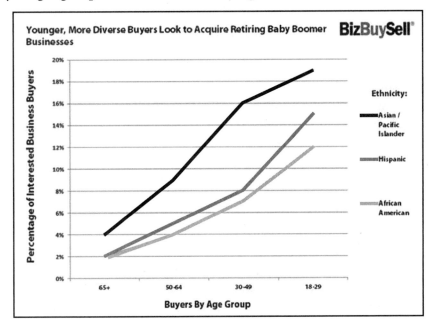

Source: "Report: Younger, more diverse buyers look to acquire retiring baby boomer businesses," *Business Journal*, February 18, 2014, http://www.bizjournals.com/bizjournals/how-to/buy-a-business/bizbuysell/2014/02/more-minorities-buying-businesses.html?page=all.

A rule of thumb in buying a well-run operation is the money you expect to make per year should be equivalent to what you are putting as your down payment to buy the company. As an example, a $100,000 a year salary should have you putting down $100,000 to buy the business. This would be an excellent deal and is called "buying a job." This job acquisition is only after you have moved out the seller and have learned the ropes. For the first ninety days after the sale, you should have the seller on board and most likely will be paying the seller as a consultant during this transition time. This dollar-for-dollar arrangement would be a great goal but not necessarily the right ratio if the company has a lot of assets or real estate. This "down-payment salary ratio" is not all the compensation either. In these smaller transactions, there is almost always a fairly heavy level of sub debt or earn out that could comprise up to 50 percent of the total valuation. This cash over time can be paid to the seller for up to five years after the closing in installment payments. To continue with the $100,000 down-$100,000 salary ratio as illustrated above, these extra payments to the seller could equal an additional $300,000 over five years or $60,000 per year. Much like paying off the mortgage on a home, when these payments are finally paid, the salary of the new owner can take a quantum leap incorporating this sum ($60,000 in the example) into his or her salary.

— CASE STUDY —

One of my favorite entrepreneurs, "Big Stevie," was thrust into this role with the collapse of his longtime employer, Eastman Kodak Company. Rochester, New York, was devastated by the fall of this landmark business, and over seventy thousand employees were eventually let go in that city alone. Faced with zero employment opportunities, Big Stevie thought of his dream job and found a key role with Speedways & Stadiums, a NASCAR-related business using instant photography. Stevie had to assist in funding the company or buy his way on board with $50,000 with a low salary. However, he received an excellent stock position in the company that, if it materialized, could have retired Stevie five years down the road. This was not to be, as the company crashed and burned for a number of reasons. In hindsight, Stevie made the right move as the business was related to his days at Kodak, and he had a love for NASCAR. Stevie dusted himself off and got back into the entrepreneurial fray with another company that also failed. Undaunted and still game, Stevie has once again anteed up and now is plowing deep into his next adventure. His life after Kodak has been a roller coaster, but he has earned his stripes, and his resiliency is testament to the creative spirit of American entrepreneurship.

In many smaller deals, the buyer should be ready not to get a salary for up to six months as he weans the seller from the operation. Even in the smaller operations, the seller usually has an employee or two who have great knowledge of the operation but do not measure up to the new owner's work ethic and go-go-go mentality. These sacred cows should be put out to pasture once they have been milked of their knowledge of operations. Many key employees simply do not embrace change.

In a comprehensive study regarding entrepreneurs, David Corbett found that:

> More than half the working population of [the] United States thinks seriously about owning their own business. At least 500,000 managers are being fired every year ... Entrepreneurship is an attractive alternative that offers new independence and control, perhaps the ticket to trying something [one] has always wanted to do. The 55 to 64 year old market is also the single most affluent consumer group today and many of these affluent individuals are candidates for small-business ownership.

If you are going to roll the dice and buy a business, that often means you are not too enamored with the businesses you have worked at in the past. Or perhaps you are stifled in an industry where you know how to grow a business if you had your own firm. In buying a lifestyle business, you will find many of your competitors are not top-flight executives or entrepreneurs; these small businesses are not recreating the wheel. But you are going to bring your business into the twenty-first century by working harder and smarter.

So why not pick a business or industry you actually like?

If you enjoy clothes, fashion, and jewelry, then buy a company or franchise in this vein. If you enjoy cars and transportation, then go after a business related to the industry. For your once-in-a-lifetime shot at buying a business, try to match it to one of your interests. Widget companies can be fun, but they can also turn into mind-numbing boredom after you get the machine rolling. Many buyers plunge into new fields where they don't know the benchmarks and find out too late they are in the wrong arena. Play to your strengths and stay associated with an industry related to your work experience or at least one in which you have a basic understanding.

— CASE STUDY —

We had the opportunity to work with a top-flight CEO who founded, for the second time, an educational business that rapidly sky rocketed to $40M in sales with a $6M EBITDA. However, disaster struck when the Obama administration changed practicing guidelines for the sector and drove most industry players into insolvency. Poor timing and this change caused our client to lose a possible windfall sale, and she had to shutter the business. After going through a messy shutdown that would have taken years off any of us, she decided to make a career change and bought a small silver manufacturer of fine jewelry. She loves jewelry and the sector, as it is wide open for a creative, aggressive entrepreneur. She stepped up with little money down and purchased the business from an honorable traditional owner seeking retirement. She immediately turned over the sales force, made numerous key hires while expanding the product offerings into new verticals, and developed a web presence. All this she accomplished with little money expended, but she has perfectly repositioned the company. As she was new to the field, she could not find any bank financing. Now, as she approaches her one-year anniversary, we believe she will get her financing and continue to reposition and grow the firm to become a regional leader. She looks forward to the day when she can take a salary!

Chapter 16

Buying or Investing Internationally

MANY OF US DREAM about an exciting cross-border world where we cut deals internationally and bring business to our home turf. We hear fantastic stories of international travel and cultural experiences where exotic ports of call are on the monthly agenda. International business people are always talking about offshore accounts and overseas homes and the easy way to beat the Internal Revenue Service.

The truth, however, is very grim, and most overseas endeavors by first-time business owners end in misunderstandings and ultimately disaster. Major contributors to the problems are challenges of time, distance, and language barriers. Time kills. Even in our Skype and Internet-enhanced world, you can see days and weeks go by as "out of sight, out of mind" venders and customers do not communicate with you in a timely manner. Also, in international business, cultural relationships can trump sound business-making decisions, and loyalty to a fellow countryman can suddenly derail a no-brainer deal. It is a much-harder and more expensive proposition to secure relationships in foreign countries. You must have a sizable profit margin and seamless operation that will allow for time lags and transit costs.

Even as English has become the main international language for business, the written word of contracts remains in foreign languages, and they can become complex and rife with misunderstandings. Exactly how does one enforce a breach overseas? There are a hundred lawyers out there who would like you to use them to find out!

To plunge into an international business without prior experience in the sector or strong in-country relationships is ill advised. This is especially relevant if the new owner has to put forth considerable cash to buy goods or secure contracts.

However, if the business is a service business with no money at risk, then one can take the time and chance without great loss should the venture fail. Being a middleman, broker, or service provider can be a lucrative livelihood if one understands the parameters and risks involved in getting paid. But these opportunities usually develop for business people in the trade. Here is an excellent example of being a successful middleman or service provider in a foreign country.

— CASE STUDY —

Tedd Tennis is a now glowing success story of applying American know-how to a new land. Without knowing the language, Tedd plunged into Panama as an ex-pat of no strong international distinction but armed with selling skills and charisma that know no borders. Tedd became a novice real estate broker in a rural peninsula. For years, he trudged sweaty hills and was boxed out by local customs. Tedd gradually earned the trust of the community, squared off against the other gringo real estate baron in the region, and eventually defeated him on all fronts and now sits in this vanquished opponent's hacienda! Tedd is fluent in Spanish, plays in a touring rock band, and owns numerous mountaintop retreats. You can see him hosting *House Hunters International* with their 2.5M viewers. Tedd is a classic success story of burning your boats like Cortez on the beach and plunging inland to entrepreneurial success.

YOUR INTERNATIONAL PARTNER

It is highly advised that any sizable cross-border operation have a foreign national on the other end that is a part owner of the business. Many of the government and regulatory issues with their delays and fines evaporate when your in-country partner "handles" the issues. You have to have a deep level of trust for these participants as they literally control the lifeblood of your business. They should not be non-vested employees or paid poorly as they truly are key employees a stateside operator becomes dependent upon. These partners are very difficult to replace as they control their end of the business and pose a threat in being able to set up a competing firm if not treated fairly.

I have been blessed in having my partner José Goldner in Panama as a man for all seasons. I met José through the Internet when surfing for an in-country host. I brought down fifty high net-worth individuals that José hosted in a myriad of events, ranging from fishing tournaments to taking us through the epicenter of Carnival week. As like-minded entrepreneurs in different lands, José and I made a pledge, which we have kept, to build a bridge between Panama and the United States. We started off slowly by me bringing down investors to buy land and do developments. This took time, but eventually, José and I, as well as other partners, have accumulated magnificent beachfront properties that will someday be prime development parcels. We have opened up bull breeding and cattle ranching on these oceanfront parcels and expect to capitalize over time. José and I have built a bridge that has brought commerce both ways. Many crash-and-burns and cultural misunderstandings have occurred, but we are making excellent progress in our grand plan. Literally, hundreds of people have benefitted from our trusting relationship, and hundreds more will follow!

Most international entrepreneurs are in the foreign business because they love the travel and cross-cultural experiences. Having an international partner with little or no cash to contribute can lead to their working into a sweat equity position. Your new partner will take great pride in having an American partner and will look to have the same international experience stateside as you are having in his or her country. Being lavishly hosted, having memorable international experiences, and establishing foreign networks have no price tag. Better to be riding a horse on a beach with your partner discussing issues than sweating out traffic or dealing with a snowstorm. Better to break even abroad than at home!

OFFSHORE ACCOUNTS AND MYTHS

With tracking technology, the IRS and other governing bodies in the States and abroad have taken away much of the benefits of overseas tax shelters and operational benefits. The Cayman Islands used to be a huge haven for offshore, nameless accounts, but the Obama administration has virtually shut down this option and is putting tremendous pressure on other offshore hosts, such as Switzerland and Panama, to disclose all US nationals' overseas bank accounts. IRS offices are springing up around the globe, and there is a huge crackdown on these havens.

The standard rule of having to declare more than $10,000 in cash in entering the United States is being strictly adhered to. There is no limit to the amount a US citizen can bring into the United States, but if it exceeds $10,000, the person must declare it on a special form to the US government. Woe to the traveler that has $10,001 without filling out the form. This will lead to a trip to an immigration office and a quick grilling about overseas business endeavors. Even if one can explain away the oversight, the violator is now entered into a database that is transmitted to several agencies.

Wiring money out of the United States in relatively small amounts (less the $100,000) usually does not draw an inquiry, but bringing that same amount of money back in requires an explanation from an accountant.

The basic premise of making money overseas is that most overseas countries have a lower tax bracket than the United States. If you earn a fee, commission, or income out of country, you are supposed to pay the foreign tax on the earnings. If that tax is lower than United States federal taxes, you will owe the difference to the IRS. For example, if you earned $100,000 in Panama and the Panamanian tax rate is 10 percent, you would pay the Panamanian government $10,000 in taxes. You would calculate the taxes you would have paid the IRS, deduct that $10,000 paid to Panama, and then pay the United States the balance, which could be an additional 10 to 26 percent, or in this example, an additional $10,000–$26,000. But the fact is most people do not pay their taxes in Panama, and most overseas operators or investors in Panama put their money in an offshore account that cannot be traced back to the United States. The problem with this for the offshore account holders is they cannot bring the profits back into the United States and they must stay offshore unless they want to declare these profits and pay their full federal taxes on them. Thus, this leads to wealthy individuals building homes in foreign countries and developing overseas lives for the rich and famous.

BUYING REAL ESTATE OVERSEAS

The safest and most secure way to begin investing overseas is to buy land. There are many ways to be swindled in land ownership, but if one aligns with the right advisors with certifiable track records, an entrepreneur can break into the overseas world of business and investments. This approach, however, is not usually a full-time job and does not pay a salary or dividends. Your pay comes over long periods of time as the land is appreciated or rezoned for development or subdivisions. Most countries we like to visit for fun and sun have a multitude of real estate options to invest in. They are used to foreigners coming to their land to take advantage of hoped-for appreciation in the beautiful countryside, waterfront properties, and development opportunities.

— CASE STUDY —

I once took a very affluent and famous doctor to a third world country in his quest to buy land and make a large real estate development. He was full of know-how and bluster and was a self-proclaimed "man of the world." After a short period of time under our in-country tutelage, he struck out on his own. We heard weeks later he was crowing like a rooster about a piece of land he had purchased with a magnificent waterfall and ocean acreage for $250,000. We crossed paths and congratulated him on such a score, and he beamed with pride as he had done it on his own. To us, something smelled fishy, and upon investigation, we found he had bought a waterfall in a national park with a fake deed! Out of pride, he refused to believe our findings. Still, we went to a meeting with him and confronted the swindler. After a nasty session, the good doctor got a refund by the saber rattling of my intrepid in-country partner, and but soon enough, our wayward physician went off and bought another boondoggle!

There are always obstacles to hurdle, even in land acquisition, but if you do get clear title to the land, you can always sell it. Most overseas buyers for land are all-cash deals. There can be local bank financing, but getting a mortgage can lead to challenges with loans from banks, domestic banks accounts, citizen and work permits, as well as a host of other daunting issues. In most cases, the land-holding time needed to make a decent profit is five to seven years. A buyer/investor that cannot pay all cash does not want to be saddled with a long-term mortgage and the hassles of international payments. Any appreciation made in the acquisition would be chewed up before an exit by mortgage payments during the long hold period.

Usually these investments are made with a strategy other than just profit. Many times, the buyers want to buy and build for their own purpose or use the land acquisition as an excuse to travel to the foreign world to indulge themselves. They have already made their living and nest egg and now are using their spare cash or savings to live out a dream. But they must always watch out for the nightmare!

— CASE STUDY —

On a more successful note, I brought down and sponsored a rough-and-tumble business owner and world traveler (we shall call him Judas) and introduced him to many business opportunities, as well as land deals, with the understanding he would pay a fee for any deal that was done. To my knowledge

at the time, Judas never bought anything through my
network. Years later, I found out a different story. He
had gone back to this magnificent land and spent $3M
on strategically placed land that, over time, blossomed
in worth to $13M. Never a fee was paid me. But this
man made all the right moves, partnering in-country
correctly, and being bold with his cash. There are
piranhas on both sides of the border!

OWNING A BUSINESS IN A FOREIGN LAND

The most difficult entrepreneurial feat is a foreigner acquiring or
starting a business in a host country, especially in the third world.
In Europe and Asia, the laws of the land may be foreign but are well
laid out and can be followed with the right translations and guidance.
But in the developing world, bribes and other forms of gratuity are
perilous paths to tumble down. Trying to decipher who are really
behind the local government and paying them for the privilege of
operating a business in their arena can be a very bad mistake. One
must never borrow money from local unregulated sources, and the
foreign owner must always have emergency exit strategies. These can
range from selling to your in-country partner or friends at a great
discount or simply pulling down the blind and disappearing back to
the mother country. This could lead to avoiding unsavory issues that
may or may not be of their origin.

— CASE STUDY —

A good friend and fellow entrepreneur, Neil Evans,
an American, moved to Panama for a career change
after a successful career as a movie producer stateside.
He came to Panama with no transferable skill sets
that were in demand, but his verve and willingness
to plunge into a new world took him to the winner's
circle. He ran the gauntlet of entrepreneurship in
Panama for years and finally succeeded. Before his
success, he had developed a number of promising
businesses that were shanghaied by locals or were

still born, but he never gave up. He now owns and operates Panama Tropical Food Co., a cross-border gourmet food company selling rum cakes and coffee gifts, among other products. Big orders are flowing in, and expansion is underway. He enjoys the good life but still hasn't learned his Spanish!

Chapter 17

Creative Deal Structure

W HEN YOU HAVE NO CASH to buy or invest in a business, you have to become creative in your deal structure and have a willing and flexible seller. The buyer must also give the seller the opportunity upon default to take back the company and rescue it from troubles the new owner has steered it into. There are numerous ways to structure these types of deals, but the most common use a combination of sub debt, earn out, and rollover equity.

Leveraged buyout or LBO: using more debt and less cash to buy a company and using the company's assets as collateral (or leverage) for the loan.

An excellent example of a **leveraged buyout (LBO)** that was structured correctly but was ultimately doomed follows.

— CASE STUDY —

A well-polished and solid business executive named Bart was making between $300,000 and $400,000 annually as an industry consultant. Working long days and traveling endlessly, he sought to acquire a related business close to home where he could get a good salary plus work towards building up a company that would create equity for him and his family. The problem was Bart had only $200,000 to deploy.

Our search for Bart found a well-known family-owned print business that had adapted to the changes sweeping the industry and had revenues of $18M and an adjusted EBITDA of $1.8M. The owner also owned the 100,000-square-foot plant with well over $10M in equipment and inventory. The payables and receivables were in good order. The seller wanted a sales price of $10M come hell or high water, even if he had to take the whole sales price back over time post-closing. The seller understood Bart was ready to work sixty hours a week and, through industry connections, could bring in another $2M–$3M in sales very quickly. The two had a meeting of the minds, and Bart pledged to mentor the family members that stayed on to ensure the family name would live on.

The deal was structured such that Bart would sign a five-year sub-debt note for $3M at 7 percent interest rate. Bart went to Wells Fargo (an asset-based lender that made Bart sign personally) and secured a large loan of approximately $5M based on 75 percent of receivables and 50 percent of good inventory. Although there was a lot of equipment in the plant, this industry's resale value of used equipment was not good as the sector was flooded with companies shedding like assets. An additional earn out was structured that would, over time (if goals were met), propel the owner past his goal of a $10M enterprise value. This would be a 5.6 multiple, which was well above the 3–4 multiples being earned in this slumping sector. From the outset, the company would have to hit all its benchmarks and make headway against industry trends for the seller to hit his payout goals.

Bart, with an excellent executive package, came on board like a whirlwind and immediately energized the company and instituted wide-ranging changes that are often needed when a third generation business is sold. But trouble was brewing as the one hundred plus union employees revolted and demanded wage increases and other increased benefits that would doom the company. As Bart battled the unions, business began to evaporate, and despite a new infusion of clients, the company began to miss its benchmarks, and Bart was soon in default with the seller. The business began to fall out of covenant with Wells Fargo, and trouble was brewing on all fronts.

The seller, an experienced operator, reengaged into the business and, along with Bart, stabilized the company, but it was clear the LBO was in trouble. The seller approached Briggs Capital as intermediaries, and we negotiated a sale back to the owner. Bart was still retained as president of the firm but was no longer on the hook for the mortgages/bank notes, and the original owner infused more capital and stabilized the business.

In hindsight, the continued collapse of the industry was the true culprit of the transaction. Both seller and buyer were in accord and made a formidable team with a creative deal structure that in good times would have made wealthy men of both buyer and seller. A few years after the buy back, the company was shut down in an orderly fashion, and the seller controlled the shutdown of the business that allowed him to retire with dignity.

Below is a general overview of a successful deal that was creatively structured by a progressive buyer and seller in the lacrosse equipment sector. The negotiated deal used creative ways to obtain the seller's high and lofty sales price but in a fashion that did not burden the business with excess debt and carrying costs. This case study shows the ability of a seller to be flexible in deal terms and ride his company from a strong regional company to a national powerhouse.

— CASE STUDY —

The seller was viewed as a genius in designing and manufacturing lacrosse-related equipment. He was well off from an earlier transaction in the sector and had quickly driven sales of his company to $8M with a $3.2M EBITDA. The company was sold for an enterprise value of approximately $18.3M. There were many suitors for this well-branded firm, but he selected a group that would give him:

- $10M in cash at closing
- Money over time through a seller's note (mortgage)
- A rollover percentage of the new company.

The buyer and seller meshed on all fronts, and over a short period of time, the firm grew rapidly in a hot sector. The sales price at the time was considered high at 6.1 multiple of EBITDA, but looking back, the sales price was a bargain. After a quick expansion over several years, the company was sold again for a reported $45M with both the original operator and the private equity buyer making a large profit. In fact, this resilient entrepreneur continued with the new owner with an excellent package that included stock. For a third time, the company was sold, and this truly cagey entrepreneur scored big again doing what he loved to do. A truly remarkable trifecta!

In structuring creative deals, a seller and buyer can also use different payment vehicles to pay money over time and avoid burdening the company with monthly payouts. These vehicles include the following.

- **Phantom Stock.** This is "off the balance sheet" shares of the company that are paid only when the company is sold. It is often preferable to being granted stock because phantom stock creates a tax event only when it is exercised and not when it is granted.

Phantom stock: stock not actually owned by selected employees but that follows the price fluctuations and pays any resulting profits to the selected employees.

- **Excess Salaries.** This is another form of paying cash over time to the new owner who did not get all cash up front. This salary can be terminated if the company is not producing.

- **Performance Bonuses.** It is exactly as it sounds—monies paid for company performance and is predicated solely on excess cash flow from operations.

- **Dividends.** These are a vehicle used to pay shareholders a percentage of profits at the subjective approval of the board of directors or ownership.

- **No-show Jobs.** Many times this is used by buyers to pay sellers when the seller does not have to show up for work but still may be contributing to the well-being of the company. This allows many sellers to stay on health insurance and receive other company benefits, such as auto-related expenses.

No-show job: after the sale of a company, a position for the seller that pays but has no requirement to work or be in the office.

- **Royalties.** Buyers often pay a separate stream of revenue to sellers on a "per sale basis" where they receive a percentage of sales for their specific products developed while they were the owner. This allows the buyer to pay the seller over time for performance, as this is not recorded on the balance sheet.

- **Non-compete Clause.** Oftentimes a buyer will make a seller sign a non-compete clause to ensure the seller does not set up a competitive company and ruin the new buyer's business. The new buyer can tie a certain amount of the sales price to this contract that receives special tax considerations that are beneficial to the seller.

Non-compete clause or non-compete agreement: a seller's contractual promise not to compete against his/her old firm for a stipulated time after the sale of the company, usually three to five years;

- **Consulting Contract.** This independent-contractor vehicle granted to the seller by the buyer can be several years in length. It is a flat fee that allows the buyer to pay the seller over time. It also allows the seller, in his or her new life, to write off expenses against this consulting revenue that transaction proceeds cannot be used to do. The seller will receive a 1099 tax form at year's end.

Chapter 18

How to Approach a Business to Buy

FROM MY EXPERIENCE in assisting hundreds of buyers in their quest to buy a business and having gone through the process twice myself, my overriding belief is the following.

The buyer should be contacting companies directly that fit the buyer's profile.

A buyer can mount a multi-facetted campaign that will cover all the buckets of a classic search campaign. But the best results happen when a buyer does the homework on a sector, industry, or market vertical and *picks up the phone and calls the owner.* Of course, a call out of the blue does not usually get the caller past all the gatekeepers to the seller. The buyer must take a few intermediate steps first. The best method I have seen practiced over the years is a well-orchestrated one-on one-approach with the following steps.

1. **Have some commonality with the businesses you select.**

   The buyer should select the companies he or she wants to approach based upon his or her business experience, relationship to the industry, and personal affinity to the industry. There has to be a common denominator between buyer and seller that gives the seller confidence the buyer is not a total rookie who will make novice mistakes with the business. When I set out to buy my first company, I knew I could not buy the Yankees or Red Sox, so I set my sights on the pet food business where my love for animals and knowledge of dogs led me to talk intelligently about the industry with sellers.

2. **Be prepared in every meeting with the seller.**

   The buyer will have to spend time and energy to become conversant in the selected industry because sellers will be wary of anyone they perceive as a newcomer. In the first tense meetings, the seller will often fall back (and rightly so) in cross-examining a prospective buyer on what he or she knows. It would be a shame to get all the way to the first meeting and blow the opportunity because the buyer is not prepared.

   Digging up information about the companies and doing research is a real pain but must be done. In this process, the buyer will be learning all about the industry and the competitive matrix that will serve the buyer well in initial discussions. Obviously online research, including SIC codes and industry groupings, is a good way to start. But common sense rules in your quest for knowledge.

3. **Use snail mail to contact the buyer directly.**

   Once the buyer has a list of companies to approach, the buyer should send out a snail mail FedEx or postal overnight service letter to the owner marked "Personal & Confidential." This personal delivery that the owner's staff or assistant can't intercept can be a potentially game-changing letter. Many staff members will most likely try to be deal killers, as new unknown ownership is a threat to their comfortable existence.

In a single page, the letter should concisely summarize why the buyer is approaching, note the buyer's synergies with the seller, business, and/or industry, and state that the buyer is not affiliated with any known players in the industry (especially competitors). The seller will be deeply suspicious of leaking his information out to the industry.

4. **Call the seller two days after he or she receives the letter to set up an appointment.**

When owners receive a well-thought-out letter that they realize is not a mass-marketing approach, the note will stand out, they will be thoughtful in reading it, and they will remember it—to a point. Most likely, they will not call you, but you will call the seller two days later and refer to the letter. When you do this, the owner will recognize the proper sequence of events— the personal letter and then the call two days later. Do not wait more than two days to call, as ownership assuredly will be swept up in daily events that may have your correspondence fading away after three business days.

The follow-up call to the letter is a key juncture, and the buyer's sole goal is to be able to set an appointment. Do not make a pitch on the phone. That will only give the seller an opportunity to weed you out. The seller will be trying to screen out inappropriate buyers, will be suspicious of any buyer's angle, and will be paranoid about anyone knowing he or she is contemplating exiting the firm. So make it brief—immediately state you are not affiliated with anyone from the industry, set the appointment, and get off the phone.

5. **Gather specific information about this buyer and company.**

    Once the appointment is set, the buyer should find
    out more about the firm and industry and really be
    prepped for the meeting. If the buyer can find out any
    of the personal interests of the seller before the meeting
    and be able to discuss and develop a relationship over
    these interests, it will go a long way to gaining the
    seller's confidence.

6. **Primarily listen at the first meeting and let the buyer know
    you have the cash.**

    At that first meeting, the buyer should voluntarily give
    the seller a confidentiality agreement that will keep
    the buyer from disclosing any information the seller
    provides. It will ease the suspicions of the seller and
    show the professionalism and sensitivity of the buyer.

    The major mistake of buyers at the first meeting is
    diving into the numbers too quickly and not listening
    to the seller. This is especially true of the younger
    generation of buyers who just want to get down to
    business; they start to ask invasive questions and try
    to draw valuation summaries too quickly. One of the
    main keys to a successful first meeting is to listen and
    understand what drives the seller and his or her family.
    Learn about the seller's hobbies, relationships with the
    children, the spouse's interests, and other personal
    matters. Turn yourself into a chameleon! Morph into
    the person the seller wants you to be, and set aside
    for now all interest in the business mathematics. You
    must become the seller's confidant.

    Do not try to accomplish too much at the first meeting.
    But do let the seller know you have the cash to do the
    deal! And leave a great impression and ...

7. **Follow up with a letter and thoughtful gift ... and wait.**

    After the first meeting, immediately follow up with
    a confidential letter and perhaps a modest gift, like

a book that would flatter the seller. The gift should reflect the respect you have for the buyer and not be a display of extravagance. In most instances, the seller is busier than the buyer, so time flies for the seller and drags for the buyer. The buyer must have patience and be prepared for a long courtship. This is a major reason why a buyer should have multiple deal scenarios underway for the waiting game, for a buyer is many times a deal killer.

8. Set up the second meeting.

The buyer's goal is to set the second meeting where the two parties can begin more formal discussions related to the business. The second meeting is about facts and figures once a synergistic fit between buyer and seller is established in the first meeting. Oftentimes, the buyer can send an agenda to the seller asking for certain information to make the meeting more productive. This second meeting should happen no later than two weeks after the initial one. Out of sight out of mind for the seller!

9. Ask about the business at the second meeting without criticizing.

At this second meeting, the buyer will be drilling into and understanding the business. It is very important at all times at this early stage that the buyer not overly criticize, critique, or point out obvious flaws in the seller's company or management style. Most sellers take great pride in their operation. Time tends to warp companies into a unique operation, bent to the seller's idiosyncrasies. The buyer should keep quiet about his or her plans for change, including any thoughts on employee cuts.

Before you begin the hunt to find a business or approach owners with your intentions to buy their business, you have to be prepared to be cross-examined. The buyers must be ready with a series of documents that will position themselves as good candidates who can execute a transaction. These are the documents needed.

- **Personal Bio/Buyer Profile**

  A classic résumé is not appropriate for buying a company. A résumé given to an owner by a prospective buyer would immediately put the buyer at a strategic disadvantage. Buyers are not seeking employment but rather asserting and presenting themselves as a commanding officer that the seller would be willing to turn over his life's work to. The buyer must appear to be a respectful executive or manager with prior work experience that makes this acquisition a good hand-off for the seller. In reading the document, the seller must have confidence in the buyer's skill set.

  Depending upon the size of the company the buyer is seeking, the buyer may form an LLC for $500 that will be the buying entity. In having the LLC done, the buyer looks prepared to proceed immediately on an acquisition and shows he or she knows how to go about the acquisition process. Most sellers have owned their business for a long time and served in some lesser role to earn their spurs before becoming an owner. The age of the typical seller usually ranges from fifty to sixty-five. Most of their careers spanned the non-social-media world, and they appreciate old-world formalities such as the printed profile they can show to family and advisors.

  Buyers should include a picture of themselves on the one-page profile, done on high quality glossy paper. Also make this document available as a PDF for online distribution.

  At right is the buyer profile I have used to represent myself in the marketplace.

SAMPLE BUYER PROFILE
Rod Robertson

BCI has recently been formed by Rod Robertson in his quest to acquire a controlling interest in an operating business. Rod currently owns and operates Briggs Capital (www.BriggsCapital.com), a mergers and acquisitions firm serving small to mid-size companies. For the past decade (after successfully building and selling his own business), Rod has enjoyed assisting buyers and sellers to reach their goals. Rod has successfully quarterbacked over forty transactions, and his firm has been a cornerstone in the M&A marketplace in New England. Rod also acts as consultant to over twenty firms to advise on growth strategies and operational efficiencies.

At Briggs Capital, Rod is a veteran of adapting to new businesses and developing growth strategies for multitudes of companies in the States and abroad. His experience ranges across all sectors, and he is seeking a business that has strong upside potential that may need growth capital or infusion of new hard-driving management. Rod plans to work at the business on a full-time basis. He also would be interested in a sector where acquisitions of competitors or synergistic companies would make for dramatic growth. Rod would consider coming on as a partner and bring his cash and ability to lead a company through rapid growth in an acquisition. He is willing to develop a unique compensation package to a seller that could make for repeated pay days over time, in addition to cash at closing. Rod is a qualified buyer and is affiliated with numerous funding sources.

Before Briggs, Rod bought and then built before successfully exiting (in five years) Great Eastern, a consumer products company. He also held numerous executive roles ranging from CEO to VP of sales of private and small public technology companies. Earlier on, Rod had a successful career as a real estate developer in the Boston area.

Rod enjoys traveling and has visited over fifty countries. He has served on numerous boards and given guest lectures at the Harvard Business School and Babson MBA program, among other venues.

To learn more about Rod, please visit www.BriggsCapital.com or on LinkedIn.

- **Team Sheet**

  The buyer should also have a team sheet that outlines the service providers the buyer will use in the transaction. You should have hard copies of this, as well as a PDF version. The team members should consist of a lawyer, accountant, due diligence team members (apart from the lawyer and/or accountant). The sheet also should list references that can be called by the seller at the appropriate time with prior notification. These references should include former business owners or managers, as well as commercial bank officers that are lined up to provide senior debt. These team players should be delighted to be part of your acquisition team, as they will provide their services.

  By making this commitment to these team players, you also can recruit them as "search engines' in your quest. They should come from firms that have multiple advisors who will have more bodies from their firms keeping an eye out for acquisition targets. Using old friends and one-man shops who are jacks-of-all-trades does not bring you potential business. Instead, use a source that can hunt for you.

  If possible, your team also should have a high-profile individual from the community that would add credibility to your team with the sellers.

- **Published Information about You**

  If you have any articles, trade publications, or relevant information on yourself that sets you forth as an industry expert, you may present them as supporting documents.

- **Business Card**

  The potential buyer should have a business card made up with the specifics of the buyer's new company to distribute to literally hundreds of folks during his or her quest.

- **Online Presence**

  It is key to have your buyer profile and team sheet as a PDF that can be sent online to a multitude of parties. You will be surprised at how widely circulated your documents go, and this is all good for your quest. You also will want to have different versions for individual approaches to different industries and even specific buyers. It is worth the time and effort to tailor-make each document for each specific seller you meet with. It is very difficult to find a ready, willing, and able seller, and when you have your chance, you have to present yourself in the most relevant and salient way possible. Many potential buyers who are seeking decent-size companies (over $5M in sales) set up a website that includes their buyer profile and team sheet. It can be a static page, but is a great reference point and shows to the community the commitment of the buyer, as well demonstrates the buyer being up with the times.

INVESTMENT BANKERS AND BUSINESS BROKERS

For every one qualified seller, there are at least twenty buyers making approaches from many angles. Intermediaries that represent sellers are deluged with buyers almost on a daily basis. We at Briggs Capital receive a minimum of ten buyer inquiries a week from people from all walks of life. There is rarely a seller inquiry. The sellers are the sought-after commodity in our business, and they can literally be worth their weight in gold. Many buyers think they are a valued customer to the intermediary, which is a fallacy. Most brokers will take the buyer's name and contact information and dump that into a database for when a company comes up for sale. They then can be part of the big email blast that goes out to hundreds of prospective buyers. But in most cases before the big public launch, the selling company has been quietly shopped and vetted to well-positioned buyers of the broker. If a search for buyers goes out to the public domain, you can be assured at least five strong motivated buyers from that sector have turned down that offering. The goal is to be one of those insider buyers that gets first call and look. To be in that inner circle, the buyer must exhibit certain qualities, as well as provide solid documentation to the intermediary:

- A buyer profile and team sheet
- Experience as a manager or business owner
- Confirmation of cash on hand to complete the transaction
- Ability and intention to move quickly through due diligence
- Being a closer and not a tire kicker
- A personality that meshes with the seller's
- The knowledge of how to value a company

The buyer must reach out to many brokers via email setting his or her criteria forward. Buyers must also tell the intermediary that they are willing to pay the intermediary a fair market fee if he or she generates a seller that is not officially being marketed. Most good brokers and bankers have at least ten companies they are in contact with that could be sellers at a later date. A buyer's approach and style could trigger the broker to approach a potential seller that is percolating on the broker's back burner. With certain buyer/seller synergies made clear to the broker and the broker knowing he or she is getting paid by the buyer, the intermediary may approach a prospect earlier than intended. In many cases, it is out of sight, out of mind with the brokerage community, so keep pinging them and take the time to call each and every one on your list. Buyers should not make the mistake of assuming they are a coveted asset to the broker.

The most successful way to get bankers' or brokers' attention is to pay them a monthly retainer in a search campaign. Many buyers do not have the skill set or the time to hunt correctly. Time is money in many ways, so you do better to link up with a proven broker who knows you're serious by your paying him or her than spending months and months searching on your own as an uneducated hunter in the refined game of acquisition. The fees can range from $1,000 to $5,000 per month. These fees should be offset against the commission the buyer pays to the intermediary at the closing. The ability to secure meetings with multiple companies will be greatly heightened, especially when the broker can tell the prospective seller that his or her broker's fee will be paid by the buyer. The seller will then know this is a serious buyer lined up with the right industry professionals.

NETWORKING

Buyer have to be committed to the process and pull out all the stops in their campaign. They must make everyone around them aware they are on the hunt. The Internet allows buyers to use social media and connect with multitudes of influencers. Buyers must make all these people aware in their network that they would gladly pay a finder's fee for just introducing them to a company. As most of these networking people are not mergers and acquisitions specialist, they are only being asked to make the introduction and sit back and hopefully make a substantial fee. Hunters should be alert at all times in their daily life to what people around them are saying about their businesses. Is their company growing? Is it faltering? Is ownership asleep at the switch or out of touch? Does Junior not want to take the company over? Has the owner suffered an illness? Are the partners fighting? Many deals are done by someone introduced by an employee who can give the inside scoop. Spies are always welcomed!

Following is my letter seeking help via networking.

SAMPLE NETWORKING LETTER

Dear XX,

How goes the battle?

With over a decade at the helm of Briggs Capital (www.BriggsCapital.com), I have decided to make a career change and leave the ranks of investment banking to acquire and operate a business. It has been a fascinating tenure here at Briggs, and the firm will continue to supply M&A services, but like Cortez, I am burning my boats on the beach and plunging forth on my quest to run a business.

To this effect, I have formed Briggs Capital Investors (BCI) and have the right set of advisors and multiple equity sources behind me to close a transaction. I know the buy-side drill as well as anyone and am confident I will source and close a deal over time. I am flexible on size and sector, but a range of $10M-$50M in sales with a $1M plus EBITDA is my strike zone. My preference would be to acquire a firm that needs or has a marketing and sales emphasis.

I would ask you to keep my hunt in mind and forward this correspondence to associates and anyone in your network whom you feel could turn me onto a possible seller. I am pleased to pay fees and/or retain service providers that have assisted me. The attached document gives more background to my campaign.

I would like to thank you in advance for your thoughtful assistance in my quest.

As always,

Rod Robertson

CONSULTING

Keeping in touch and developing relationships with different consulting groups can lead to getting multiple looks at businesses in transition. Consultants are needed when a business seeks to perform better or become more efficient. Both of these signs lead to cash flow issues that, in turn, could lead to ownership examining their exit options as well. Becoming a consultant yourself in the sector can lead to many interesting opportunities. Most consultants in small to mid-size companies deal with ownership in some fashion. It is an excellent way to become a known and trusted entity.

CLOSING TIPS

Let us say a buyer has successfully located a business and negotiated an acceptable price and now is entering upon the perilous path of due diligence. This often leads to a close 90 to 120 days after the signing of the letter of intent. Before the Great Recession, approximately 75 to 85 percent closed within ninety days. With the financial meltdown of the recession, this closing percentage has decreased to approximately 65 to 75 in our experience.

The costs associated with due diligence and closing have also increased for buyers and can range from $50,000 to $500,000. It is always more expensive for the buyer than a seller to get to close, and the ratio of buyer's to seller's dollars spent can be as high as three to one. Many buyers make the mistake of letting their lawyers and accountants take over the deal, and these advisors can run rampant in creating and defending what-if scenarios that will ultimately never affect the deal. Most buyers (and sellers) are not familiar with the deal process, but it behooves them to become deeply enmeshed in the process, as it will save them time, money, and aggravation with the seller. Here are some worthwhile tips for a buyer.

- Select advisors with deal experience.
- Stay in the game and learn about the process.
- Understand the cash flow of the target company in great detail.
- Interview key employees early on in diligence and make key allies.
- Do not take on poor or troublesome employees.
- Set up a board of advisors with different experience to draw on.
- Stay in touch with the seller—don't let advisors isolate you.

- Count the inventory at close.
- Check with the big customers just before close.
- Go through ALL accounts receivable and payable before close.
- Override your lawyers and accountants when need be on business issues.

Chapter 19

Post-closing Growth Cycle and New Reality

FIRST DAYS ON THE JOB

THE INTENSITY OF ACTIVITIES for closing on the sale of the business can derail a buyer's plans for day one and beyond at the newly acquired company. There does not need to be a momentous game changing announcement post-closing. However, a press release, prepared in advance of closing, should be immediately sent out to all major venders, customers, employees, and related parties that interact with the business. All these organizations and individuals most likely have heard rumors swirling about. The truth often gets distorted, and a crisp factual communication to all must be sent outlining who the new buyer is and that all business practices will remain the same for the near future. Personal communication lines should be open to all that have the new owner listening and being sympathetic to past wrongs and slights. Assurances should be given that all grievances will be addressed over time. The new owner should meet one-on-one with as many key players as possible to learn the real truth about the business.

As mentioned before, the owner has the right not to hire or retain any employees and must extend an invitation that offers ongoing employment. This is done seamlessly, and most employees are not aware of this rehiring issue. In larger organizations, very rarely is this invoked, but with smaller firms where every employee has a significant impact on the operations of the company, this is an excellent window of opportunity for the new owner to cut out slackers, antiquated employees, or the old guard of prior ownership. Just trimming the roster for cost-cutting is reason enough. This also sends a message to the employees that the new ownership has done their homework and made preemptive moves that will benefit the company. These non-rehirings are usually silently approved by the rest of the employees who can see why new ownership took such drastic steps at the close. The good employees should respect ownership for making these moves that will strengthen the company and thus their own employment scenarios. Once that threshold of time elapses for rehiring, new ownership will have to deal with any troublesome personnel on a more equal footing.

AMBUSHES FOR NEW OWNERSHIP

There are a thousand stories of new ownership nightmares. They range from the problems with the books to bad or obsolete inventory. The most dangerous time for the well-being of a company is the first six months after a sale and change of ownership. To weather it, especially for a small or lower market business, *get an immediate grip on the day-to-day cash flow of the business*. In taking over a new business, the biggest error we see new owners make is running out of cash before they know it. Problems that can cripple a business often arise quickly. Here are several such problems and suggested solutions to each.

- Your new bank or existing old bank can balk due to covenant breaches overlooked but now enforced under new ownership. Make sure you are personally aware of all terms and conditions and sit with your bank before the close to make sure there are no snags.

- Your customers may balk at paying you to test your resolve or ask for extended terms that could lead to cash flow issues. Your customers can see this opportunity, and you must be on top of your accounts to ensure payment and many times reel in over extended accounts that had developed with the last owner.

- Your accounts payable may want to get paid up or start fresh with you and set different, more stringent terms that could lead to having to pay overdue or even on-time payables from the last owner. Brace yourself for these approaches and say it is business as usual unless you want to extend terms, or threaten to drop their account.

- Key employees can come to you demanding raises and try to hold you hostage during your rookie phase. Buy time with them. Listen sympathetically to their complaints and veiled threats but tell them you have a sixty-day moratorium on any changes.

- Your customers can approach you individually or on a united basis to give them better terms or they will move their business elsewhere. If it is a united approach of many customers, ignore the whole approach as these loose confederations disintegrate rapidly. Deal with them one at a time.

- Your competitors can try to steal accounts or take your lines of business elsewhere. It is an ideal time to make contact immediately with all your key accounts and sniff out if there are issues with raiding competitors. You can strike back or even contact your competitors to warn them off.

- Key employees may try to spin off and set up a competitive business. If the company is large enough, a new buyer should consider making an equity pool of free stock that these key employees can earn into over a three- or five-year time frame. This should derail a spin-off. When they sign their equity or new upgraded employment package, have a solid non-compete clause in place.

A NEW SHERRIFF IN TOWN

At around the thirty-day mark, after the new owner has listened, learned, and assimilated the culture of the new organization, ownership should make operational changes in the business if needed. After the observation period, new ownership can now adroitly implement striking changes set forth operationally before expansion plans are rolled out. Any changes in pricing, terms with customers, venders, or any related operational efficiencies that need to be implemented should be ironed out. With the new house in order, ownership can look to their growth plan.

GROWTH STRATEGY

A key issue that applies to many buyers is that they do not have enough cash to ramp up the business after the closing. This is for a variety of reasons, including extended due diligence, poor financial forecasting of closing costs, and **capital expenditure** issues. New ownership should implement its new growth strategy and begin to have buy-in from employees and other parties associated with the game plan for growth.

Capital expenditure: also CAPEX; money spent by a company to acquire or upgrade fixed, productive assets, such as trucks, office computers, buildings, etc.

A rule of thumb for new business ownership in the $1M-$10M enterprise value range is to have approximately 20 to 25 percent of the down payment amount on the business set aside for growth capital. As new buyers are usually increasing debt on the company to pay out the seller and have accumulated other expenses against the business, many times they are not capitalized enough. It is not good to step into the driver's seat and have no gas. Most acquired businesses have earn outs, sub debt payments, etc. that call for more cash flow until the business can grow enough to handle these new cash-flow burdens. To make the acquisition worthwhile, the business obviously has to grow well beyond these new expenses.

If new ownership does not have cash set aside for growth, do not buy the business! There is nothing worse than buying a business that barely can pay its bills and being assaulted with all kinds of new ownership issues that could cripple a company out of the chute. Taking cash from a bank can be okay for temporary cash-flow issues, but adding long-term debt to solve near-term issues will lead to more problems later. One of the main premises of buying a business is to grow the company so the buyer will have equity in the company and a possible nest egg at the end of the road. But no growth capital means no growth!

Let us say the buyer has worked through the turbulent first sixty days on the job and has the company stabilized and ready to go forward. It is a natural inclination of new ownership to watch every dollar going out the door, but owners must step back and let go of this inclination and spend money for growth in a detached and professional manner. They should run the business like a hired manager. This is exactly why ownership should bring in outside advisors with their domain expertise. They can see the playing field correctly and not be swayed by the fears and concerns of ownership.

New owners should have strategic reasons for buying the company and making it grow. They should then cross over their related knowledge of the business and industry with what they have learned during due diligence and the first months of ownership. Then they should develop a growth strategy based upon a solid strategic plan by current employees and subject-matter experts. The associated consulting fees paid to these advisors for laying out the plan are usually money well spent. These consultants can actually mature into future employees and leaders of the firm as it grows in size and stature within its industry vertical. Many owners going through their company's growth cycle do not take salaries. They lead by example in sacrificing their personal needs for the betterment of the machine. The employees and advisors will gladly work with an owner who denies himself or herself to pay others to help the company flourish. The whole organization should be excited at expansion and change, for those that clung to the old ways have most likely been banished.

Most companies acquired with new operating debt must grow, or they will languish; they have no middle ground to rest upon. As most sellers have founded their business and have a lower bank debt than new buyers, the new owners need to generate more cash immediately to pay the higher bank notes. In today's fast-paced Internet and social-media-driven world, proactive growth is a necessity. If the new company is not seeking out all angles for growth, rest assured the competitors are.

BUILD THE NEWLY ACQUIRED COMPANY TO SELL

If there are two companies for sale that a larger player is looking at, the buyer will go for the company that is built to be sold and can be easily integrated into the buyer's organization. Larger strategic buyers should be the sought-after exit for entrepreneurs who have acquired a business from another individual. They historically pay more—time is of the essence for them as their investors/shareholders want growth to come both organically and through acquisition. These professional buyers usually have the bigger war chest to close on a deal than do other entrepreneurs.

Here are reasons to sell to strategic buyers.

- They usually pay more.
- They usually pay more cash up front and avoid earn outs and such.
- They have professional acquisition teams lined up.
- They do not need financing like individual buyers.
- They are industry players who have expertise in running the company in their sector.
- They are usually profitable.
- The seller's newly acquired employees will find a safer employment haven in strategic buyers.
- If the seller has to take money over time, it is better coming from a bigger organization than a tapped-out entrepreneur
- Strategic buyers are ready for due diligence and are buying because the seller is in the sector.
- It is less of a personal or emotional deal than with individuals.

The mergers and acquisitions marketplace is always full of stories of why a strategic buyer chose one company instead of another. Many times the smaller firm with less profitability trumps the larger firm in being sold. Even if a buyer has recently purchased a firm, he or she should build the business so that one day it will be a target for acquisition. Many buyers swear their business is not for sale, but when a big strategic comes calling, their tune can change as they may be one of those lucky business owners who get a deal they can't refuse.

A business owner should always run the business in a professional fashion and avoid the temptation of running it like a private fiefdom. Shoddy books in a sales process will bring deep concerns to a buyer and lead to a deeper dive into the numbers by the buyer's advisors. These deeper inquiries may turn up even more corner cutting and questionable business practices of the seller. Big buyers will shy away from a deal that post- closing could turn up financial irregularities. If these unorthodox business practices are carried on year after year, they compile years of financial misrepresentation that can have serious consequences for both a buyer and a seller.

If you are looking to sell your newly acquired business, be aware of several factors that attract the attention of strategic buyers and affect its ability to command a high price. The best ways to build a sound foundation for a company to be acquired at a later date involve the following factors.

- **Audit your financials.** Everyone realizes it is expensive to audit a firm's financials. But to try to save the time and expense by avoiding an audit will haunt you when it comes to selling. The larger the company, the more the need to have audited statements. This yearly event will keep you honest and apply discipline to how the firm is run. If a buyer demands audited statements, you may have to go back at least two years to comply.

- **Use mid-size companies for advisors.** For the audit and other related practices (legal), you should use mid-range firms, as documentation prepared by small shops will not pass muster with larger players.

- **Be a clone.** Look into the future and analyze who could potentially buy the company in five years if you treble its size. Then understand how they operate and see if they have acquired any companies in the recent past. Understand the potential buyer's idiosyncrasies. For instance, if your potential buyers do not have a strong sales force, build one for them. If they do not have strong IT, build your own for them to adopt. Whatever their weakness is, make your firm strong in that arena. Compensate for a buyer's weakness.

Audited financials: an independent CPA firm's highest level of review of a company's financials; more thorough than reviewed financials oar compiled financials.

- **Have proper legal work.** Make sure you have competent legal counsel. Most firms that choose to become a C corporation (C corp) in small business end up bitterly regretting that election. Incorporated companies have to pay double taxation when they sell. Check on the difference between a Sub S and an LLC. Understand which to select and how the earnings flow through to the partners. Always ask your attorney if you should be registered in Delaware. If not, find out why.

- **Limit your commitments to employees.** Try not to have any long-term employment contracts. This habit can cause issues in a future transaction. The least number of full-time staffers and related benefits will allow the future buyers more flexibility to incorporate your overhead into theirs.

- **Bank and investor debt.** Be careful on your bank loans as well as investor terms. Make sure there are no prepayment issues with your bank when you pay the note off. Best to see if you can structure an assignment of your loan so the new buyer can step into your program and not have to go through the huge hassle of setting up a new banking relationship. Make sure your investors have no say if you decide to sell for whatever reason. They may very well want to have you keep on chugging, but do not make them party to your subjective decision-making. Limit the information you provide to them at all times.

- **Keep out unions.** If you have a union, try to disengage (good luck with that!). If you do not have a union, under no circumstances let one on board, as most every buyer will shy away from their conduct and demands.

- **Secure signed supplier contracts.** If you inherit "hand shake" relationships, gradually work them into a contract. Even if the contract is month to month, it is better than having only a verbal agreement in telling a future buyer that these companies are still going to honor your arrangement. These open arrangements usually lead to the seller having to take more money out in earn outs until the new owner is comfortable with the arrangement. Why should a buyer pay for something that could evaporate?

- **Identify potential future buyers early on.** Analyze the field of play and make a list of possible future targets to sell to. Over time, find a way to make the acquaintance of their management and keep a steady stream of positive information flowing by them. Try to build your business to be of service to theirs.

- **Know your competition.** Spend the time, energy, and effort to understand your competitors. Learn everything about them from the history of ownership to their pricing and operating habits. You never know what is happening behind closed doors at these firms. They could be seeking an exit—and you could buy them. They could be in financial trouble—and you could drive them out of business. Or you could do joint marketing and sales together. Better to have the respect and open lines of communication than operate in a void and make bad decisions.

- **Make your company's presence known.** It pays dividends for others to know about your company. If it doesn't already, you must immediately give your company a strong web presence and other social-media strategies that place the firm in the midst of the new generation.

- **Practice best practices!** Learn from the big boys in the sector. Poach employees, conduct market research and information gathering, and do not recreate the wheel. Do what they do but be more nimble and tailor-make it for your arena.

QUICK TO MARKET

It is essential for all companies, newly acquired or not, to ramp up their sales and marketing campaigns using multiple deployment vehicles. A buyer or new owner can become too absorbed in getting in the saddle and tinkering with the company. Running the business and growing the business are two separate functions. Ownership has to focus on growing the business, as day-to-day functions can absorb everyone's time. One always has to be aware of the passage of time. Always assume there is someone somewhere in competition with your firm doing something creative that could eclipse your efforts.

Chapter 20

Timing: When to Buy, When to Sell

BELIEVE WE ARE ALL GUILTY at some level of "coveting thy neighbor's success." Anyone with ambition is a competitive person, and competition breeds a multitude of conflicting emotions as we view others in business. This is especially true for those that we perceive as having lesser skill sets than we do; we think the smarter, more clever, more knowledgeable operators should succeed above others less so. But money begets money, and those that inherit wealth or a family business have a huge jump-start over the toiling masses that come from meager or modest means.

In many ways, however, the playing field is leveled with these "lucky sperm club" members. The stories and statistics are endless about second and third generation business owners who do not have the drive, ambition, or skills to capitalize on business like the ambitious entrepreneur. Most entrepreneurs come up the hard way and are the best and the brightest, or at the very least, the most driven. Working for the family business owner or keeping track of family businesses in one's domain can lead to a great acquisition that may not be driven entirely by money for the seller.

We all know timing is everything in life. That is true in business, and especially, timing matters in approaching instant ownership possibilities.

Understanding timing takes great practice and concentration on macro and micro events. Opportunities abound and to see them, you must recognize the events creating them all around you, from the overall big picture of world events sliding down to the general business picture.

For instance, consider interest rates. As it climbs and falls, the interest rate is a key indicator of value. If a company needs large operating cash, then it usually has a large asset base, which means big bank loans. A spike in rates can lead to a default or perhaps an owner who may want to fold his cards and sell. Troubled banks call in loans. New technology in a given sector could cause a ripple effect that would spook an owner into selling. A death in an owner's family or a health issue to an older owner is a telltale sign that a buyer should make a rapid approach. People sometimes feel it is a bit ghoulish to approach a troubled owner, but many times the owners are looking for their white knight.

Like a surfer scrutinizing the swells, the buyer has to know which wave to catch. A botched approach and emersion into the wrong company can be very damaging financially, as well as time consuming. The average entrepreneur or buyer searching full time usually has a one-year window to close a deal. More than one misfire can lead to the exhaustion of time and resources of a wannabe buyer. Having a long period of time to look is crucial. Or, if you lack the time, consider having intermediaries look for you. That, however, calls for a search-side firm and a retainer. Usually one has the time or the money, but rarely both.

If there are no fish under the boat, don't go fishing.

The heyday for buying was the run-up before the Great Recession. The aftermath for eighteen months was Death Valley. In 2014 and forecasted through 2016, the M&A world is for crafty survivors and people who are buying in sectors they understand or have experience in. General hunting across all sectors is a dangerous undertaking. Getting up to speed on a new industry is a risky business, as potential buyers are blind to changing dynamics and short- and long-term threats.

The same skills for knowing when to sell are equally relevant. Many owners on the sell side make a decision not on industry developments but rather personal problems or concerns. Most owners have been at the helm for years, and they have made their money. However, the majority of the money is locked up in their business, so they need to get at their wealth.

A NEW OWNER SHOULD ALWAYS BE READY TO SELL

A first-time buyer must always be ready to sell. Certain industries are so turbulent and ripe for change that fortunes are made quickly or other firms can be irrelevant before the new buyer is aware of seismic shifts in value. Better to make a quick risk-reward assessment and unload while you can if the industry dynamics have shifted ominously. The new buyer does not want to be the last in the know.

The company should have its books in order and its strategy and plan laid out. Ownership should have the ability to impress an unknown third party that the firm is the correct one to buy. When a competitor comes knocking, the firm must be shipshape and exhibit all the hallmarks of a progressive firm that can be added on or rolled up. It would be wise to have an executive summary on the company available at all times. It can be updated and deployed when needed, but trying to draft such a document over a short period of time will most likely not show the company off to its best effect.

Timing in and timing out can save an owner thousands of hours of work with the swipe of a pen. But, by cutting the right deal at the wrong time, the buyer may win the battle but lose the war. Great deal terms will be muted and possibly meaningless if the firm is operating in a shrinking or obsolete marketplace.

But selling when the shrewd owner sees the trade winds shifting is a key to riches. If an owner can see over the horizon or understands shifting industry dynamics—and acts upon such insight—he or she will sell in a timely fashion and receive as much cash up front as possible.

Caveat emptor!
Buyer beware!

Chapter 21

Selling Your Business

HUNDREDS OF BOOKS and thousands of articles cover how to sell your business. In this book, I will highlight the selling process and give a buyer/entrepreneur insights into the thinking of a seller.

Once a business owner has acquired, grown, and is ready to exit his business in an orderly fashion, he or she should *always be prepared to sell*. Month after month, year after year, as time flows buy, the seller should accumulate knowledge that will assist in the plan to sell and compile the information in specific files. Such a disciplined and conscientious approach will save time in the end and increase the seller's likelihood of selling well. Here are files the seller should maintain from the start.

- **Closing Bible.** This file contains every possible legal and accounting document needed when the company is put on the market. It should include all the documents used in the run-up to the initial purchase that could be of interest to the new buyer or for supporting info for the next seller in a pending sale.

- **Industry M&A File.** This notes all mergers and acquisitions activities in the sector that are relevant to the company.

This can be extremely valuable when it comes time to sell because digging up information in a short period of time can be difficult for small privately held companies. Investment bankers and brokers always have a hard time finding information from comparable or like-sales. But if the owners/operators of a business always keep abreast of industry developments, they can buttress the valuation of the business in many ways. They can track sales of larger companies or big players in adjacent verticals that will give tracking data for all concerned. Sellers in aggregating this data will also be assisting their eventual banker or broker when they are scrambling for market data. In firms large and small, as well as venders in the sector, this file could hold the name of the eventual strategic buyer who will acquire the firm for larger multiples.

- **General Industry File.** This file tracks news in the sector. The data will allow the seller to accumulate knowledge and build a story that shows growth and trends in the industry and why their company is worth so much more. One can build matrixes and story lines backed up by years of relevant (if selective) data. This information can cover, competitors, new product lines, new technology deployed, macro and micro trends, as well as a host of other relevant issues. A case can be built from this data alone that could greatly heighten the value of a business. It also shows the new buyer that the owner has good industry intelligence and will not be ambushed by swift changes in the sector.

- **Operating History of the Business.** This will include month-to-month entries on a wide range of issues. It should have subsections covering such topics as employee conduct and wage history, vender pricing, manufacturing costs over time, capital expenditures, as well as any relevant data on the company.

KNOW THE VALUE OF YOUR BUSINESS

A business operator should always have an understanding of the value of his or her enterprise. Over the years, the most shocking revelation I witnessed in case after case was owners' failure to have a clear understanding of the worth of their business. The majority of small to medium-size privately held or family-owned businesses have up to 70 percent of their net worth tied up in the business. It only makes common sense for estate planning, or at least personal-financial planning, to understand what the value is and how this affects a family's cash flow and future cash flow needs. These expenses can range from college tuitions to weddings or even the ability to add on to the company through growth or expanded product offerings. As any financial planner or wealth manager says, it is risky business to have the majority of a family's wealth tied up in one enterprise—especially when that business can't be sold or liquidated quickly. A need for quick cash and a forced sale of a company usually does not bode well for the seller financially. Sitting on a "cash machine" does not mean that the machine can be sold quickly. Many times, it is worth more as a running institution than as a fast sale.

Family and friends almost universally heap praise on a business owner and, in their naïveté and bluster, spout out huge valuations of the business. The delighted owner always basks in these discussions, and after hearing them repeatedly from a chorus of well-wishers, the seller subconsciously holds these bloated guestimates as a benchmark for the value of the company.

Business operators are almost gun-shy to find out the true value of their business because they are afraid their bubble will be burst. In most cases, they are correct, and when reality fails to meet the hype of family and friends, there is a time of deep consternation and disbelief. This mental readjustment can be harsh medicine for an owner and lead to a waterfall of other financial repercussions to the financial planning of the family. Reality, however, cannot be ignored, and it is best for all not to operate under an illusion of wealth. For bankers and brokers, the unveiling of their professional estimate of the company's value can lead to a real "truth or consequences" time. In ancient times, the messenger bringing bad tidings to the king was often slain. Today, woe to the industry professional who bears bad tidings!

THE DREADED NET-NET VALUATION

Once a seller has been given a valuation of the business that he or she was not previously aware of and wants to continue to explore an exit strategy, there are many hurdles to get by. In my estimation, approximately 50 percent of sellers have a general awareness of their company's valuation before a sales process starts. As the process unfolds and the seller is given a general valuation summary and the seller still would like to proceed into obtaining offers in the marketplace, a new hurdle looms ahead. At some juncture after offers are received but not yet responded to, intermediaries greatly encourage would-be sellers to examine the true "net-net" they will receive when the dust settles on a sale. The net-net often is a depressing waterfall of payouts, payoffs, and tax scenarios that must be accounted for. This cascade of diminishing returns for a seller may consist of the following payouts:

- the deal team of brokers, accountants, and lawyers
- existing accounts payable
- bank loans
- investors
- employees or partners
- corporate taxes if a C corp
- **capital gains** if an S corp or LLC
- taxes on an individual tax bracket for earn outs
- higher taxes paid on 1040 income to consultants versus lower capital gains tax at closing

In simple terms, the net-net can kill a deal. If a seller is transacting because of health issues, adverse market conditions, operating fatigue, or any other issue that is forcing a sale, then the net-net is a bitter pill to swallow. If a seller is selling for pure financial gain, the net-net will give him or her pause to reconsider a sale. This crucial hurdle in the sales process almost always has sellers pondering if they should just continue to run the business and get their yearly pay and owner's benefits.

Capital gains: profit from the sale of a business or investment; taxed at a lower rate than other income taxes.

Many times, potential sellers on the cusp will consider bringing in professional management. This should lead to a steady gain in value and revenues while increasing the owner's cash flow substantially, even if the owner steps back in the operating role. This is a true point of consideration—what owners would not like to have their company throw off more cash as they work less while turning the reins over to possible successors?

At this juncture, some owners close to selling can see the difficulties ahead to get to a close and may not have the stomach for the process and due diligence. Perhaps they are tormented at leaving their loyal employees to a heartless new owner or are afflicted with a myriad of issues. But many also realize they are now tantalizingly close to unlocking the wealth they have accumulated over the years, and most sellers plow on to a close, despite the disclosures of the net-net.

Chapter 22

Pearls of Wisdom
By Russell Robb

Russell Robb Russ is a twenty-plus-year veteran of mergers and acquisitions and past president of the Boston Chapter of ACG with over eleven thousand industry professionals. Russ has also been a successful business owner who practices what he preaches. He is a cornerstone of the investment banking world in New England and has assisted legions in their quest to business ownership. Russ is also a horseman and a country squire. His two books, Buying Your Own Business *and* Streetwise Selling Your Business, *are great readings that complement this book. Russ can be reached at rrobb@TullyAndHolland.com.*

THROUGHOUT THIS BOOK, different issues involved in buying a company are addressed in separate chapters. Cumulatively the text should be helpful to you in completing a transaction. In this chapter, however, I have brought together the important nuggets of information; hence its title.

From an experienced dealmaker's perspective, Andre Laus, managing director of the Recovery Group in Boston, a firm specializing in turnaround and corporate improvement, has the following comments for buyers:

> Profits, profits, profits: Like the analogy of the ingredients for successful real estate acquisitions, location, location, location, companies with consistent profits over a long period are usually the best acquisitions. Reliability of earning, year in and year out, is more important for most buyers than the total magnitude of earnings if the earnings are inconsistent. A very successful group with which I was previously associated acquired over a dozen midsize companies in less than ten years. Part of their success is attributed to the majority stockholder's criterion of acquiring only companies with ten years of unbroken profitable earnings. Such standards place a greater burden on the acquisition process, but the post-acquisition results have been most rewarding.

Additionally, the corporate culture that no cost is too small to address cumulatively results in noteworthy profits. From a buyer's perspective, continuous cost management results in more profits, just as increasing sales usually result in greater profits. Management should focus on both items with equal emphasis.

THE QUALITY OF WORKING CAPITAL

Working capital (current assets less current liabilities) should be viewed skeptically and beyond the immediate implication of the numbers. For example, if there is an excessive amount of receivables over ninety days, it may be indicative of the industry, the quality of the customers, or the company's own lack of financial discipline. Either way, the extent of this item may cause a buyer to reconsider the potential acquisition.

Also, inventory is an important component of working capital. Most businesspeople analyze inventory with regard to annual turnover, but few people focus on the equally important issue of what percentage of the orders are shipped complete or if a system to measure customer order fill exists at all.

STRONG CUSTOMER ORIENTATION

Many of us have read Tom Peters and Thomas Waterman's famous book, *In Search of Excellence*, which keeps focusing on the importance of the customer in the eyes of all employees of the company. Some progressive companies have a customer council that meets quarterly. Buyers should be looking for companies that are customer-driven, as this is indicative of future success.

STRONG EMPLOYEE ORIENTATION

Employee training programs, employee empowerment, and employee respect are all indications of a company that probably believes its most important asset is its people. Not a bad philosophy! An incidental tip is to look at the company bulletin board, which reflects how management feels about its employees. And, above all things, look at the men's or women's washroom. If it isn't clean, reconsider buying the company. The employees probably do not take pride in their company, their product, or themselves—and the company accepts it.

COMPANY WITH NO PROBLEMS

Within reason, buyers should try to avoid buying companies with serious problems. Of course, all companies have some problems, but before a new owner can start growing his new acquisition, he should heed the advice of Roy Little, the famous capitalist and owner of Narragansett Capital. Before seeking ways to grow a company, first concentrate on avoiding catastrophe, and second, be sure to keep the ship on a straight course. After those two points have been achieved, then one can focus on ways to grow the company.

PEARLS OF WISDOM

1. A buyer should be talking with at least four or five potential sellers at any one time and actively negotiating with two or three.

2. Write a memorandum to oneself on each meeting. Details about the points discussed in minor or major meetings and matters agreed upon are invaluable in keeping discussions on course.

3. Avoid introducing your attorney into discussions with principals before the elements of the business deal have been agreed upon. As soon as the buyer introduces such an expert into the discussions, the seller does likewise. Since attorneys must protect the technical aspects of their client's positions, more transactions have failed because of premature introduction of such specialists.

4. Don't make ridiculously low offers that will insult the owner.

5. Don't negotiate complex deals.

6. Don't count on assets being always leveraged for a cash flow buyer. I understand sellers look at fixed assets, while buyers concentrate on cash flow.

7. Keep the buying process as fast as possible. The buyer should be able to keep making rapid analyses and decisions that will benefit the momentum.

8. For any given deal, there is a limited window of opportunity. If you spend too much time raising equity after the target company is in play, the window will close.

9. If you're having difficulty raising the necessary equity to complete the transaction, suggest the seller keep the accounts receivable, the real estate, or even the machinery. If you plan to borrow money against machinery and equipment for your acquisition financing, your banker will need to have an official liquidation appraisal on the machinery and equipment. Anticipate this and have the appraisal done early instead of later so the momentum of completing the deal is not lost.

10. Predetermine your acquisition borrowing power so your financing will not come up short at a critical juncture of the transaction. For example, the following percentages are normal borrowing ranges:

Accounts receivable 90 days or less	70 – 85%
Inventory not work in progress	25 – 60%
Machinery and equipment (liquidation)	50 – 80%
Land and buildings (market price)	60 – 80%

11. Remember the rule of one third: after an equity investment of one third of the purchase price, the cash flow must provide the CEO/owner's salary, a return on investment, and enough money to service the debt.

12. Besides profitability, some successful buyers often concentrate on the following ingredients: strong and committed management, steady and predictable business in a non-cyclical industry, substantial market share, and admirable corporate culture.

13. Agree at the outset that the party that is acquiring the business will draft all the documents and the selling party will then review and make comments. Not only does this sequence provide order for the transaction, but it's also to your advantage as the buyer to draft the documents based on your understanding in your own language.

14. When buying a company, target an industry, product, or service that is on the upswing. Conversely, few acquisitions succeed if the industry, product, or services are on the downswing.

15. The announced reason for the sale of companies is rarely the real reason. Investigate, take your time, and listen carefully. If you're getting bad vibes about the deal, get out of the transaction quickly.

16. In order for your attorney to be a deal maker instead of a deal breaker, don't expect him or her to win every point in contention.

17. Sellers are often selling their legacy, so the dynamics of the sale are often more important than the top bid. The preferred buyer, in the eyes of the seller, is not necessarily the highest bidder but rather the one who has the best intentions. Buying a business goes beyond the numbers. Unfortunately many buyers drop the ball in romancing the seller.

18. A buyer's insensitivity to the owner of the selling company can destroy a deal. Be sensitive to the seller's attachment to the company and its employees, customers, and vendors.

19. Most deals take time to complete, usually two to five months after the letter of intent. While you have to exercise some degree of patience, remember that 50 percent of all deals fail to close after reaching the letter-of-intent stage. It's very important to keep the momentum going, and it is imperative you retain experienced counsel in closing deals. Most sellers, somewhere along the line, get cold feet, and so buyers must maintain the seller's interest.

20. Non-negotiable items should be pointed out early in the negotiation, such as asset versus a **stock sale** or that the seller's paper will be subordinate to the bank.

Stock sale: sale of a company with all liabilities and assets.

---

21. For companies without audited statements, make sure you substantiate their financials with their tax returns. You can justify paying less for a company if the statements are not audited because the figures are not verified by the accountant.

22. The older the business, the better established it is and the stronger its customer and supplier relationships.

23. The more industries in which the company sells its product, the more protection it has from the ups and downs of a single industry.

24. The tax objectives of the buyer and seller are at opposite ends of the spectrum in an acquisition. The seller's goal in structuring a buyout is to maximize the after-tax cash in his or her pocket, while the buyer's goal is to maximize the seller's assets that can be depreciated or amortized.

25. The best growth companies of a reasonable size (over $10 million in sales) usually are heavily pursued by numerous private-equity groups that have an overabundance of capital to invest.

26. Buying companies is usually cheaper than trying to grow them from scratch.

27. From a buyer's standpoint, a business is worth less if it is a subchapter S corporation because of the lower book value resulting from the earnings flowing through to the owners. A lower **book value** is also going to reduce the leveragability of the transaction.

Book value: net worth of a company; assets minus liabilities.

---

28. Try to get very close to the seller because there is a strong possibility that his or her advisers are not expert in mergers and acquisitions. Additionally, the potential seller is apt to receive opinionated advice from friends that invariably increases the seller's insecurity about the deal. Meeting along with the seller, even during the final negotiations, will frequently improve the chance of not having a deal derailed by the seller's advisers. If the buyer is not receiving information that was

requested from the seller, it may indicate a cover-up of facts. The buyer should consider other companies instead.

29. A critical issue in buying a business is access to capital.

30. Management: the most important issue you need to consider is whether the owner is the reason for the success of the business. If the owner leaves, can you fill this role?

31. Seller financing is a popular means of structuring the deal and is used in over half of the transactions completed.

32. Be sure that the CEO has the legal authority to sell the business as this authority may rest with the board of directors, a majority stockholder, a bank with a lien on the business, etc.

33. Knowing the strengths of the business is at least as important as understanding its weaknesses. Focus on the company's competitive edge.

34. The art of the business-acquisition process begins with techniques to find a large number of business deals before they come on the market.

35. Many people do themselves a disservice by looking at all deals that might be interesting. Instead, narrowing the search by targeting specific industries, types of businesses, size, and geographic location makes research more efficient and more likely to succeed.

36. It is imperative that you follow up with anyone who gives you a referral. Report back to the person giving the referral, indicating what transpired. Not only is this professional courtesy, but it also will lead to more referrals from the same source.

37. Make generous use of appraisers (i.e., corporate, real estate, equipment, etc.). The appraisals will keep you from overpaying.

38. Price doesn't kill deals—terms do.

39. From a seller's perspective, if the deal falls through, much confidential information has been given to the wrong people. Therefore, the more discrete the buyer is with confidential information, the more confidence the seller will have with the buyer.

40. Act with absolute clarity in all your negotiations so the potential deal breakers surface as early as possible and can be dealt with for as long a period as possible, rather than at the eleventh hour.

41. In negotiations concerning a promissory note, the interest rates and payment schedules are key issues. Interest rates often will track rates of commercial lenders. Parties also should evaluate various amortization options, including interest-only periods and balloon payments in the loan payments, as alternatives to equal installments of principal and interest over a given term.

42. In negotiating, if the seller wants a stock sale instead of an asset sale for tax reasons, the buyer should request a lower selling price. If the seller wants a fully collateralized note from the buyer, then the acquirer should negotiate at a lower interest coupon.

43. The biggest deal breaker is usually the disparity of the price between the buyer and the seller, and the negotiation is usually a colloquy to bridge the difference. To broach this, the buyer could say, "This is the way I see the valuation. What do you see?"

44. As a buyer, ask the seller these three provocative questions:

- How did you grow the company?
- What is the company's competitive advantage?
- If you had a million-dollar windfall in the company's checking account, what would you do with it?

Chapter 23

The Winners' Circle

Let us fast forward to a buyer who has executed on his goal of buying a business and is making strong headway a few years into ownership. Let us assume wealth is being created through increases in sales, new products, and a host of other good news in the company. Many of the fears and perils of rookie ownership have been circumvented, and the company has a bright future.

CREATING WEALTH FROM AN OPERATING BUSINESS

Without the ability to acquire competitors or significantly increase productivity by investing heavily in the business, the opportunity for creating wealth will be a long organic process. It will be one sale at a time, one new product announcement, and a slow process of creating wealth. This is how most new buyers and entrepreneurs make the winners' circle.

However, for those buyers/operators that have a war chest of cash to buy competitors or fund steep growth, they may propel themselves along more quickly. In this day and age, time is truly accelerated in business marketplaces and land grabs, footprints, and other rapid expansion plans trump the "one brick at a time" syndrome. The path to the winners' circle is more often than not led by the bold who stretch and risk huge setbacks.

FIRST TIME ON THE FIELD? HOW ABOUT A SINGLE?

If an individual wants to become a serial entrepreneur and is wedded to fast action and not so much the company, then most likely, he or she will seek an exit and a return to the playing field with another acquisition. For the lucky business owners who can create more wealth by continuing on with their current regime and not having to go through multiple exits, their path is more clearly defined. But for all operators, when do you sell?

This question is first addressed by the operator examining the risk-reward of continued ownership. If the company is steaming ahead and all looks well, then the owner should continue ownership and not consider a premature exit. But, if the owner/operator has scraped together all available money, his or her wealth and well-being are tied directly to the operating business, and trouble is looming ahead, he or she should always consider an exit. Going down with the ship is a noble but unnecessary course of action. Cashing out and doing what is called a "full cycle" really consolidates the entrepreneur as a veteran of business ownership. If the owner can take enough chips off the table and begin to play with house money the next go around, this option should be always considered.

SECOND TIME AT BAT? SWING FOR THE FENCES!

Virtually all business people do better and make sound operating decisions when they do not have dire repercussions for every major move they make. First-time owners often have their primary residence as collateral and have brought in friends and family to make the acquisition. These obligations/liabilities are a huge mental burden and often inhibit sound business decision-making.

Second-time owners can have an advantage in running their business if they often do not have such burdens and can make decisions apart from personal concerns. It has been proven time and again that the operator who steps boldly up and makes aggressive pragmatic decisions, despite fearful consequences, usually wins the day. A successful entrepreneur, who has unencumbered personal assets or has exited successfully on a business, now can step into a new company with a better track record for possible investors, or perhaps even shed all investors. A successful operator coming off a sale of his or her business will garner strong following from many members of the business community ranging from bankers to future partners. There is a world of difference between a rookie and a successful business owner who has run the gauntlet for a successful full cycle.

THE GRAND MASTER

Those who have successfully exited from two separate full cycles we call Grand Masters. Many an operator can acquire a company and stumble into the winners' circle, carried by momentum from blind luck or, better yet, other people's skill sets. But doing it twice erases all doubts of the entrepreneur's capability.

Each business ownership cycle should last a minimum of three years, but more people tend to exit at the five-year mark. The longer stay allows the new owner to take the company through its most perilous time of the first year and then hit high gear implementing a growth strategy. Putting the growth strategy into effect can take up to a year, which means the firm will need three years of operating time to create new wealth. Once this growth program has generated consistent performance, the company will be able to show a trailing EBITDA track record of three years. This leads to developing an exit strategy that could take up to a year. This pattern leads to a five-year program:

- one year of orientation and strategy
- three years' growth
- one year to sell

This is especially relevant when there are investors on board who are looking for an exit. If a seller has three years of year-over-year growth, then it will be difficult for any would-be buyer to cast aspersions on the company's valuation matrix going forward.

The Grand Masters, with their victory on the playfield, can now dictate terms and conditions to many less renowned players in their next undertaking. Many Grand Masters do not want to get in the trenches again and would rather conduct strategies and orchestrate events that are much more fun and intellectually stimulating than the day-to-day grind. Each Grand Master has his or her strengths, be it sales and marketing, operations, or finance, and can play to his or her strength and have others as the workhorse. Most important, Grand Masters do not have to sign personally with the bank to guarantee the loan.

TAKING CARE OF YOUR TEAM

A fascinating saga often unfolds that tests the moral fiber of many sellers. They wonder, "How do I reward my long-toiling, loyal employees?" Must owners have a cadre of important managers or key employees that they have become dependent upon over the years and have made pledges and promises that when the company is sold, "you will be taken care of." This is the proverbial kiss of death, as most sellers develop amnesia for these long-suffering workers when they cash out. The new owner often inherits angry and wounded employees, stung by being passed over for a piece of the financial rewards that the seller has reaped. The new owner now has to deal with these sullen individuals who have learned that verbal promises bear little weight in a change of ownership.

But what if the seller or a new owner wants to take care of these key employees? Several options are available.

- The seller can pay an employee one to two weeks' salary for every year employed.

- The seller can pay a cash bonus equal to 25 to 50 percent of the last year of the employee's salary.

- The seller can give stock from his or her rollover equity in the new company as incentive for employees to work hard and cash them both out.

- The seller can pursue the new ownership to give key employees stock in the new company during the course of negotiations.

- The new owner can set aside a block of stock, up to 15 percent, for key employees to earn over three to five years.

- The new owner can designate a certain amount of the profits as profit sharing for the retained key employees.

- The new ownership can set individual goals and bonuses for key employees.

Chapter 24

What's It Like to Be Rich?

W E ALL REALIZE THAT BEING RICH is a relative term. When you have nothing, rich can mean having enough money for food. To those higher on the economic scale, being rich can mean leaving a sizable cash legacy for the next generation. In our business of representing buyers and sellers, we like to have clients think hard about what their magic number is after the net-net. Combining this with other personal net worth holdings leads to a total net worth. Without this exercise, some high rollers find it hard to reconcile the lifestyle they have come to expect and the reality of what their business will bring them in a sale. This case study shows that bad planning can also lead to a lavish lifestyle that can turn into a trap.

— CASE STUDY —

We recently had high-living clients in Florida who owned a chain of retail outlets. They had a $4M mortgage, boats in the water, a multitude of luxury cars, and a high vacation budget. Their yearly expenses were approximately $700,000. The stores kicked off about $700,000 in net income, so they were about breakeven. But the business was worth only

> 3.5X EBITDA, so the clients' value on the business was $2.5M. After closing expenses and paying off the business loan and the taxman, the net-net would be about $1.5M, or enough to pay for only two-plus years of living. The clients have found themselves on a treadmill they can't get off unless they cut their debt and drastically reduce their *Miami Vice* lifestyle. We don't think this story will have a happy ending.

With this net-worth goal in mind, a buyer, seller, or business operator can back into numbers that would achieve their goals. In our industry, we always banter about what would we consider the minimum threshold of being rich or well off. That number used to be $3M, but now has climbed to $5M. This number is obviously higher in areas with a high cost of living and pricey real estate. In our informal arena, we say that one would need $3M liquid cash as a bottom line plus an equal amount in real estate to make it in the winners' circle.

We often ask our clients to do a personal budget and balance sheet so they can see what their monthly expenses are. This can impact the payout on a sale as the seller may ask for a higher price to be able to live comfortably post-sale. Most new small-business owners rarely take a salary for the first six months as they figure out the new landscape. If buyers are putting in all their cash and have no cash reserves on the home front to carry the family unit for a year, they should take serious pause about proceeding to a close. Running out of cash and scrambling on the home front is not where anyone wants to tread. We also suggest this budget be shared with the buyer's significant other so everyone knows what he or she is getting in for. The stories are legion of some unsuspecting spouse seeing a for-sale sign being planted in the yard or a repo man dragging away the company car.

MOVING BEYOND ENTREPRENEURSHIP

On the good side, if one is free of earthly concerns, the opportunities are endless for an individual or a couple to become active players in their "field of dreams." Successful entrepreneurs do not have to roll the dice again and try to double down for further success—although most successful business owners that have sold their business have to restrain themselves for throwing themselves back into the game. Successful people are programmed to keep on succeeding. Rounding out one's life by pursuing a good cause and foregoing another roll of the dice can be a meaningful end in the autumn of life.

Successful sellers are great players in their area of expertise but can be a bit timid outside their domain. The blocking and tackling and clear decision-making that made them wealthy can be applied to the field of dreams. These new financially independent folks do not have to plow huge amounts of money into their chosen personal-interest endeavor. They can drop a certain amount of money (say $50,000–$100,000) in a non-profit and take a leadership role in raising cash for it and going forward. Most non-profits or socially responsible organizations lack hard-charging, clear-thinking business leaders and welcome the mental horsepower as much as the cash invested. These organizations want to trade off of successful people's networks and continually expand through introductions. Spreading the excess cash from a sale into noble pursuits can be very rewarding and stress free.

Thought leader: an individual who creates new products or strategies for a business.

To make the metamorphosis from a hard-driving and successful business owner operating in a narrow industry vertical to a public figure speaking about and representing a non-profit takes a new set of skills. Migrating away from hands-on control to becoming a **thought leader** is a process that has to be worked on daily but, once achieved, opens many new doors.

Chapter 25

Promoting the New You!
By Marsha Friedman

Marsha Friedman is the CEO of EMSI Public Relations (www.EMSIncorporated.com), a national firm that provides PR strategy and publicity services to businesses, professional firms, entertainers, and authors. She is a renowned expert on assisting people to magnify their message in all forums ranging from personal branding to corporate public relationships using all modems of communication as a business owner. Marsha is the author of Celebritizing Yourself *and can be heard weekly on her Blog Talk Radio Show, "EMSI's PR Insider," every Thursday at 3 p.m. EST. Follow her twitter at @MarshaFriedman. Marsha can be reached at mfriedman@EMSIpublicRelations.com.*

"CELEBRITIZE" YOURSELF TO GAIN VISIBILITY
AND CREDIBILITY FOR YOUR BUSINESS

Entrepreneurs, other business leaders, and their companies can benefit tremendously from seeking publicity as an expert in their field or industry. Becoming a media go-to source for information relevant to your field not only helps market your business; it also builds the brand—for both the business and the entrepreneur. It provides visibility, credibility, and positioning as a trusted authority in the public eye. It can also help down the road when it's time to sell your business.

Launching a public relations campaign is an affordable, effective means of promotion. Unlike advertising, there isn't a price for publicity, also called earned media. You don't have to pay journalists, talk-show hosts, and social media followers to help spread your message—you just have to get them interested in it.

And how do you do that?

By "celebritizing" yourself!

That's my term for branding yourself as an expert. It's how you make yourself a source of information for the media by providing journalists, show hosts, and social media users with information and insights they find useful. In return, they may invite you on their show or quote you in an article, providing you with a mass-media audience.

Think creatively about the various facets of expertise you possess. Obviously, you know a lot about the product or service you provide, but there are probably a number of related topics you can address as well. Does your business deliver top-notch customer service? That's a challenge for many companies whose owners and managers might welcome the practical advice you can provide.

Is your product green or sustainable? Is it affected by politics or the economy? Does it have ramifications for a particular industry, group of people, or geographic area?

These are all ideas to consider as you look for ways to plug yourself into newsworthy topics and national conversations and gain media exposure. You don't have to be a Hollywood star, a university professor, or an elected official to get the media interested in you; regular people do it every single day. However—and this is critically important—you do have to provide valuable, engaging content. A sales pitch does not qualify! When you give a radio, TV, or print interview or post on social media, you will not engage audiences by saying, "Here's why my business is fabulous and why you should buy our products!"

By providing content that helps people solve their problems, you'll gain exposure in a more subtle and valuable way, as "Joe, the guy who owns Tools R Us, the company with all those cool whatchamacallits."

Here's a step-by-step guide to start celebritizing yourself, including identifying your audience, crafting your message, and pitching yourself to the media.

WHO IS YOUR AUDIENCE AND WHAT IS YOUR MESSAGE?

First thing's first: You have to identify your audience(s) because that will influence everything, from the message you convey to how you choose to publicize it.

Does your audience include older adults? The bulk of people reading newspapers, online or in print, are aged 45 and older. Are they men? Slightly more men than women listen to talk radio. Women? More women than men are watching TV talk shows. Are they using social media? Facebook, Google+, and Twitter are the largest social networks.

As you consider your audience, think about who these people are and what types of problems they have. What mother with young children isn't looking for ways to save time? Retirees may be frustrated by the learning curve involved with using new technology. These insights can help shape your communications. People want to solve their problems!

Now it's time to work on crafting your message. To do that, first identify:

1. **Your expertise.** What are your business's specialties, and what relevant knowledge do you have that can help others, whether it's consumers or other businesses? A company that develops apps for organization and efficiency might have a CEO who can share insights on new technology or tips for personal organization.

2. **Your passion.** What is it that got you this far? What made you want to spend the time and effort to acquire your business? Maybe you want to help people with their finances. Or to contribute to making our planet cleaner. Or you're a fitness buff, and your tool will inspire more people to get off the couch. Identify what it is that makes you passionate about the product or service you provide because that's what you'll love talking about. Your enthusiasm will not only be contagious; it will also energize you and fuel your drive to get your message out.

3. **What others need from you.** What solutions or insights are people looking for, and what do you have in your arsenal of information to meet their needs?

Combine the answers to these questions—your expertise, your passion, and the information that your audience needs—into your message. For example, the message for my company, EMSI Public Relations, is: "At EMSI, we create visibility and credibility for our clients using a pay-for-performance model that guarantees media exposure and sets us apart from our peers."

GETTING PUBLICITY

By definition, publicity is not advertising; it's coverage by the media of people, events, and issues deemed to be of interest to their audiences. Getting publicity by celebritizing yourself is just one prong of your business's overall marketing plan.

What does publicity do for you? I'll share a story. A colleague of mine who's a former newspaper reporter knew a savvy attorney. He'd tip her off whenever he had a particularly juicy case *if* she promised to include his name alongside that of his client in her story. He'd figured out that having his name in the paper bought him something no amount of advertising could: credibility. Whether he won the case or lost it, people remembered his name.

The endorsement of traditional media, even if it's simply mentioning your name, is marketing gold. And thanks to the Internet, the value of that gold is through the roof. Potential customers have more choices than ever before. They also have more scammers and con artists to worry about. What makes one business more trustworthy and appealing than another? The endorsement of its CEO by TV and radio shows, newspapers and magazines—and now, bloggers, news websites, and followers on social media.

When the media recognizes that you have something important to say, you gain credibility. When you have hundreds or thousands of people following you on Twitter, Facebook, or LinkedIn, you have a stamp of approval from the general public. Both forms of recognition give others confidence that you—and your business—are as good as you say you are.

But the return on investment usually isn't immediate, which can be frustrating to people who expect a surge in website visitors or sales with every media interview. That used to happen more often in the old days—way back in the '90s—when a radio talk-show host might chatter with you for thirty minutes, and newspapers had twice as many pages to fill. Sometimes, when the timing of an interview aligned perfectly with an urgent public problem, the person's expertise, and solution-oriented content, the businessperson could hit the jackpot.

More often today, marketing through media exposure is a strategy that pays off over time—with effort from you. How do you grow your investment?

- **Display your endorsements prominently on your website.** "As seen on CBS," "Featured in the *Louisville Gazette*," "Heard on WTUT radio." Don't forget to mention your 12,000 Twitter followers and all those Facebook fans, too.

- **Attract visitors to your site by continually posting new, useful, and entertaining content, perhaps via a blog.** Keep building contacts and allowing people to get to know you by interacting on Twitter, LinkedIn, and other social networking sites, and look for more opportunities to be an expert source for TV, radio, and print.

PITCHING THE MEDIA

If you can get a journalist or talk-show host interested in your story idea, you might be interviewed for an article, asked to write an exclusive article, or invited to be interviewed as a guest on a radio or TV show.

A media pitch is your written communication to editors, reporters, bloggers, and TV and radio producers and talk-show hosts telling them what you have to offer their audiences. It can include a short news story describing the problem and some helpful information that readers can apply to it that doesn't involve buying your service or product. Once again—*this is not a sales piece!* Avoid adjectives that make your pitch sound like a product review: "fabulous time-saver every working person needs!"

Instead, remember your message. What's your expertise? Your passion? What information do people need that you can provide? Be objective, factual, and concise.

You'll have much more success with this if you pay attention to timing and/or the news.

- **Timing.** What are the seasons, holidays, national anniversaries, or events, such as elections, that might be relevant to your business or expertise? The media will be looking for fresh new ways to tell these recurring stories, and you might just hold the ticket!

- **News.** The mass media, including trade publications, are focused on issues and events in the news today, so you're much more likely to get publicity if you can speak to something going on now. That's not as difficult as it sounds, but it does require creative thinking. If your company sells door locks, a spate of home burglaries in the news would be a good time to suggest an article or talk-show segment about the safest types of doors, locks, and other home-security measures. A device that helps parents anticipating the birth of a child might make you the perfect person to talk to about tricks for easing labor pains when the next celebrity's pregnancy makes the headlines.

When you send your pitch, be sure your contact information is clearly visible and accurate. Don't weave it into your pitch, and don't rely on your recipient hitting the email reply button. Include a telephone number that you can answer at any time, or one for daytime and another for evenings and weekends. You may get just one call from the editor or producer interested in your pitch, and if you don't answer, he or she may very well lose interest.

Make sure your email is free of typos, grammatical errors, and other mistakes that make you appear less than authoritative.

REMEMBER—PUBLIC RELATIONS IS ABOUT *RELATIONSHIPS*

PR is not sales. It's about developing the relationships and gaining the visibility that brings you prospective customers and helps keep existing customers coming back. It requires all the creativity, persistence, and focus you put into acquiring and running your business.

But it doesn't have to be drudgery. Becoming a media celebrity is a lot of fun. It's gratifying to help people solve their problems, it feels good to be recognized as an authority, and the relationships you develop can be deep and meaningful.

To be successful, remember the critical elements.

1. **Know your audience.** Think about all who have a stake in your business, identify their problems, and tell them how you can solve them. That way, you'll reach your target audience.

2. **Give the media what they want!** Be creative about tying into seasons, news, and anything timely and topical. The media are hungry for fresh angles, sources, and great information. If you move quickly, you can be the person who provides that.

3. **Share your publicity on your website.** Links to radio and TV interviews and mentions in print publications give you credibility. The implied third-party endorsement of those journalists and talk-show hosts is marketing gold! They make you stand apart from the competition

and tell visitors, "This is someone the media go to for information. If they think this person is good, well …"

Staying in front of your audience means that getting publicity is not "one and done"—one great story in a magazine or on TV isn't enough. It needs to be a sustained effort.

You'll enjoy the benefits as you're growing your business, and you'll continue to reap them when and if the time comes to sell it. The credibility and familiarity you generate through the celebritize method will make your company that much more appealing to prospective buyers.

Chapter 26

The Mad Scientist Syndrome

WE HAVE ALL HEARD about these madmen and kinetic women, vibrating with excitement over their breakthrough technologies or inventions. We all marvel at the creator of the next app and the ease that millions are rained down upon these wunderkind. The stories are legion of the toiling worker who suddenly lays the golden egg and is propelled to wealth and stardom. This is the fool's gold that keeps us all driving forward and alert for that one-in-a-million opportunity. Those of us that are not the inventor or the creative force but rather the sound-thinking strategist to bring this opportunity to realization have to team up with these thought leaders. The mad scientist is most always devoid of business sense, and we business people are devoid of creative genius, so a matching set we are!

Where do the two worlds collide? Like worker ants massing around the egg-laying, inert body of the queen, our society covets the brain power of our most productive entrepreneurs. But these people are also vulnerable to the predators and usurpers of the business world. The ideas and prodigiously developed products of these creative ones must be brought to market through existing channels. Between the drawing board and the cash register are thousands of days of peril and roads fraught with danger. These madcap days have many dangerous fronts, from internal expectations to the realities of the mercantile system.

Managing expectations is the key to success.

THE MAD SCIENTIST

Hyperkinetic, mad scientists resonate with energy and capability. They have a distain for traditional business and believe they have fostered a paradigm shift in their niche. This often can be true, but these dreams and assertions often die on the infertile plains of reality. We mere mortals are not ones to judge the true application of their new breakthrough technology, but rather, we must become the implementer of their dreams. It is the goal of the scientists' handlers not to bog these creative individuals down with routine blocking and tackling of business but to free their time to allow them to continue on their visionary path.

Yet, the scientists or inventors must understand they cannot take their new product or service to market; they must rely upon tried and true industry professionals. The creative ones must understand their limitations and overcome them to reach success.

- Time is flowing by, and there is someone somewhere working along the same lines, so speed to market is essential to success.

- The inventor must trust someone quickly with the right connections that can move the product into the mainstream. Suspicion of all comers is healthy only to a point for it can stall out the process.

- Scientists cannot be rude or impatient with those supporting them and their venture. Today's workers or partners can quickly become tomorrow's competitors as they learn more about the inventor's product set.

- Fostering loyalty through distribution of stock is a must. This should be done in the time-honored fashion that gives significant shares for certain benchmarks of services rendered by key team members. These benchmarks can be for achieving goals or time served.

- To receive funding, a proper team must be ready to be deployed with their duties as well as compensation spelled out.

- A timeline must be adhered to by all parties to get the product to market by the deadline. A cash-flow model must be tied to the timeline to ensure that investors and workers alike understand the torturous path ahead.

- The raising of funding must supersede all other efforts, for without operating income, the machine will grind to a halt.

- This cash focus now means enacting the full business plan and bringing key personnel on board.

- Placing a realistic valuation on the company at certain checkpoints is a must. Untold entrepreneurs have seen their potentially explosive product go to the dustbin over inflated dreams and spooky spreadsheets.

If the mad scientist does not heed time-tested protocol of the business world, those in the know will begin to spread the news of a troubled operation that needs to be jump-started. The vultures will soon follow, and the inventor will find himself or herself confronted with deeply disturbing options.

— CASE STUDY —

Several years back with the advent of telemedicine, a brilliant inventor of new technology of Indian extraction was on the precipice of a true market breakthrough. Kishor, the inventor with his clipped English accent and mile-long list of academic and technological credentials, clearly had the brain wattage and know-how to develop cutting-edge technology. He had all the classic synergies lined up of the inexpensive back-end offshore engineering department in Delhi to a veritable who's who of Harvard and MIT brainpower surrounding him. We met several times, and I was caught up in this first-to-market twist on telemedicine. I immediately began the Chinese fire drill of calling on potential strategic partners and possible team members to quickly join up.

But the warning signs of a long painful death were there from the beginning. Kishor agonized over his spreadsheet showing huge growth and valuation and cagily hedged on dribbling out stock option offers to key management figures while hoarding his Golden Fleece. There was a buzz created around his company by my efforts and like-minded handlers who could see the value. But Kishor's presentations were too long and technical; he hogged the ball and droned on endlessly missing the cues from his audience and not communicating clearly. The shame of it all was he was in the forefront of his industry but there was only smoke and no fire. He was cash strapped and miserly, and soon his team began to dissipate. The first-class team he had assembled began to grumble as he continued to pitch off-mark. He had his moment in time (actually six months) and blew it. If he had listened correctly and set aside his own idiosyncrasies, he would have had his day in the sun (far more than six months). Instead, he relentlessly carried on, spending himself into poverty, and his team drifted away. He is an honorable man whose inflexibility and steadfast desire to hoard all his chips led to a painful death of his dreams.

THE MAD SCIENTIST'S BUSINESS PARTNER

For those of us who are not a creative genius or visionary, we must realize our limitations and stay to our strengths. We must recognize greatness in others and understand their flaws as well. For greatness always seems to cohabit with deep defects. When industry professionals hear about this new invention or set of products or breakthrough methodology, they quickly migrate to the inventor behind it. Then we all must be able immediately to grasp the breathtaking opportunity of the mad scientist. At these initial meetings, we must pour gasoline on the fire and fan the flames of far-reaching potential. But at the same time, we must send cautionary signals of impending trouble to the inventor if he or she keeps on a helter-skelter path. For all of the brainpower and wattage, mad scientists too often show no business discipline and ignore the realities of the marketplace.

The questions that you need to ask yourself before you hook your wagon to inventors or new technology lists are the following.

- Are they a honorable people, ones to keep their word?
- Are they ruthless enough to succeed?
- What drives them? Money? Fame?
- Have you checked other industry players for the validity of the offering?
- Are they control freaks? Are they controlling in areas out of their expertise?
- Are they willing to hand over the reins at some future date?
- Have you done a thorough background check? Academic and business?
- Are they reasonable about their current worth? What is their financial condition?
- Are they reasonable about the invention's or new technology's future worth?
- Who has been guiding them to date?
- Can you team up, or will you just be replaced someday soon?
- Will they listen to advice?
- Can you really contribute to this endeavor?
- Is it out of your strike zone?
- Do you have the fortitude to learn a new world and not get paid until funding arrives?

STRUCTURING RELATIONSHIPS BETWEEN CREATIVITY AND BUSINESS

The business partner must show his or her worth in a series of meetings. If the endeavor is steaming along frantically, then the business executive must take the initiative to outline his or her understanding of the company and proposed role to the inventor.

Do their thinking for them!

Inventors, the thought leaders, will not have the time or the clarity to understand or assess you properly. They are besieged with multiple problems at all times. You are there to bring clarity and not to become another riddle to be solved. The business partner is there to unload problems from the shoulders of the thought leaders and constantly take on more roles and burdens. Business partners must demonstrate their ability to see an issue and then solve it. They must not pose the problem without a series of solutions for the distracted thought leader to choose from. Business partners should be bold and make recommendations and stay away from becoming a yes-man for the inventor. Use the following guidelines in working—or thinking of working—with inventors:

- Work in the beginning without a deal or getting paid.
- Make yourself as irreplaceable as possible.
- Once a clear picture of company value is understood, cut your financial deal with the inventor.
- Be committed for long irregular hours with no traditional sanctuaries.
- Be careful in committing all your time to a risky undertaking.
- Build your own spreadsheets and understand when you should get paid.
- Welcome change and new team members.
- Be ready to get canned at all times!
- Understand these opportunities are not usually long-term employment.

When a mad scientist is cutting a deal with a business partner, the two sides often have a tremendous gap in valuation on the company. Creative ways can be found to eliminate this difference.

— CASE STUDY —

In a recent negotiation between a technology founder and an experienced business manager, the two faced a wide bridge in valuation. The founder thought he was generous in offering 5 percent of the company to the manager over a five-year period. The founder believed the company would be worth $100M in five years, although its current condition of $1M in sales and understaffed team would lead most to deeply question this valuation. Such an enormous gap in technology companies' perceived value between visionary ownership and hired hands can almost become ludicrous and calls for creatively negotiating without insulting the owner.

A simple solution was reached that can be applied in most other cases as well. The manager agreed to take a sliding scale of ownership, based on the value of the business:

$1M–$10M of enterprise value:	10%
$10M–$20M of enterprise value:	5%
Over $20M of enterprise value:	2.5%

In this case, the pragmatic manager gets a big payout for the company on a conservative growth projection (up to $10M) while the founder keeps the majority of the payout on his home-run scenario. Only time will tell, but the safe assumption is that the wily manager will cash out very nicely if the company is even moderately successful while the founder will be left fuming having to stroke such a check.

Chapter 27

Crash and Burns

A S WE HAVE DISCUSSED, the statistics are daunting for an individual to seek, locate, buy, grow, and eventually resell a business. The trials and threats along this torturous path can come from a multitude of sources. However, during this full life cycle of a business, entrepreneurs can greatly stack the odds in their favor by preparing themselves for the worst-case scenarios. But what if the company takes a torpedo in the engine room or ownership simply runs out of gas? As the skipper on the bridge, ownership must be aware and prepared for troubled waters and should try not to go down with the ship!

The major issues from my standpoint that confront ownership and lead to dire straits or loss of enterprise value at the wrong time are flushed out below.

SELLING TOO EARLY

Many owners simply sell their business before the most advantageous time. The most difficult part of buying a business is the vision to pick a winner and then get it through year one. Once the company has its footings and is gathering momentum by deploying the new ownership's growth strategy, the heavy lifting and anxiety of stumbling out of the chute has passed. But oftentimes, exhausted ownership suffers a malaise and has been spooked by the difficult journey to date. These owners can suffer from a case of the nerves, perhaps understanding they are not made out for the stress or the industry. Or they simply may want to pull the ripcord for a nice return for their short time as owner. For whatever reason, if they have decided to exit, they should pause to rethink. This is the time for a good set of advisors to step in and counsel wisely that the firm should gather momentum and begin to create real value for an exit. These advisors should frame everything in a finite time where ownership knows they will get their pre-ownership life back. If ownership has lost their will to continue, they should be urged on by their handlers and key employees to carry on as long as possible. The years three through five are when over 65 percent of the EBITDA is created, and it is not a good plan to leave this wealth on the table for the next lucky buyer. A spooked seller is a buyer's dream!

SELLING TOO LATE

Selling too late is oftentimes much worse than selling too soon. Besides the additional wear and tear of years gone in leading the company, ownership that miscalculates its timing to sell can be doomed for an awkward slide into a trough of depression. New technologies, as well as new methodologies, even in the most staid business sectors, can lead to a company's being eclipsed without owners even knowing it.

Business owners must have an extensive network at all levels of their industry so they can be aware of and understand the threats to their business. When these threats are identified, action must be taken to correct the company's position in the industry, or the firm should be sold in a rapid sales campaign. These quick sales driven by market conditions must mask the true intent of why the seller is moving on.

Most times, forecasting drastic changes in a business or industry sector without solid evidence are false alarms and a gamble by the potential seller as a reader of the future. This can leave the seller selling too early. An example of acting upon shaky predictions would be a business owner believing that a new technology will come out in three years and make his business obsolete. After he rushes into a sale, he later sees that this threat was only a mirage, and he should have held firm to guide the business through the daily challenges. On the other side of the buyer-seller equation, a buyer should seek out such a seller who can be spooked into a sale.

Selling too late can lead to a long terminal slide for the company. Ownership must be ready to step in and take immediate action if they realize they have held on too long. Once the company's management realizes crippling changes are at hand, the value of the business has plummeted. The sale cycle alone can take six to twelve months, and by then, any issues bubbling on the horizon have risen for all to see. Having early warning signals for impending threats known and unknown can be the key to salvaging the enterprise value of a firm in a sale. Being able to quickly deploy and get underway a sales process for the right reasons to outsiders can be a key ingredient in timing. Having the executive summary brushed off and ready to go, the right broker lined up, as well as possible buyers, can cut months off the process. Selling too late often means a reduction in value, but still, an overall intact exit for the company is better than a crash and burn.

TERMINAL IMPACT

Watching a company crash and burn is like watching a slow-moving train wreck. For the informed advisors or even management inside the company, the impending crash can be seen from a long distance away. Owners often refuse to believe the end is at hand, and they plow on making the crash even more devastating. It always seems as if owners take drastic action only after the crises is full blown. They have the most intimate knowledge of the company and the world in which it operates and would be expected to understand and interpret what is happening to their doomed company, yet they refuse to recognize the signs. They often scoff and believe they once again can keep the company solvent.

As a company begins to dissemble, the ownership seems always to be operating on outdated financial news. During normal operating conditions, a company can be run on examining prior month's financials with a fifteen-to-thirty-day lag time in updating these key monthly reports. This data lag time has been a tradition and necessity over the years for many owners. However, with today's new accounting systems and Internet connectivity, a company can be run on instantaneous financials and reports updated daily when needed.

During a terminal slide, money is needed to pay for the essential heartbeat of the company—payroll, fuel, etc. The owner must have a systematic shutdown program with enough cash in reserve to pay for vital shutdown procedures.

As terminal impact looms closer, the owner must be aware of the issues that will change this situation from a financial wreck to a potential personal criminal offense. The major issues to be watched are:

- **Employee Salaries.** The owner is always responsible through the company and *personally* to pay the salaries of the employees as long as they work. Even if the employees in some fashion agree to go along and keep the ship afloat, the onus for the payment of these salaries and related benefits can be charged against the owner personally as a federal offence. If a company has fifty employees with an average salary of $40,000 per annum, one week's wages can amount to more than $38,000. Many companies in dire straits are waiting for a bail out or even a bottom-feeder buyer to save them. Ownership is often desperate to keep the company afloat as are the employees, but the risk can be severe and catastrophic. At this stage, the white knight rarely appears.

- **Lawyers and Accountants.** The end game always has the lawyers in play. It is crucial to have the right ones and have money to pay them. As the company grinds to a halt, it will be the lawyers that bail out ownership. Fees for the accountants also must be set aside, as they perform vital forensic functions that will arm the lawyers to mount a plausible defense against all creditors.

- **Key Employees.** Ownership must have a roster of key employees that can assist with the shutdown or whatever functions the company requires as the firm is disassembled. There should be a set aside as well as "combat pay" for these folks who will be working amidst the ruin of the company.

CUTTING BAIT

As a company is declared terminal and has no salvage value beyond hard goods or its lease, owners must be willing to cut bait and have an orderly closing to avoid many of the issues as outlined above. Owners need to have set cash aside and now access it to cover key expenses, including, as mentioned before, employee salaries. Then owners must make a general announcement to all concerned that the firm is ceasing activity. This announcement will bring angst and emotions down upon the owners, but they must be prepared to weather this storm and follow the right procedures.

YOU CAN'T JUST WALK AWAY

The aftermath of a failed business goes on and on. One cannot just throw the keys at the place and expect it to wind down by itself, even through a Chapter 7 shutdown. It usually takes a minimum of ninety days for a business to be shut down. For the distraught owners, their trial by fire can continue for up to a year—or longer as the following story shows. Only the lawyers win!

— CASE STUDY —

Briggs orchestrated a merger between two $25M companies and believed that 1+1=3. Everyone in the industry saw this merger as an excellent move for both firms to consolidate a leading position in the sector. Textbook synergies could be seen—closing a 50,000-square-foot location, combining and reducing sales and marketing personnel, keeping only the best employees, cross selling with more product lines going into each company's respective marketplace, and more. The list of positive moves was endless. However this $50M company filed for bankruptcy a year after the merger. Lawsuits have blanketed all participants, and five years later, this quagmire is staggering through the court system to the glee of the participating lawyers and the chagrin of everyone else. In retrospect, it is still difficult to believe these companies failed in this no-brainer merger, but the aftermath continues.

MANAGING YOUR FAMILY'S EXPECTATIONS

Business owners usually have an elevated standard of living. Their spouses and offspring have developed a pride in the family business that becomes part of their personal identification with their community as well. This life of privilege can be destroyed quickly and with disastrous financial consequences for the family unit. Many owners have blocked news of this impending disaster from loved ones, and its ruinous appearance can be devastating. Owners should tell those around them of the situation as it becomes apparent what is in store for the failing company. Both owners and family will need support and sometimes counseling for what is coming their way.

PERSONAL ASSET PROTECTION

When buyers of a company set forth on an acquisition hunt, they must begin the process of protecting their personal assets from creditors if the company they acquire dissolves. Even though this scenario may not unfold, it must be prepared for from the very beginning.

Becoming judgment proof up front as much as possible is a prudent plan. When people go to buy a company or take on debt from other regulated or personal lenders, they usually must supply these future creditors with their personal balance sheet that outlines their personal assets. Not to include assets is a breach with the banks. Borrowers can exclude only certain assets with the lender's prior written acceptance of these exclusions. Thus, what buyers put on this balance sheet is what they risk if their company defaults. Any new assets gained by a personal note signer, however, are also fair game for note holders, whether the assets are disclosed on a personal financial statement or not.

If potential buyers want to protect assets, such as their home and savings accounts, they must protect them up front. Many cagey note signers transfer the full value of their house or major holdings to their spouse. This, of course, puts the spouse in full control of those assets, but the individual signing on the loan can, through a court process (e.g., divorce) hopefully, get back 50 percent of the assets. Signing over assets to non-spouses starts a future borrower down a risky path.

If the future borrower signs (hides) too many assets away and shows too little in collateral, then he or she will have difficulty securing a loan. It is a tightrope that must be walked by all parties concerned. Most of us recall when O. J. Simpson was on trial. The family of the deceased was suing him for his assets, but he declared himself bankrupt. He has a large NFL 401(k) and Keogh retirement account that are untouchable by any creditors. This rule applies to all of us (outside of divorce)—these retirement accounts are untouchable. If a bank or lender understands a borrower's balance sheet is light but the spouse is loaded, the bank will oftentimes give a loan it would not usually do as it knows the tricks of the trade (hiding and switching out assets) and realizes the spouse will most likely bail out the borrower in case of default.

Once the personal financial statement has been submitted to a lender/bank and a loan has been made based upon that balance sheet, the borrower can't remove large sums from the balance sheet without informing the lender. But many borrowers do slowly bleed personal assets off their personal financial statement as the company performs better and banks can turn a blind eye to enforcement. As an example, a borrower for estate planning purposes could move a summer home into a spouse's name that would remove it as a guaranteed asset over time.

When asked for the rule of thumb in obtaining personal guarantees, a former senior vice president of U.S. Trust in Boston responded: "The rule of thumb is always get them."

Naturally, the banker's objective is different from the borrower's. Russell Robb, author of *Buying Your Own Business*, set forth the following thoughts and guidelines on how to negotiate with a bank on personal guarantees.

1. If the company has a strong financial position or personal reputation, shop around for a bank that will not require a personal guarantee. While this may be unlikely at the outset, the borrower may at a later date reduce the borrowing base from 75 percent on receivables to 50 percent.

2. Establish at the outset that a personal guarantee will be a pivotal issue. If you sign a loan agreement with a guarantee, it will be your objective eventually to release you from that obligation.

3. Sign the personal guarantee but place restrictions on the extent and limits to which the bank can collect from the personal guarantor, such as $200,000. One does not want to sign a joint or several guarantees, which allow the bank to collect the bank note simultaneously from the business and the individual signer. An indemnification guarantee restricts the bank from suing individual guarantors of the business when it fails to pay its obligations.

4. Arrange a scenario that will trigger when the guarantee will go into effect. Personal guarantees will go into effect if you are late on more than three consecutive loan payments when working capital falls below a specified amount.

5. Alter the loan provision, make sure the grace period is extended, for example, from a week to fifteen days.

6. Shares of personal guarantee liability reflect the percentage ownership of the major stockholders. For instance, the 20-percent owner of the company would be responsible for 20 percent of the guarantee liability.

7. Write an agreement stating that the bank will let you off the personal guarantee when the note is 70 percent paid off. The bank will use certain benchmarks that must be obtained, based on either the income statement or the balance sheet.

Chapter 28

A Lawyer's Perspective
By Dan Murphy

Attorney Dan Murphy has practiced business law domestically and abroad for over thirty years. He specializes in small business mergers and acquisitions, as well as business litigation. Dan started his legal career working for a large firm but now manages his own firm, the Murphy Law Group. He is adept with start-ups, and his expertise covers the full spectrum of legal services. Dan has always received the highest peer reviews by Hubbel Peer Review. Dan can be reached at djm@mlgllc.com

WHEN AND HOW DO I INVOLVE AN ATTORNEY?

Before consummating terms of a transaction, it is important to identify and retain a lawyer that you have confidence in and intend to use to close the transaction. Preferably, this occurs before signing a letter of intent. It is important for your attorney to discuss with you the various aspects of a purchase and sale agreement ("purchase agreement") from either the buyer's perspective or the seller's perspective. While this article touches upon transactions from both perspectives, its focus is from the buyer's perspective.

CHOOSE THE RIGHT LAWYER

First, choose the right lawyer. Ask friends and colleagues for referrals. Use the Internet to check lawyer websites. Check to see if and how they are rated. The most reliable rating system is provided by Martindale-Hubbell. The Martindale-Hubbell Peer Review Ratings help buyers of legal services identify, evaluate, and select the most appropriate lawyer for a specific job.

The Martindale-Hubbell Peer Review Ratings are an objective indicator of a lawyer's high ethical standards and professional ability, generated from evaluations by other members of the bar and the judiciary in the United States and Canada. The first review to establish a lawyer's rating usually occurs three years after his or her admission to the bar. The Martindale-Hubbell Peer Review Ratings reflect a combination of achieving a very high rating of a general ethical standards and the legal ability numerical rating. A threshold number of responses is required to achieve a rating. The general ethical standard rating denotes adherence to professional standards of conduct and ethics, reliability, diligence, and other criteria relevant to the discharge of professional responsibilities. Those lawyers who meet "very high" criteria of the general ethical standards can proceed to the next step in the ratings process—legal ability. Legal ability ratings are based by performance in five key areas, rated on a scale of one to five (with one being the lowest and five being highest). These areas are:

- **Legal Knowledge:** lawyer's familiarity with the laws governing his or her specific area of practice

- **Analytical Capabilities:** lawyer's creativity in analyzing legal issues and applying technical knowledge

- **Judgment:** lawyer's demonstration of salient factors that drive the outcome of a given case or issue

- **Communication Ability:** lawyer's capability to communicate persuasively and credibly

- **Legal Experience:** lawyer's degree of experience in his or her specific areas of practice

The numeric ratings range may coincide with the appropriate certification mark:

- **AV Preeminent (4.5 – 5.0)** is a significant rating accomplishment, a testament to the fact that the lawyer's peers rank him and her at the highest level of professional excellence.

- **BV Distinguished (3.0 – 4.4)** is an excellent rating for a lawyer with some experience. A widely respected mark of achievement, it differentiates a lawyer from his or her competition.

- **Rated (1.0 – 2.9)** demonstrates that the lawyer has met the very high criteria of general ethical standing.

Meet with prospective lawyers before committing to their services. It is important to know your lawyer and for your lawyer to know you. Communication is the key component of any attorney-client relationship. In order for your lawyer to protect you and to deliver maximum results, he or she needs to understand your goals and expectations. Make sure you feel comfortable with the person you choose as a lawyer. Protect yourself from surprises in your lawyer's billing. Ask your lawyer what his or her hourly rate is and what it will likely cost to do the legal work for the transaction. Ask your lawyer if he or she will be doing the work or it will be delegated to others.

UNDERSTAND THE BUSINESS YOU ARE ACQUIRING

As a buyer, you must understand just what it is you are purchasing and how you are going to make the purchase. Use your attorney to make sure the agreement you sign provides you with the time and information necessary to complete the transaction.

Make sure your attorney interacts with your accountant. Many times, businesses can be acquired with very little cash coming directly from the buyer. The buyer may finance most or all the purchase but will not be able to ascertain the financing available until the value of the company has been established. You may also explore having the seller provide part of the financing or enter into an earn out, where the purchase price is paid in part from future profits over time. Accordingly, the financial condition of the company needs to be examined at an early stage. This can be accomplished by using a competent accountant to review the company's books and records for a sufficient period of time. It may also require some forecasting of expenses and revenues. Your attorney needs to be involved early to make sure the seller agrees to provide the information necessary to value the company and to provide the buyer with as much flexibility as possible when exploring financing to complete the transaction.

DUE DILIGENCE

Your lawyer should help you understand the business you are purchasing. It is important to understand the components of what makes the company work. Explore the viability of the company's staff. Part of the value of the company will be the talent of the staff as well as the consistency of employment and the commitment going forward. The status of key employees needs to be evaluated and valued just as does the hard assets of a company. As an example, do key employees have non-competition agreements? These things need to be addressed during the due diligence period. Your attorney should provide you with the time you need to assess the viability of your purchase. A due diligence period should be negotiated at the early stages of a transaction. Due diligence can occur at any time prior to closing. Closing the transaction, however, should be subject to proper due diligence.

ASKING PRICE

As a buyer, you need to understand how the seller developed the asking price. If the company is in a market that typically reaches a value based upon a multiple, it will be important to test the data used in the seller's formula. As an example, if a seller claims the asking price was determined by multiplying annual sales times five, the strength of the annual sales figure would need to be evaluated. Will those sales be sustainable? Do you need a representation from the seller that he or she has no knowledge of any of the key (top ten) customers having any issues with the company going forward? These types of issues need to be accomplished during the due diligence period.

The seller, on the other hand, has to evaluate the strength of the buyer before committing to the sale. The last thing a seller wants to do is to commit to a buyer that is financially incapable of completing the transaction. The seller should have an attorney retained before committing to a particular buyer for a sale. The attorney can not only help evaluate the strength of the prospective buyer but also make sure any agreements entered into are significantly safeguarded to protect the buyer.

REPRESENTATIONS AND WARRANTIES

The "representations and warranties" section of any purchase agreement is typically the most critical section of the contract. The purchase agreement will contain certain representations and warranties. Some are relatively standard; others will be unique to the particular purchase. Buyers and sellers will negotiate and compromise what is contained in this section of the agreement. Sellers, for example, will want to limit their warranties to areas not available to the buyer during due diligence. A representation is a statement of fact that induces a party to enter into a contract. The statement, made before or at the time of making the contract, is of a past fact or existing fact or circumstance related to the contract. As an example, a standard representation would be that the "seller owns full legal and equitable title to an asset that is the subject of the sale."

A warranty is a promise that a proposition of fact is true. Where a representation covers past and existing statements, warranties cover existing and future statements. An example of a warranty would be that the seller warrants that it is not involved in any litigation nor has it received notice of a potential claim. When a contract uses the terms "representations" and "warranties" together, they blend the past, present, and future together within the terms of the contract.

In a typical acquisition, representations and warranties are given by both parties to disclose material information. The seller's representations and warranties tend to be more extensive because they include information about the target company or business and the stock or asset and liabilities being transferred. The representations and warranties allocate risk between the parties and will act as the basis for an indemnification claim based upon a breach or inaccuracy.

The attorney for the buyer will do his or her best to get the seller to commit to absolute representations and warranties. The purchase agreement will include representations and warranties that survive the closing and others that will expire at closing or at some time thereafter.

An example of the topics for a typical seller's representations and warranties in an asset sale agreement would be as follows:

1. Due organization and qualification
2. Authority to execute and prepare agreements
3. Financial statements
4. No material adverse change
5. Tax matters
6. Compliance with laws; permits
7. No breach
8. Litigation
9. Employment matters
10. Contractor matters
11. Contracts
12. Real estate
13. Title
14. Conditions and sufficiency of assets
15. Intellectual property
16. Products and inventory
17. Customer and supplier lists
18. Undisclosed liabilities
19. Accounts receivable and accounts payable
20. Employee benefit plans
21. Insurance
22. Operation of seller
23. Environmental matters
24. Sales practices
25. Affiliate relationships
26. No broker

As you can see, the representations and warranties of a seller are exhaustive. They are the meat of the agreement. Buyer's counsel will insist that some are absolute while seller's counsel will attempt to limit the representations and warranties by adding "to the best of seller's knowledge" as a modification to the representation or warranty.

Asset purchase: the payment for some or all the assets of a company and usually not the liabilities.

On the other hand, the buyer's representations and warranties are not nearly as exhaustive. After all, the most important part of the buyer's commitment is that either his or her cash is green or the financing is in place. The following would be topics for a typical representations and warranties of a buyer in an **asset purchase agreement**:

1. Due incorporation
2. Authority relative to this agreement and ancillary agreements
3. No violation
4. Absence of litigation
5. Product liability insurance
6. No broker

Asset purchase agreement or APA: an agreement between a buyer and seller that finalizes the details of buying some or all the assets of a company.

Make sure you understand the representations and warranties. Go through each with your lawyer to assure your understanding of exactly what is and what is not being represented or warranted. If the seller wants to modify certain representation as "to the best of the seller's knowledge," make sure that is acceptable to you. In representing you as a buyer, your lawyer will not allow the seller to modify all representations and warranties. A good example of a representation that cannot be modified would be one that represents the ability to convey good ownership to the buyer.

Just remember, your lawyer is your teammate. You need to work with him or her to succeed. Communicate freely with your lawyer. The attorney/client privilege protects you and allows you to have frank discussions with your lawyer. Work with your lawyer to establish reasonable outcomes, both in the result of the transaction and in benchmarks leading to closing. Never allow yourself to be guessing about the progress of your transaction. Talk to your lawyer throughout.

Chapter 29

A CPA's Perspective
By Bill Mahony

Bill Mahony is a CPA and tax attorney who has run his thriving practice for over thirty years. Bill specializes in small-business ownership and consults on tax consequences for buying and selling businesses. He takes his practice one step further by integrating business ownership into a client's personal net worth and advising how to protect one's assets and accumulated wealth. Bill can be reached at bill@wmahony.com.

A CPA SHOULD BE an integral part of any buyer's purchase of a business, be it large or small. A CPA can explain the tax effects of purchasing the business, the most tax-effective way to purchase the business, and the different types of entities available when owning a business. Hiring a CPA experienced in M&A will ensure that you get what you paid for when you buy a company and that you take advantage of all tax-reduction methods, not only in buying the business but also in running the business in a tax-efficient way on an ongoing basis.

A CPA CAN SAVE YOU

You can recoup CPA fees many times over by saving tens of thousands of dollars on a wide variety of deal points. The way that a business is purchased can have a dramatic effect on a purchaser's ongoing tax liability and cash flow for years to come. Typically, a buyer will want to engage in an asset purchase, as opposed to a **stock purchase**, for a number of reasons, such as the following:

- In purchasing the assets of a company, the purchaser is absolved of any unknown liabilities inherent in the business. If the purchaser were to buy the entity itself (stock sale), any unknown liabilities carry over to the new owner.

- If buyers purchase the assets of the business, they get a new depreciable basis for the assets purchased, which will reduce their tax liability over the coming years. If, instead, they purchase the entity, they are stuck with the depreciation basis of the existing company, which most times is very low.

Stock purchase: buying the stock of a company that includes liabilities as well as assets.

ESTABLISH VALUATION

Although there may be other members of the purchaser's team who will place a value of the company to be purchased, an experienced CPA can add a second set of eyes as to the appropriate valuation based upon his or her knowledge of reading financial statements and tax returns. Particularly with the purchase of a small business, the CPA can identify any personal items being paid for by the company that, if removed from the valuation, make the business more valuable to the purchaser. The CPA can also assist in judging if a company is too big for the purchaser or if cash flow will be an issue for the amount of cash the buyer has. An experienced CPA can run cash flow projections on both a pretax and post-tax basis to ensure that the buyer has the necessary resources to carry the business in bad times, as well as good.

SET UP YOUR SELECTED COMPANY TO GET FINANCING

A CPA experienced in M&A can ensure that the books and records of the company to be purchased are understood by and show the business in the best light to any lending entity the buyer is considering for financing. Most CPAs also have relationships with banks that provide financing to small businesses. The existence of such a relationship adds a layer of trust between the prospective lending institution and the company, not only in the initial purchase phase but also should the company require a credit line or additional financing down the road.

ESTABLISH PROPER BOOKS AND FINANCIAL STATEMENTS FROM THE BEGINNING

Having a CPA set up proper financials ensures you receive top value if you ever think of selling the company or bringing in investors. In most cases, when prospective purchasers or investors analyze companies, they find the books and records maintained by the company are not adequate to do a proper valuation. In many cases, this leads to a reduced purchase price or the failure of any lending institution the prospective buyer is utilizing to finance the purchase from doing the proper due diligence to provide the funding. Therefore, it is imperative that any business have the proper accounting system in place so the records are maintained in a proper way and the necessary documentation is available to any purchaser or investor. A qualified CPA can also provide advice as to the proper presentation of financial statements to the prospective purchaser or investor.

HAVE YOUR CPA AT YOUR SIDE WHEN SELLING YOUR BUSINESS

When you have grown your business and are ready to sell it, your CPA is the best person to discuss the valuation of the business, the terms of sale, and all other important financial matters involved in the sale. At that point, your CPA should have an intimate knowledge of the financial details of your company, most likely more than you do. During your ownership of the business, a good CPA will meet with you on a regular basis to ensure that your business is being run properly from a financial standpoint and is always in a financial condition that will look the best to a prospective purchaser. Your CPA should be a critical team member sitting at the negotiating table to provide all the details of the financial ins and outs of the business, be it a temporary drop in revenue, any increased expenses, or events on the horizon that may increase the value of the business. Your CPA hopefully will have set up your company so it is desirable for a buyer from a tax perspective and the transfer can be done in the most tax-beneficial way for both parties.

COMPILED, REVIEWED, AND AUDITED FINANCIALS

There are three different levels of financial statements that a CPA will prepare for a business: compilation, review, and audit. The difference is the level of service, which is determined by your needs and what your prospective buyer or investors require.

Compilation

- This is the most basic level of service CPAs provide with respect to financial statements.

- The accountant does not obtain or provide any assurance that there are no material modifications that should be made to the financial statements.

- The CPA must comply with Statements on Standards for Accounting and Review Services (SSARSs), which require the accountant to have an understanding of the industry in which the client operates, obtain knowledge about the client, read the financial statements, and consider whether such financial statements appear appropriate in form and free from obvious material errors.

- A compilation does not contemplate performing inquiry, analytical procedures, or other procedures ordinarily performed in a review; or obtaining an understanding of the entity's internal control; assessing fraud risk; or testing of accounting records; or other procedures ordinarily performed in an audit.

- The CPA issues a report stating:

    - The compilation was performed in accordance with SSARS.
    - The accountant has not audited or reviewed the financial statements.
    - It does not express an opinion or provide any assurance about whether the financial statements are in accordance with the applicable financial reporting framework.

Compiled financials: the most rudimentary review of a company's financial statements, neither audited nor carrying any opinion about their quality.

Review

- Reviewed financial statements provide the user with comfort that the accountant is not aware of any material modifications that should be made to the financial statements for the statements to be in conformity with the applicable financial reporting framework.

- A review engagement involves the CPA performing procedures (primarily analytical procedures and inquiries) that will provide a reasonable basis for obtaining limited assurance that there are no material modifications that should be made to the financial statements for them to be in conformity with the applicable financial reporting framework.

- The CPA designs and performs analytical procedures, inquiries, and other procedures as appropriate, based on the accountant's understanding of the industry, knowledge of the client, and awareness of the risk that he or she may unknowingly fail to modify the accountant's review report on financial statements that are materially misstated.

- A review does not contemplate obtaining an understanding of the entity's internal control, assessing fraud risk, testing accounting records, or other procedures ordinarily performed in an audit.

- The CPA issues a report stating:
  - The review was performed in accordance with SSARS.
  - Management is responsible for the preparation and fair presentation of the financial statements in accordance with the applicable financial reporting framework and for designing, implementing, and maintaining internal control relevant to the preparation of analytical procedures, inquiries and other procedures, as well as fair presentation of the financial statements.
  - A review is substantially less in scope than an audit and that the CPA is not aware of any material modifications that should be made to the financial statements for them to be in conformity with the applicable financial reporting framework.

Reviewed financials: outside review by a CPA of a company's financials; a step down from audit.

Audit

- Audited financial statements provide the user with the auditor's opinion that the financial statements are presented fairly, in all material respects, in conformity with the applicable financial reporting framework.

- In an audit, the auditor is required by auditing standards generally accepted in the United States (GAAS) to obtain an understanding of the entity's internal control and assess fraud risk.

- The auditor corroborates the amounts and disclosures included in the financial statements by obtaining audit evidence through inquiry, physical inspection, observation, third-party confirmations, examination, analytical procedures, and other procedures.

- The auditor issues a report stating:

    - The audit was conducted in accordance with GAAS.
    - The financial statements are the responsibility of management.
    - An opinion that the financial statements present fairly in all material respects the financial position of the company and the results of operations are in conformity with the applicable financial reporting framework (or issues a qualified opinion if the financial statements are not in conformity with the applicable financial reporting framework).

Audited financials: an independent CPA firm's highest level of review of a company's financials.

C CORPORATIONS, S CORPORATIONS, AND LIMITED LIABILITY COMPANIES (LLC)

If you are purchasing the assets of a new company, you will need to establish an entity to own the assets. There are basically three options for business organization and formation—a **C corporation**, an **S corporation**, and a **limited liability company** (**LLC**).

C corporation or C corp: designation of a business as a corporation that is taxed under US income tax law separately from its owners; an entity usually more appropriate for large business and not for small companies.

A C corporation (**C corp**) and an S corporation (**S corp**) are exactly the same in respect to liability protection. The difference is in how you are taxed. A C corp has what is referred to as a double taxation. First, the corporation itself is taxed on the profits it makes, and second, when those profits are distributed to the shareholders as a dividend, the shareholders report the dividend as income on their individual tax returns. So essentially, you are paying taxes twice on the same money your corporation makes, thus the double taxation.

S corporation or S corp: corporate structure popular with small businesses because it provides the liability protection of a corporation with the tax benefits of a partnership; also called subchapter S corporation, sub S corporation, or sub S corp.

An S corporation is a tax election a C corporation can make to eliminate the corporate-level tax. This allows the earnings to pass through the corporation to the shareholders. You pay taxes only once on the earnings. This is a great tax advantage, possibly cutting the taxes on a corporation's profits in half. Also, when income is passed through to the individual shareholders, it adds to the shareholder's basis. This can be a significant advantage when the corporation is sold. All things being equal, an S corp will generally have less capital gain than that of a C corp due to income being passed through to the S corp's shareholders and thus increasing their basis.

However, you must qualify in order to elect to be taxed as a sub S. The essential requirements are:

1. The corporation cannot have more than 100 shareholders.

2. All shareholders must be either a US citizen or permanent resident.

3. The corporation can only have one class of stock (i.e., no preferred stock, but you may have voting and non-voting common stock).

Even though you do not pay income taxes for the S corp, a tax return must still be filed on behalf of the corporation.

Limited liability company or **LLC:** not a corporation; a legal form of a company with liability protection for the company members; frequently used vehicle to buy small to medium-size businesses.

An LLC can be more flexible than a corporation. Owners of an LLC (called members) have the choice of being taxed as a corporation or as a partnership. Most LLCs choose to be taxed as partnerships due to several advantages over corporations. With an LLC, anyone can be an owner, including another LLC or corporation or a foreign citizen. The LLC is a pass-through entity, meaning there is no corporate-level tax return. All the income and expenses are passed through to the owners who report their share of the income and expenses on their individual tax returns. Members of an LLC also can agree to divide the profits differently from time to time, rather than split the profits according to share ownership. This is known as special allocations, and this cannot be done in a corporation in which the shareholders must share a proportional amount of the profits based on pro-rata ownership. Additionally, there is no limitation to the amount of passive income an LLC can earn.

Finally, partnership accounting offers another major advantage to LLCs taxed as partnerships. Most debt incurred by the LLC will add a proportional amount to the basis of the members. This increase in basis is an advantage for utilizing pass-through losses, which are subject to the at-risk rules. You need to be careful that there is no piercing of the corporate veil of an LLC. And you must follow corporate formalities, such as preparing annual minutes each year to be in compliance.

PERSONAL FINANCIAL STATEMENT

In purchasing a company, more times than not, a lending institution will want a personal guarantee of the purchasing individual(s), that is, a personal financial statement that shows the guarantor's ability to repay the loan should the company default. This statement asks for all the personal assets and liabilities of the prospective purchaser(s).

A SALE: YOUR TAX RAMIFICATIONS AND NET-NET

In the sale of a business, a qualified CPA should make you aware of the obvious tax ramifications, such as capital gains tax, and some hidden, not so obvious taxes that can also be imposed. Examples may include many possible recapture provisions under IRC (Internal Revenue Code) Section 1231, which is the sale of property held for the production of income or property that is used in a trade or business. Depending on how the sale is accounted for, individual assets that were being depreciated may have a portion or all of that prior depreciation recaptured. In that case, that income will be taxed as ordinary income. There may also be recapture provisions imposed on property that had been expensed by the company under section 179 of the IRC. Even the sale of appreciated inventory can have special taxes imposed under Section 751, which is known as the hot assets. For the business owner to know the true net-net amount to be realized and to make an informed decision about the sale, all these details need to be presented.

Chapter 30

Women and Minority-owned Businesses
By Rebecca Hicks

Attorney Rebecca Hicks is the managing partner of Hicks Law Group in Dallas, Texas. Respected as a leading attorney in the state of Texas, where she counsels women and minority-owned businesses, she is viewed within her industry as a thought leader and has been awarded over a dozen coveted designations and awards, including SBA Women in Business Champion. She is a featured personality on many media outlets and has authored or given over seventy industry presentations. Rebecca can be reached at RHicks@HicksLawGroup.com.

ADVANTAGES OF WOMEN OR MINORITY-OWNED CERTIFICATION

DEPENDING ON YOUR BUSINESS TYPE and target customers, there may be certain advantages to becoming certified as a women, minority-owned, or disadvantaged business. Diversity is a hot topic in all aspects of the business world, and there are several formalized programs targeted at helping diverse or disadvantaged business owners get ahead. For example, the federal government and many state and local governments have diversity or women and minority-owned inclusion programs. Many private companies also set diversity goals for their procurement and have formal programs to help ensure that women and minority-owned businesses get a fair shake in the procurement process. Keep in mind these programs are not a free ride. Your company must provide a good product or service at a competitive price. The certification process is stringent—women or minorities generally must own at least 51 percent of the business and control the day-to-day operation of the business. But, if you qualify, the rewards can be considerable with access to sole-source and limited competition contracts and mentoring programs with some of the largest, most successful companies in the world.

Programs to support women and minority-owned businesses have their roots in the Civil Rights Movement of the late 1960s. Based on historical discrimination, **minority-owned business enterprises (MBEs)** were severely underrepresented as providers of goods and services to the US government. General opinion held that if given priority treatment by the US government, these MBEs could not only become good suppliers to the US government but also competitive businesses in the private sector. With this reasoning in mind, President Nixon signed Executive Order 11458 on March 5, 1969, which required government agencies and their contractors to contract with minority-owned companies and report the results against pre-established goals. This executive order is the foundation for subsequent governmental diversity programs, such as 2011's Women-Owned Small Business Federal Contract Program, and the inspiration for diversity programs in private industry.

Minority-owned business enterprise or **MBE**: a business at least 51 percent owned, operated, and controlled on a daily basis by American(s) of ethnic minority classifications as specified by the US government.

This chapter will provide an introduction to several prominent business diversity programs that may be of benefit to your business.

FEDERAL GOVERNMENT DIVERSITY PROGRAMS

The US government is the largest consumer of goods and services in the world, so if we want to level the playing field for women, minority, and disadvantaged businesses, inclusion in federal procurement is a great place to start.

Several federal government programs are targeted for including MBEs and women-owned businesses (WBEs) in procurement. The US Small Business Administration (SBA) manages and administers most of these programs, although individual federal agencies may also have their own specific programs. Founded in 1953, the SBA assists and encourages small business development and growth in the United States. A growing part of this mission has been providing specialized outreach to women and minority-owned business enterprises, specifically by certifying these businesses according to federal procurement standards and then providing direct procurement assistance to these certified businesses. SBA certifications can provide a tremendous, direct benefit to your business. If your company seeks to do business with Uncle Sam, getting certified makes sense. A brief discussion of the major diversity programs benefiting M/WBEs for federal procurement are discussed below.

SBA 8(a) BUSINESS DEVELOPMENT PROGRAM

The SBA 8(a) Business Development Program, or 8(a) BD, was created to assist qualifying socially and economically disadvantaged businesses in gaining a foothold into government contracting. Under this program, the SBA enters contracts with federal agencies and then subcontracts that work to 8(a) BD certified businesses. In 2012, SBA awarded more than $16 billion in federal contracts through 8(a) BD.

Eligibility requirements are strict. The business must be at least 51 percent owned by one or more socially and economically disadvantaged individuals. Social disadvantage usually means membership in a designated group (African American, Hispanic American, Native American, and Asian American) but can be conferred by certain other extenuating factors that created a social disadvantage. Economic disadvantage means that your ability to compete in the free-enterprise system has been impaired due to diminished capital and credit opportunities as compared to others in the same or similar line of business who are not socially disadvantaged. The business owner's net worth, exclusive of business equity and home, must be less than $250,000 and must remain less than $750,000 for the duration of the program. SBA also requires that the business possess reasonable prospects for success in the private sector. Therefore, the company must have at least two full years of business operation in its industry classification prior to the application date.

The 8(a) BD Program runs for nine years, and you are required annually to demonstrate your continued eligibility. You also must make significant progress in obtaining non-8(a) projects, especially during the final five years (known as the transitional stage) of the program, or else face restrictions on future awards or even termination from the program.

8(a) BD MENTOR-PROTÉGÉ PROGRAM

The 8(a) BD Program also provides significant advantages with the Mentor-Protégé Program. The purpose of the mentor-protégé relationship is to enhance your capabilities, assist you with meeting your SBA-approved business plan, and improve your ability to compete successfully for contracts. The 8(a) BD also allows the mentor to form joint-venture arrangements with your company in order to compete together for other government contracts. These joint-ventures allow your business to participate in contracts beyond your normal scope of expertise and give the mentor access to sole-source and limited-competition small business contracts.

Currently, more than 7,000 firms participate in the program. Overall, the SBA 8(a) BD program, if you qualify, represents an excellent opportunity to expand your business into federal contracting.

SBA 8(a) BUSINESS DEVELOPMENT PROGRAM CERTIFICATION PROCESS

The complete 8(a) Business Development Program application instructions and pre-application checklists are available on the SBA's website at www.sba.gov/category/navigation-structure/how-apply. If you answer yes to all of the following questions, you may be eligible to participate.

1. Do all principals show good character?

2. Is the firm organized as a for-profit business?

3. Is the firm a small business that meets the SBA size standard?

4. Has the firm been conducting ongoing business for at least two years?

   a. Does the firm have established filings (i.e., articles, permits, etc.) with the state, county, and city where it does business and are the fillings signed, dated, and stamped by the state that issued them?

   b. Does the firm have tax returns and financial statements that show its growth and potential to succeed?

5. Does one or more socially and economically disadvantaged individuals:

   a. own a majority (51 percent or more) of the firm?

   b. serve as the highest officer?

   c. manage the firm?

   d. control the board of directors?

   e. run the firm's daily business operations?

   f. receive the highest pay from the firm?

Keep in mind that your local SBA office provides free one-on-one counseling to assist you in preparing your application package. Online pre-application training is also available via SBA's website: www.sba.gov/tools/sba-learning-center/training/pre-8a-business-development-program-training-series. Firms owned by an entity (rather than an individual) have different requirements. Eligible entities include Alaska Native Corporations (ANCs), Native American Tribes, Native Hawaiian Organizations (NHOs), and Community Development Corporations (CDCs).

SBA HUBZONE PROGRAM

Established in 1997, the SBA Historically Underutilized Business Zone (HUBZone) program is designed to help small firms in certain disadvantaged communities gain access to federal contract opportunities. The federal government has designated certain geographic areas (low income, high unemployment, Indian reservations, and military base closure areas) as HUBZones and has charged the SBA with providing assistance to qualified firms in these areas. The goal of the program is to increase employment opportunities, economic development, and investment in the HUBZone.

The federal government has set 3 percent government-wide prime and subcontracting goals in these communities with a 10 percent price evaluation difference under a full and open competition contract, meaning your proposal can be deemed price competitive even if it is up to 10 percent higher than competing bids. If your business's principal offices are located in and at least 35 percent of your employees reside in a HUBZone, you may qualify. The SBA provides a detailed map of designated zones on its website www.sba. gov/content/hubzone-maps. To be eligible, your business must be owned by and controlled by at least 51 percent US citizens, and you must be a small business by SBA standards. You also must have been in business for more than two years.

As a HUBZone firm, your business can also qualify for higher SBA-guaranteed surety bonds on construction and service contract bids.

SMALL DISADVANTAGED BUSINESS CERTIFICATION

The federal government wants to encourage and increase the participation in federal procurement of small businesses owned by socially and economically disadvantaged individuals. To this end, the Small Disadvantaged Business (**SDB**) designation has been created. SDB certification has two main advantages. First, an SDB can qualify for up to 10 percent price in evaluation adjustment when bidding on federal contracts in certain industries where there has been ongoing discrimination. Second, prime contractors receive evaluation credits if they achieve SDB subcontracting targets, increasing the subcontracting opportunities for SDBs.

If at least 51 percent of your business is owned or controlled by one or more socially and economically disadvantaged persons and you meet the SBA's size standards as discussed above, you may qualify to self-certify as a SDB. You may self-certify by registering your business in the System for Award Management (SAM) at www.sam. gov/portal/public/SAM.

SDB: Small Disadvantaged Business; a US government designation for a business at least 51 percent owned or controlled by one or more socially and economically disadvantaged persons.

Keep in mind that if you qualify for SDB status, you may also qualify for 8(a), HUBZone, Women Owned, and/or Service Disabled status.

WOMEN-OWNED SMALL BUSINESS (WOSB) FEDERAL CONTRACT

There are two classifications of women-owned small businesses germane to this program: (1) women-owned small businesses (WOSBs) and (2) economically disadvantaged women-owned small businesses (EDWOSBs). Both must be at least 51 percent unconditionally and directly owned and controlled by one or more women who are US citizens. The EDWOSB simply requires that the women owners also be economically disadvantaged.

The Women-Owned Small Business (WOSB) Federal Contract program, established in 2011, is aimed at expanding federal contracting opportunities for women-owned small businesses. The federal government must award at least 5 percent of its prime and subcontract dollars to women-owned small business, and each federal agency develops diversity goals in addition to this 5 percent. The WOSB program enables federal government contracting officers to meet these goals by specifically limiting, or setting aside, certain contracts or opportunities for competition solely among eligible women-owned small businesses. A contracting officer may set aside a requirement for a women-owned small business if:

- The North American Industry Classification Systems (NAICS) code assigned to the solicitation, invitation for bid, or quote is in an industry in which SBA has designated that WOSBs are substantially underrepresented.

- The contracting officer has a reasonable expectation that two or more WOSBs will submit offers. This is sometimes referred to as the "rule of two."

- The anticipated award price of the contract does not exceed $6.5 million in the case of manufacturing contracts and $4 million in the case of all other contracts.

- In the estimation of the contracting officer, the contract can be awarded at a fair and reasonable price.

NAICS: (pronounced "nakes") North American Industry Classification Systems; the US government's categorization of businesses by the goods or services they produce or activity they engage in.

The SBA has identified eighty-three NAICS codes where women-owned small businesses are either underrepresented or substantially underrepresented. You can visit www.sba.gov/wosb to see which NAICS codes are underrepresented. If your business provides goods or services within one of the eighty-three underrepresented NAICS codes and it is a women-owned business, you should take a careful look at the WOSB Federal Contract program. You can look on the Federal Business Opportunities website (www.fbo.gov) to find federal government solicitations that may be set aside for WOSBs or EDWOSBs. The announcement and solicitation will state that the agency is limiting competition to either EDWOSBs or WOSBs eligible for the program. In addition, the solicitation should contain certain FAR (Federal Acquisition Regulation) clauses, which explain that it is set aside for competition.

SERVICE DISABLED VETERAN-OWNED BUSINESSES (SDVOB)

Service-disabled veteran-owned businesses require no federal certification. SDVOB owners self-certify. To be eligible, you must be able to produce an adjudication letter form the VA or a Department of Defense Form 214 stating that you have a service-connected disability. If you qualify, you may be eligible for certain sole-source and set-aside contracts. The benefits are similar to those of SDB.

The Veteran's Administration has established the Vets First Verification program, which gives priority to SDVOBs in contracting. More information on Vets First is available at www.va.gov/OSDBU/index.asp.

DISADVANTAGED BUSINESS ENTERPRISE (DBE)

Recognizing the need for greater participation of disadvantaged businesses in state and local procurement, the US Department of Transportation created the Disadvantaged Business Enterprise program. For the DBE entity, you have an opportunity to compete fairly on federally funded transportation projects in a manner similar to SDB set-asides but without price-evaluation considerations. The program requires state and local transportation agencies that receive federal funds to establish goals for DBE participation and to review large prime contracts in order to establish contract-specific DBE subcontracting goals. State and local agencies are also required to certify the eligibility of DBE firms to participate in DOT-assisted projects. The DOT has wisely chosen to create a DBE Unified Certification Program (UCP) that greatly simplifies certification across multiple state and local agencies. Once a DBE is certified anywhere in a state for any DOT-assisted project, that DBE is certified for all DOT-assisted projects in the state. More information is available at http://www.dot.gov/osdbu/disadvantaged-business-enterprise/dbe-uniform-certification-program-ucp.

OTHER FEDERAL DIVERSITY PROGRAMS AND CERTIFICATIONS

Many federal agencies, such as the Department of Transportation, have separate certifications, set-asides, and Offices of Small Disadvantaged Business Utilization. If you are targeting a specific government agency, make sure to look for small-business and disadvantaged-business programs for which you might qualify.

STATE AND LOCAL GOVERNMENT PROGRAMS

Most state and local governments have diversity programs. This includes city government, school districts, and transportation departments. The governments set inclusion goals for MWBEs (minority and women-owned business enterprises) and implement programs to help meet those goals. These programs can include mentor protégé programs, policies of giving points for procurement bids that include a certain level of MWBE subcontractors or suppliers, or allowing bid points for a joint venture where a MWBE is a meaningful participant.

Eligibility requirements and certification processes vary by state and by municipality so make sure to enquire about the availability of these programs before you begin the bidding and proposal process.

PRIVATE BUSINESS DIVERSITY PROGRAM

As the evidence mounts that diversity is good for business, big business has formalized its diversity efforts, not just internally in hiring practices but also in procurement. Companies set goals for procurement from diverse businesses and seek out MWBE companies to do business with. Usually, these companies require you to register directly with them as a diversity supplier, but they often accept or require national certifications, such as those from the Minority Supplier Development Council (MSDC), the Women's Business Enterprise National Council (WBENC), and the SBA. As bidding opportunities arise, these personnel work to match sourcing and procurement teams with registered diversity suppliers. Businesses often have one or more employees charged with managing the supplier-diversity program. The company's supplier-diversity professional can help guide you through the procurement process and be your internal cheerleader, so that relationship can be key.

Many of these supplier-diversity programs rely on MBE or WBE certification obtained through a third-party organization. The certification process generally involves payment of a fee, usually in the range of $200 to $500, completion of an application, submission of paperwork regarding the company's structure and control, and a site visit and interview with the company's principal. The certifying organizations take their responsibility very seriously, and any irregularities or omissions in the application and supporting paperwork can delay certification, or even cause denial of certification. A discussion of the general requirements for MBE and WBE certification is below. When determining the type of certification to apply for, you should always start with the question, "What type of certification do my current or potential customers look for and accept?"

WOMEN'S BUSINESS ENTERPRISE (WBE) CERTIFICATION

WBE certification is designed to ensure that a business is legitimately owned, managed, and controlled by women. This gives companies or state and local governments looking to do business with women-owned businesses the assurance that your company truly is owned by women.

Generally speaking, the following criteria must be met to qualify for WBE certification:

1. At least 51 percent ownership by a woman or women;

2. Proof of daily management and unilateral control of the business by the women owner(s);

3. Documented evidence of contribution of capital and/or expertise; and

4. US citizenship or permanent legal resident status.

WBE certification can be obtained from several national and local or regional entities, so check with your customer or potential customer to see which certification he or she accepts. The most commonly recognized organizations that provide WBE certification widely recognized on a national level are:

- Women's Business Enterprise National Council (WBENC), www.wbenc.org

- National Women Business Owners Corporation, www.nwboc.org

- US Women's Chamber of Commerce, www.uswcc.org

- El Paso Hispanic Chamber of Commerce, www.ephcc.org

MINORITY BUSINESS ENTERPRISE (MBE) CERTIFICATION

Similarly, MBE certification is designed to ensure that a company is truly owned and controlled by one or more minorities. The general requirements for certification are:

1. Your business is a for-profit enterprise.

2. Your business is physically located in the United States or its trust territories.

3. Your business is at least 51 percent ethnic minority-owned. Ethnic minority-owned is defined as any business having owner(s) belonging to the following minority groups:

   a. African-American having origins in any black racial groups of Africa (not of Hispanic origin)

   b. Hispanic whose origin is from Mexico, Puerto Rico, Cuba, Central and South America, or Hispanic cultures or descents

   c. Asian and Pacific Islanders whose origin is from Japan, China, the Philippines, Vietnam, Korea, Samoa, Guam, US Trust Territories of the Pacific, Northern Marianas, Laos, Cambodia, Taiwan, India, Pakistan, and Bangladesh

   d. Native American having origins in any of the American/Alaskan Indians, Eskimos, Aleuts, and Native Hawaiians. All American/Alaska Indians must be documented members of a federally recognized tribal entity.

4. The minority/ethnic owner(s) of the business are US citizens.

5. The minority/ethnic owner(s) of the business must be active in management and daily business operations.

6. The minority-owner(s) shall possess the power to direct or cause the direction of the management and policies of the firm and shall possess the capability of making day-to-day as well as major decisions on matters of management, policy, and operations of the firm. There shall be no restriction on the minority-owner's ability to control that would prevent the minority-owner from making a business decision without the cooperation or vote of a non-minority person. Such control shall be known or at least tacitly acknowledged in day-to-day operations by employees and business references of the business. Where licenses are required to perform the functional mission of the company, such licenses shall be held in the name and/ or independent control of minorities.

7. The minority-ownership and control shall be real and continuing and not created solely to take advantage of special programs aimed at minority business development.

8. The minority-owner(s) shall enjoy the customary incidents of ownership and shall share in the risks and profits and shall have contributed capital, equipment, and/or expertise to the business commensurate with his/her percentage of ownership.

The National Minority Supplier Development Council (MSDC) provides the most widely recognized MBE certification. More information can be found about the NMSDC at www.nmsdc.org.

DO YOUR HOMEWORK BEFORE APPLYING FOR CERTIFICATION

If you determine that one of these diversity programs may benefit your business, then you need to make sure the documents governing your company will support certification. Ownership must be properly reflected, and governance and control must meet the requirements of the certifying entity. You should consult your attorney to ensure that the requirements are met. Any irregularity in the corporate documentation, bylaws, minutes, etc. can delay or even cause denial of certification.

After certification, if your company decides that a joint venture is a good business decision, then make sure the joint venture agreement meets the requirements to receive advantages of the MWBE participation. For example, there are very specific requirements regarding the form and content of the joint venture agreement for a joint venture to be able to participate in the SBA 8(a) Program.

When selling your business, keep in mind that if contracts were procured based on MBWE status, that will need to be addressed since a change in ownership can impact the certification and thus the contract. Any purchase or sale documents need to be reviewed with the MWBE certification requirements in mind.

Chapter 31

Our Fork in the Road

THE YEARS SLIDE BY for all of us. We all are constantly assessing what our life's ambitions are. We see our friends and associates who have secured their dream job and are merrily paddling through life as the lucky souls. For the rest of us—most of us—who are incessantly working and striving to get ahead, business ownership can be the winner's cup. But we cannot just watch the field of play and hope to grasp that prize. Merely sitting on the sidelines means we are making a decision to be a non-participant in the most rewarding game of life: entrepreneurship.

Winning at Entrepreneurship is both a call to action and a reference tool to give you a heightened chance of success if you take the plunge. It provides you with the language to speak coherently and confidently about the mechanics of transactions and the matrices used by all. Keep it on hand as a guide to reference as you progress through buying, building, and selling your own business.

The dividing line separating work from play is becoming increasingly blurred, and the lucky ones have removed the division altogether—their work is their play. How do you even begin? Develop an alternative game plan so you are ready to seize a once-in-a-lifetime opportunity when it pops up. When the situation arises, it must be immediately assessed and acted upon if it fits within your parameters because windows of opportunity close quickly. Increase your odds of such serendipity by attending fairs, seminars, and webinars on subjects that interest you. Talk to people in that industry or line of work. Gather data and read about it. Even if you are not actively looking, being connected to a sector of interest can create unexpected opportunities.

Winning at Entrepreneurship has allowed me to share my insights, the wisdom of my contributing writers, as well as mistakes made in the pursuit of entrepreneurship. I hope you, too, can stand in the winners' circle. Good luck!

Appendix A

Forms

DOCUMENTS ARE CORDIALLY SUPPLIED by Russell Robb from his book, *Buying Your Own Business*. These documents are in a sequence from the beginning of an acquisition search to the closing documents. They provide an excellent, full-spectrum source of critical documents in searching for and acquiring a business. These are the forms in this appendix.

- Confidentiality Agreement
- Fee Agreement with the Intermediaries
- General Proposal Letter
- Term Sheet
- Letter of Intent
- Purchase and Sale Agreement

CONFIDENTIALITY AGREEMENT

It is customary for the owner or CEO of the prospective selling company to require you to sign a confidentiality statement. Unless the seller is actively selling the business, he or she will not have such a form in the file. Therefore, I recommend that you carry your own confidentiality agreement in your briefcase in order to expedite matters. The format is fairly standard.

Confidentiality Agreement

In connection with our interest in purchasing the assets and/or stock of _____ ("the Company"), we have requested that we be permitted to examine the financial and other business records of the Company. We understand and agree that the information contained in these records is of a confidential nature and that it will be used by us solely for the purpose of making an offer for the assets and/or stock of the Company. We will not disclose, nor will our agents, servants, employees, or attorneys disclose, any of the information contained in these financial and other business records, including the identity of the Company, to any other person except to such investors, bankers, attorneys, or other persons necessary to consummate the sale to the undersigned.

Signed by: _____
                               (Printed Name)

                    _____
                               (Signature)

Date: _____

FEE AGREEMENT WITH THE INTERMEDIARIES

Intermediaries, of course, have their own fee agreements, but if they do not have a signed agreement with you and they do not have one with the seller, you will not hear about the deal from them. I urge you to be proactive and tell intermediaries that you will be pleased to pay intermediaries' fees. In fact, go one step further and send the intermediary your own version of an agreement. You can simply mail the signed form to every intermediary with whom you want to do business. It will show the intermediaries that you are aggressive, anxious, professional, and ready to review deals. Here is a form you might want to consider using.

Letter to an Intermediary

My Company, Inc.
Address
Date

TO: XYZ Intermediary

We are agreeable to paying you and/or your associates a fee based on the purchase price or other consideration for any company, agency distributorship, or other business entity or organization, whether expressed in cash or stock or any other remuneration; whether payable at closing of transaction or on extended payout; and regardless of which party pays the remuneration, when you are instrumental in helping us to purchase, sell, or acquire any substantial interest in such company that we agree to accept. Of the purchase price, the fee to you and/or your associates would be:

5% of the first $1,000,000
4% of the second $1,000,000
3% of the third $1,000,000
2% of the fourth $1,000,000
1% of the value thereafter

The payment of this fee shall be due and payable in cash at the time of closing.

My Company, Inc. will confirm in writing any introduction or referral.

If any of the principals of the parities introduced to My Company, Inc. become involved in a transaction that is consummated, an intermediary's commission will be due XYZ Intermediary, irrespective of who conducts the negotiations.

This agreement shall be binding upon both parties hereto, their administrators executers, heirs, successors, or assigns, any corporation and other entities now existing or to be formed having substantially the same principals as either of the parties hereto.

If you accept this understanding, kindly countersign and return the enclosed copy of this agreement.

Sincerely,

_____
(signature)
Printed name and title

Accepted by XYZ Intermediary

By: _____, _____, _____
    (Signature)   (Printed Name)   (Title)

Date: _____

GENERAL PROPOSAL LETTER

While most buyers prefer to talk out their general proposal with either the CEO of the target company or their intermediary, an alternative is to send a letter that broadly describes the proposal. Here is an example of such a letter.

Sample General Proposal Letter

My Company, Inc.
Address
Date

John Smith
President
Big Time, Inc.
Address

Dear Mr. Smith:

The following is a proposal to acquire the assets of Big Time, Inc. ("the Company"). This letter is an outline of a proposed transaction and is not meant to be binding on any party at this time and is subject to the signing of a mutually acceptable, definitive purchase and sale agreement. In addition, this offer is subject to the requisite due diligence effort normally attendant on a transaction of this magnitude. With the aforementioned kept in mind, our offer is as follows:

Transaction
A new corporation ("Newco") will be formed by My Company, Inc. to acquire the assets of the Company with terms and estimated purchase price of $4 million to $5 million cash at closing. We would be willing to purchase the Company without the real estate and enter into a lease at current market rates and terms. In this case, our offer would range between $3.5 million and $4.5 million.

Conditions of Transaction
   1.   We anticipate that a transaction could be consummated and closed within 120 days.

2.   This proposal is subject to financing commitments satisfactory to us. We are happy to provide you with references regarding our ability to finance the transaction.

3.   Representations and warranties of seller with respect to accounts receivable, inventory, fixed assets, disclosure of liabilities, litigation, labor matters, corporate existence, etc., will be required.

4.   We would anticipate completing our due diligence process within thirty to forty-five days, whereupon we would want to move immediately to the execution of a purchase and sale agreement.

5.   If in the due diligence process and prior to the closing, we, in our sole judgment, wish to excuse ourselves from this transaction, we may do so without any liability, fee, penalty, or cost.

6.   All fees and expenses of this transaction, including but not limited to legal, investment banking, accounting broker, and due diligence, will be paid for by each of the respective parties.

Should you have any questions regarding this proposal, please do not hesitate to contact me at (000) 111-2222.

Very truly yours,

TERM SHEET

If you and the potential seller have verbally agreed on the price and terms of the transaction, then it would be helpful to put the basic financial arrangements on one piece of paper before you go directly to the letter of intent. Such an example would be as follows:

Sample Term Sheet

Carlisle Corporation
Outline of Preliminary Proposal for an Asset Purchase

Gross purchase price	$5,000,000
Less debt assumed *	($500,000)
Net purchase price	$4,500,000
Form of consideration	
John Smith (50 percent owner)	
Cash	$1,850,000
Four-year consulting and non-compete agreement ($100,000 annually)	<u>$400,000</u>
John Smith's consideration	$2,250,000
Joe Doe (30 percent owner)	
Cash	$675,000
Carlisle stock	<u>$675,000</u>
Joe Doe's consideration	$1,350,000
Employment contract for Joe Doe: Three-year contract for $100,000 annually with additional annual bonuses of $50,000, provided company's annual operating profit of $700,000 is maintained.	
Mary Jones (20 percent owner)	
Cash	$450,000
Carlisle stock	<u>$450,000</u>
Mary Jones's consideration	$900,000
Employment contract for Mary Jones: Two-year contract for $70,000 annually	
Total Consideration Paid	$4,500,000

*interest-bearing debt (usually bank debt)

LETTER OF INTENT

My experience is that it is best to draft an agreement of one or two pages that is not legalese. The simplicity of such a letter of intent makes it less threatening in the eyes of the potential seller than a document with legal jargon and lengthy qualifications. The letter of intent has two contractual elements—that the seller will take the company off the market for a specified period of time and that both parties (particularly the buyer) will keep all confidential information confidential. All letters of intent should specifically state that this is a nonbinding agreement and the price, terms, and whether the purchase is an asset or stock transaction. It is customary for the buyer to draft the letter of intent as well as the purchase and sale agreement. This is a sample of the letter of intent.

Sample Letter of Intent

Esterbrook Corporation Incorporated proposes to purchase all the assets of Mercury Security Corporation (MSC) of Boston, Massachusetts, including goodwill, customer list, and all other intangible and balance sheet assets, to be substantially the same as those set forth on the balance sheet of MSC as of _____, 20XX (Exhibit A).

1. **Purchase Price**. The purchase price for the assets will be $_____, payable in cash at closing.

2. **Noncompetition Agreement.** The principals of MSC agree not to compete directly or indirectly with the business of Esterbrook as it pertains to MSC in any of its markets for a period of five years after closing. For such consideration, Esterbrook will pay $_____ per year for five years to John Smith.

3. **Lease of Building Space.** It is agreed that MSC will use its best efforts to transfer the lease to Esterbrook at current or market rental as permitted by lease.

4. **General and Specific Liabilities.** Esterbrook will assume the liabilities as shown on the balance sheet dated _____, but will not assume any other liabilities past, present, or future.

5. **Audit.** Esterbrook will cause an audit to be conducted by Esterbrook's auditors at Esterbrook's expense as of a date to be selected.

6. **Expenses.**

   a. The stockholders, Esterbrook, and MSC will each pay their own expenses, including legal expenses, up to the time of the closing.

   b. Esterbrook and MSC agree that no intermediary is involved in this transaction other than _____ of _____, whose compensation is the responsibility of MSC.

7. **Letter of Intent.** This letter of intent is nonbinding and may not be constructed as an agreement on the part of any party. In the event that the parties are unable to agree on a mutually satisfactory definitive agreement providing for the transactions contemplated by this letter of intent, none of the parties shall be liable to any other part or to any other person. The conclusion of any definitive agreement will be subject to the following:

   a. approval of all matters relating thereto by counsel for Esterbrook and MSC;

   b. review of all business, legal, and auditing matters related to MSC, the results of which are acceptable to Esterbrook;

   c. approval of all matters related thereto by the board of directors of Esterbrook and MSC and the voting shareholders of each company, if required;

   d. completion of such financing as Esterbrook may require to effect a closing;

   e. preparation and completion of all closing documents; and

   f. the closing date to take place in or within 90 days of the execution of this agreement.

8. **Continuing Obligations.** Until termination of the letter of intent, MSC shall not and all MSC's officers, directors, employees, agents, or representatives (including without

limitation brokers, advisers, investment bankers, attorneys, and accountants) shall not, directly or indirectly, without prior written consent of Esterbrook, entertain negotiations with or make disclosures to any corporation, partnership, person, or other entity or group in connection with any possible proposal regarding a merger, consolidation, or sale of capital stock of MSC.

9. **Confidentiality.** Both Esterbrook and MSC agree to maintain complete confidentiality of all confidential material each company exchanged with each other as outlined in separate confidentiality agreements.

All documents in respect to this transaction will be prepared by an attorney or law firm selected by Esterbrook, subject to such documents being reviewed by an individual being acceptable to legal counsel for MSC.

Mercury Security Corporation   Esterbrook Corporation Incorporated

By_____   By_____
Printed Name _____   Printed Name _____
Title_____   Title_____
Date_____   Date_____

PURCHASE AND SALE AGREEMENT

In the book, *The Art of M&A: A Merger Acquisition Buyout Guide*, authors Stanley Foster Reed and Alexandra Reed Lajoux write: "It is very important for the buyer to protect its customary right to control the drafting of the documents. It is the shortsighted buyer who tries to save legal fees by letting the 'other guys' do the drafting."

The purchase and the sale agreement, or acquisition agreement, has the following characteristics:

1. It is a legal, binding agreement.

2. The buyer will seek to protect himself or herself in such areas as pending litigation, undisclosed liabilities, and environmental problems.

3. The seller rarely sells for all cash, leaving the buyer leverage to hold out on further payments if the transaction is not what the seller represented it to be.

4. The seller may opt for a lower price at closing for all cash rather than risk post-closing adversity.

5. The conditions section of the agreement lists issues that must be satisfied before the parties become obligated to close the transaction.

6. The indemnity section relates to discoveries after the closing.

7. The representations and warranties section assures each party of the other's legal and financial ability to consummate the transaction.

8. The covenants section of the agreement defines the obligations of the parties with respect to their conduct during the period between the signing and the closing, e.g., the seller conducts the business in the ordinary manner.

Sample Purchase and Sale Agreement
(an asset purchase)

Date _____

Asset Purchase Agreement

This is an agreement among RST, Inc., formerly known as Carlisle, Inc., a Massachusetts corporation with a place of business at _____ ("Seller"); John Doe of _____ ("Stockholder"); and the Carlisle, Inc., a Massachusetts corporation with a place of business at _____ ("Buyer"). For consideration paid each other, the parties covenant and agree as follows:

1. **Assets to be sold**

    Seller will sell, transfer, and deliver to Buyer free and clear of any liens or other encumbrances, Seller's business and the assets and properties of Seller, tangible and intangible, as listed herein. Except as otherwise expressly provided in this agreement, the assets shall include only the following assets owned by Seller at the time of closing.

    a. Machinery and Equipment

    All machinery and equipment, furniture and fixtures, and the like as set forth in Exhibit B attached hereto.

    b. Tools, Dies, and Fixtures

    All tools, dies, and fixtures owned by the Seller.

    c. Inventories

    All inventory, including raw materials, work in process, finished goods, repair parts, and supplies; all inventory records; and all outstanding purchase and sales orders.

    d. Account Receivables

    The Buyer will use best efforts to collect all accounts receivable and pay those receivables as collected to the Seller within ninety days of closing in accordance with an agreed-upon list of such receivables as found on Exhibit E as of the date closing. Upon demand of Seller, Buyer will reassign for collection of uncollected receivables ninety days after the closing.

    e. Corporate Name and Trade Names

    All processes, patents, patent applications, trademarks, signs, advertisements, trade names, copyrights, drawings, and logos, including the name "Carlisle, Inc."

f. Customer Lists and Contracts
All customer lists, files excepting accounting records, licenses, permits, contract rights, and sales backlog as found on Exhibit C, and the telephone and fax number _____. Seller will provide buyer with access to Seller's accounting records upon reasonable notice for customary business purposes.

g. Goodwill
The goodwill of the Seller.

Excluded from the sale shall be all cash, bank accounts, utility security deposits, and prepaid expenses and the land and building, which shall be leased to Buyer by Seller in accordance with the Lease attached hereto as Exhibit A.

2. **Liabilities**
Buyer agrees to assume up to $_____ of accounts payable in accordance with Exhibit. Buyer is specifically not assuming any other liabilities whatsoever of Seller, including without limitation, all taxes of whatever kind or nature, accrued or payable by Seller to any taxing authority prior to and including the closing date, all of which the Seller agrees to pay.

3. **Closing Date**
The closing date will take place no later than 1:00 p.m. on _____, at the offices of the Seller or at such time and place as the Buyer and Seller may hereafter agree upon. Adjustments and prorations shall be made effective at the end of business.

4. **Purchase Price**
a. Price
The purchase price to be paid for the assets is five hundred thousand dollars ($500,000), which sum shall be paid as follows:

Certified or bank check as closing	$200,000
Buyer's promissory note per paragraph 6	$200,000
Accounts Payable per paragraph 2	$100,000
Total	$500,000

b. Allocation
The purchase price for the assets shall be allocated as follows:

Inventories	$100,000
Machinery and Equipment	$200,000
Goodwill	$50,000
Accounts Receivables per paragraph (D)	$150,000
Total	$500,000

5. Personnel Agreement: Non-competition Agreement
Stockholders will enter into a non-competition agreement with the Buyer, in the form attached as Exhibit D.

6. Buyer's Note at Closing Date
In part payment of the purchase price, Buyer shall make and deliver to Seller at the closing date a negotiable promissory note in the amount of two hundred thousand dollars ($200,000), bearing annual interest at eight (8) percent for sixty (60) months and requiring equal monthly installments of interest and principal beginning thirty (30) days after the closing contemplated herein. Such note shall be secured by a first security interest in machinery and equipment acquired and shall be personally guaranteed by Buyer in the form attached as Exhibit B. The form of said note and security agreement, and UCC financing statements are attached hereto as Exhibits F and G.

7. Seller's Use of Name
It is understood and agreed that Seller will not use the name "Carlisle, Inc." to pursue any business interests nor will Seller sell, lease, or convey usage of its name to any entity or individual.

8. Seller's Representations and Warranties
a. Corporate Authority
Seller is a corporation duly organized, validly existing, and in good standing under the laws of the state of Massachusetts and has the right and authority to enter into this agreement and carry out the terms and conditions hereof applicable to it, and the execution, delivery, and performance of this agreement will not violate or conflict with the provisions of the articles of organization or bylaws of the Seller.

b. Agreement Default

Seller as a result of the closing will not be in default under any agreement or other commitment to which it is a party or by which it is bound.

c. Financial Statement to Buyer

Seller has delivered to Buyer the financial statements through _____, Said financial statements are true and complete. Seller shall provide interim financial statements for the period ending _____ as soon as practicable after closing.

d. No Material Change

Since _____, there has not been, to Seller's knowledge, any material change in financial condition, assets and liabilities, or business, other than changes in the ordinary course of business.

e. Tax Returns, Audits, and Tax Payments

Within the times and in a manner prescribed by law, Seller has, and shall have through the closing date, filed all federal, state, foreign, and/or local tax returns required by law and has paid all taxes (including without limitation, income, franchise, sales, use, meals, transfer, payroll, and ad valorem taxes), assessments, and penalties due and payable with respect to the Business of the Seller. The Seller is not delinquent in the payment of any other governmental tax, assessment, or other charge.

f. Marketable Title

Upon the transfer of the assets at closing, Buyer shall acquire title to such property free of all liens and encumbrances and free of all claims of third parties.

g. Good Condition

To Seller's knowledge and except to the extent disclosed to Buyer or known to Buyer, all Seller's equipment and similar tangible personal property are in good condition and repair, consistent with the age and remaining useful life thereof, and their use is in conformity with all applicable laws, ordinances, and regulations. The Assets are being sold in "as is" condition, and any and all warranties from manufacturers or dealers in existence at date of sale are included in the sales price. Buyer acknowledges that Buyer has been provided a full and complete opportunity to inspect the Seller's machinery and equipment and similar tangible personal property, is satisfied with the results of all such inspections, and that the Seller and

Stockholders have made no warranties or representations with respect thereto.

h. Customer Commitments

Attached as Exhibit C is a list of all presently existing customer commitments to which Seller is a party or by which it is bound. To Seller's knowledge, all such commitments are valid and enforceable in accordance with their terms.

i. Litigation

To the Seller's knowledge, there is no pending or threatened action, arbitration, suit, notice, order, real estate tax contest, or legal, administrative, or other proceeding before any court or governmental agency, authority, or body, against, or affecting Seller, either directly or indirectly, with respect to the Assets pending or threatened that will survive the closing. There is no order, writ, injunction, or decree of any federal, state or local, or foreign court, department, agency, or instrumentality that directly or indirectly relates to the Assets. Seller has complied and is complying in all material respects with all law, ordinances, and government rules and regulations applicable to it and its properties, assets, and business.

j. No Untrue Representation

To Seller's knowledge after inquiry, no representation or warranty by Seller in this agreement, or certificate furnished or to be furnished to Buyer pursuant hereto or in connection with the transaction contemplated hereby, contains or will contain any untrue statement of material fact.

k. Continuation of Truth

The representations, warranties, and covenants set forth in this Agreement will continue to be true in all respects as of the closing date and shall survive the Closing.

l. Licenses Obtained

All government licenses, permits, and authorizations necessary for the ownership of Seller's properties and the conduct of its business as currently conducted are listed on Exhibit I, and the Seller has all such licenses, permits, and authorizations.

m. Liabilities

At the closing, there will be no liabilities, commitments, or contingencies of Seller whether accrued, secured, or determinable that encumber the assets, other than those expressly assumed by Buyer under the terms of this Agreement.

n. Continued Business
    Seller is not aware of any reason why its customer, subcontractors, or suppliers will not continue to do business with the Buyer after the Closing in the same manner in which they have done business with the Seller prior to the Closing. This does not assure or imply that the existing customer base will be retained after the Closing.

o. Stock Ownership
    The Stockerholder named herein owns one hundred (100) percent of the outstanding stock of the Seller.

p. Absence of Certain Changes
    Since the date of this Agreement as of the Closing, there shall not have been any:
    i. Transactions by Seller affecting the Assets except in the ordinary course of business.
    ii. Material adverse physical change in the Assets.

q. Profits Pending Closing
    Profits from the date of this agreement up to and including _____, shall be the property of the Seller.

9. Buyer's Representations and Warranties

a. Corporate Authority
    Buyer is a corporation duly organized, validly existing, and in good standing under the laws of the state of Massachusetts and has the right and authority to enter into this agreement and carry out the terms and conditions hereof applicable to it, and the execution, delivery, and performance of this agreement will not violate or conflict with the provisions of the articles of organization or bylaw of the corporation.

b. Agreement Conflict
    This Agreement does not conflict with the Buyer's bylaws, corporate charter, or any other internal requirement of the Buyer. _____ individually and collectively, are subject to no agreement or other constraint that conflicts with their carrying out the terms of this agreement.

c. No Government Approvals
    The transaction contemplated by this agreement does not require any state, local, or federal government approval.

d. Inspection of Assets

Buyer acknowledges that he or she had an opportunity to inspect and actually did inspect all the assets sold under this agreement and is satisfied with the results of such inspection.

e. No Untrue Representation

Buyer's warranties and representations contained in this Agreement are true as of the date of the Agreement and shall continue to be true in all material respects up to and including the date of closing. This provision shall survive the closing.

10. Indemnification

The Seller hereby agrees to indemnify, defend, and hold the Buyer harmless of and from and all debts, liabilities, costs, and expenses of any and every nature whatsoever resulting from the breach or violation of any obligations, representations, covenants, or warranties of the Seller contained in this agreement and from any liability or obligation of the Seller arising out of the Seller's ownership or sale of the assets or the Seller's operation of the business, except for those accounts payable assumed by the Buyer pursuant to paragraph 2 of this Agreement and as specifically identified in Exhibit J. Except as specifically set forth in said Exhibit J, the Buyer shall not and does not assume any other of the liabilities or obligations of the Seller.

The Seller, at its own expense, shall have the opportunity to be represented by counsel of its choosing, and control, at its expense, the defense of any claim that may be brought against the Buyer in respect of which the Buyer may be entitled to indemnifications. The Buyer shall promptly give written notice to the Seller of any such claim. In the event that the Buyer does not receive written notice from the Seller within fifteen (15) days of such written notice, the Seller shall be deemed to have waived the right to be represented by counsel.

In the event the Seller breaches or violates any provision contained herein, the Buyer shall have a right to set off against any payments due Seller under this Agreement, under a Note of even date in the amount of $200,000, or against any payment due _____ under a non-competition agreement between the Buyer and _____, an amount equal to the amount of any claim successfully brought against the Buyer as a result of said breach or violation if Seller elects to defend the claim or the amount of damages suffered by the Buyer if the Seller elects not to defend. Prior to such setoff by the Buyer, the Buyer shall give fifteen (15) days written notice to the Seller setting forth therein the reason(s) for said setoff. The buyer shall exercise such right of setoff by applying such damages against payments due the Seller as they fall due pursuant to the promissory note referred to in paragraph 6 of this Agreement and against payments due under the non-competition agreement referred to in paragraph 5 of this Agreement.

Any notice sent to the Seller should be mailed, postage prepaid, registered or certified mail, return receipt requested, or delivered by overnight carrier and addressed to the parties at their respective addresses as set forth in the Agreement, with a copy in case of notice to the Seller sent as follows:

To Seller's attorney: Name
                             Address
                             City

11. Condition of the Closing

a. Conditions of Seller's Obligations

    i. Payment
    Buyer's delivery to Seller at the closing date of payment in the amount of two hundred thousand dollars ($200,000), payable by certified or bank check without intervening endorsements.

    ii. Buyer's Note
    Buyer's delivery to Seller at the closing date as defined herein of a promissory note in the amount of two hundred thousand dollars ($200,000).

    iii. Security Agreement and Financing Statements
    Buyer's delivery to Seller of a security agreement and UCC financing statements as set forth in paragraph 6 and exhibits F and G.

    iv. Buyer's Guarantee
    Buyer's delivery to Seller of a guarantee from _____ as included in Exhibit H.

    v. Detailed Accounts Receivable Listing
    Buyer's and Seller's written agreement of the detailed accounts receivables as of date of closing as set forth in Exhibit E is included herein.

vi. True and Complete

The representations and warranties of Buyer shall be true and complete in all respects, and Buyer shall have performed and complied with all agreements and conditions required by this Agreement.

b. Conditions of Buyer's Obligations

Buyer's obligations at the closing shall be conditional upon the following:

i. True and Complete

The representations and warranties of Seller shall be true and complete in all respects, and Seller shall have performed and complied with all agreements and conditions required by this Agreement.

ii. Bill of Sale

Seller's delivery to Buyer of a bill of sale and all other instruments necessary to convert to Buyer good and marketable title to the Assets.

iii. Non-competition

The signing of a Stockholders' non-competition agreement in the form of Exhibit D.

iv. Lease

The signing of a lease acceptable to Buyer and Seller in the form of Exhibit A.

v. At the Closing, Seller will deliver to Buyer:

a) List of commitments and customers

An updated list of contracts relative to Exhibit C, which shall vary significantly from its present form except in the ordinary course of business.

b) Instruments

Appropriate instruments including Bills of Sale, and assignments transferring and conveying to Buyer, good and marketable title to the Assets.

c) Vote of stockholders

A certificate of Vote, duly executed by the Clerk of Seller, as to the due adoption by the Stockholders and the Board of Directors of Seller of a resolution authorizing the transactions contemplated of Seller by this agreement.

12. Seller's Conduct of Its Business Prior to Closing

Seller agrees that it will make no changes in the assets and will incur no liabilities or obligations between the date of this agreement and the closing date, except changes, liabilities, and obligations arising or occurring in the ordinary course of business. Seller agrees that it will use its best efforts prior to the closing to maintain and preserve its business and to retain good working relationships with its suppliers, distributors, customers, and others with whom it deals.

13. Bulk Sales Agreement

The Seller has provided Exhibit J setting forth all creditors, claimants, or others that may have claims or liens upon any of the assets to be transferred herein. Notification will be given to creditors of record. The parties agree to waive compliance with all the provisions of Article 6 of the Uniform Commercial Code dealing with bulk transfers.

14. Broker's or Finder's Fee

Buyer and Seller agree that no broker or finder is involved in the sale of assets other than _____ of _____ and _____ of_____. A broker's commission of $_____ to _____ shall be paid at the closing by Seller if the sale hereunder contemplated is consummated and the purchase price is received by Seller.

15. General

    a.   Written Notice

        All notices and other communications hereunder shall be in writing and given by delivery or mail (by overnight carrier providing a receipt or facsimile followed by first-class mail, postage prepaid) to a party at its address set forth at the beginning of the Agreement or at such changed address as a party may have furnished to the other party in writing at least ten (10) days prior to the effective date thereof.

    b   Severability

        If any provision in this Agreement shall be deemed unenforceable or void as a matter of law, such circumstance shall have no effect on the surviving portions of the Agreement, each of which shall have full force and effect. Buyer and Seller shall be required to use their best efforts to agree upon and replace any provision that has been declared legally void or unenforceable.

16. Miscellaneous

a. Binding Effect

This agreement is binding upon Seller, Stockholders, and Buyer and upon Seller's, Stockholder's, and Buyer's respective successors, heirs, executors, administrators, and assigns.

b. Governing Law

The laws of Massachusetts as of the date appearing below shall govern the interpretation and enforcement of this Agreement.

c. Modifications

No modification of this Agreement shall be binding unless in writing and executed by all parties with the same formality as this Agreement.

d. Entire Agreement

This Agreement represents the entire and integrated agreement of the parties and supersedes all prior oral and written negotiations and agreements.

e. Liquidated Damages.

Upon failure of the Buyer to fulfill Buyer's obligations under this Agreement, the deposit may be retained by the Seller as liquidated damages for any such default. Such deposit will be held by counsel for the Seller.

Effective as of _____

_____
President

_____
Witness

Appendix B

Websites

THE FOLLOWING WEBSITES contain a wealth of information and networking opportunities helpful for those looking at buying and building their own company.

- **www.BizBuySell.com:** excellent source for buying/selling small businesses
- **www.BizQuest.com:** businesses for sale
- **www.BusinessesForSale.com:** connects buyers and sellers
- **www.MergerNetwork.com:** search site for buyers and sellers
- **www.MergerPlace.com:** buying and selling businesses
- **www.Franchise.org:** excellent franchising opportunities
- **www.Entreprenuer.com:** all about entrepreneurship
- **www.FranchiseResearch.org:** insider's perspective on franchises
- **www.SBA.org:** all about the SBA

- **www.investopedia.com:** excellent knowledge source of industry and finance
- **www.BVwire.com:** Business Valuation Resources, a free business valuation weekly
- **www.SterlingPartners.com:** leading private equity group
- **www.MonroeCap.com:** a diverse private equity group; also supplies debt
- **www.Axial.net:** thousands of funding sources for acquisition
- **www.Pitchbook.com:** leading mergers and acquisition website
- **www.ACG.org:** national network of M&A professionals

Glossary

The following list contains terms used throughout the book, in addition to other terms frequently used in the world of business.

accounts payable: what a company owes to its vendors.

accounts receivable: money owed to a company by its customers.

add-back: expenses added back to the bottom line of a company's financial statement or EBITDA; usually one-time expenses, such as owners' compensation.

airball: a company with no hard assets but that has cash flow (for example, service firms); also, part of a loan with no collateral behind it.

asset-based lending: loan from a bank based on the assets of company.

angel: see **angel investor**.

angel investor: a person that invests personally in a start-up company.

APA: see **asset purchase agreement**.

asset purchase: the payment for some or all the assets of a company and usually not the liabilities.

asset purchase agreement: also APA; an agreement between a buyer and seller that finalizes the details of buying some or all the assets of a company.

asset sale: the sale of a company's assets and not liabilities; a most widely used sales methodology.

audited financials: an independent CPA firm's highest level of review of a company's financials. (See also **compiled financials** and **reviewed financials**.)

back-end synergies: financial benefits resulting when one company buys another and reduces costs in one or both companies because of redundancy.

balance sheet: a financial snapshot in time of a company's assets, liabilities, and owner's equity.

book value: net worth of a company; assets minus liabilities.

CAPEX: see **capital expenditure**.

capital: cash, equity.

capital expenditure: also CAPEX; money spent by a company to acquire or upgrade fixed, productive assets, such as trucks, office computers, buildings, etc.

capital gains: profit from the sale of a business or investment; taxed at a lower rate than other income taxes.

category killer: a company that dominates its sector, often through scale and logistics, and crushes smaller retailers (for example, PetSmart and Costco).

clawback: investors' right, specified in a contract, to have monies returned for poor performance.

cliff: a set time, usually one year from the time of employment, where the new partner who is vested is in a trial period; if the person leaves the company during this time, he or she does not take any of his or her earned equity.

C corp: see **C corporation**.

C corporation: also C corp; designation of a business as a corporation that is taxed under US income tax law separately from its owners; an entity usually more appropriate for large business and not for small companies. (See also S corporation.)

compiled financials: the most rudimentary review of a company's financial statements, neither audited nor carrying any opinion about their quality. (See also **audited financials** and **reviewed financials**.)

convertible debenture: a loan issued by a company that can be turned into stock at a given point in time; usually has a lower interest rate than otherwise because of the convertibility factor.

DCF: see **discounted cash flow**.

discounted cash flow: also DCF; a method of determining the current value of a company or asset based on the time value of money, that is, that X dollars today are worth more than the same X dollars at any time in the future.

due diligence: thorough investigation of all facets of a business to buyer's satisfaction before a purchase.

dilution: the reduction of the value of a company's stock when new investor money comes into that company.

divestment: generally, the selling of an asset; specifically, a company's selling or spinning off a division or operating unit.

earn out: part of the purchase price of a company, paid over time, that a seller must earn based upon the specified post-sale performance of the company.

EBIT: earnings before interest and taxes; an indication of a company's financial performance, or cash-flow bottom line.

EBITDA: earnings before interest, taxes, depreciation, and amortization; most-used method of assessing a company's profitability.

enterprise value: also EV; the full value of a company, including all claims against it; often seen as a more accurate evaluation than market capitalization.

EV: see **enterprise value**.

ESOP: employee stock ownership plan; a method of employee-ownership where employees of a firm buy shares in the company they work for.

family office: a private company that manages the investments for a single (wealthy) family.

fixed cost: expense of a business that is constant and independent of the number of products or services produced by the company; for example, rent. (See **variable cost.**)

founder: the individual who starts an enterprise.

franchise: a contract between a company and a franchisee to operate a business under the company's name and often guidance for a fee; for example, McDonald's.

franchisee: buyer of a franchise.

franchisor: a company that sells franchises of its business.

full ratchet: an anti-dilution clause for stock where, if the company issues an option, the investor keeps the same percentage ownership as in the initial investment.

goodwill: intangible assets of a company (for example, a brand name, customer list, patents, etc.)

indication of interest: a non-binding interest in buying a security that is waiting for approval by the SEC.

IOI: see **indication of interest.**

judgment proof: in regard to an individual's personal assets, protected and sheltered from creditors.

joint venture: two companies working together to achieve goals.

LBO: see **leveraged buyout.**

Lehman Scale: a formula for determining how much to pay a bank for handling a large underwriting or stock transfer; the sliding scale pays bankers/brokers proportionately less for larger deals.

letter of intent: also LOI; in regard to the purchase of a business, an offer to buy a specific business outlining preliminary, non-binding terms and observance of confidentiality of both parties.

leveraged buyout: also LBO; using more debt and less cash to buy a company and using the company's assets as collateral (or leverage) for the loan.

limited liability company: also LLC; not a corporation, a legal form of a company with liability protection for the company members; frequently used vehicle to buy small to medium-size businesses.

LLC: see **limited liability company**.

LOI: see **letter of intent**.

M&A: see **mergers and acquisitions**.

management buyout: also MBO; an acquisition where a company's managers buy the assets and operations of the company from its owners.

MBE: see **minority-owned business enterprise**.

MBO: see **management buyout**.

mergers and acquisitions: also M&A; concerns the strategy in buying, selling, and consolidating companies.

mezzanine financing: a hybrid of debt and equity (thus between, or at a mezzanine level of) financing, often used for the expansion of a company; also mezz financing or mezz funding.

minority-owned business enterprise: also MBE; a business at least 51 percent owned, operated, and controlled on a daily basis by American(s) of ethnic minority classifications as specified by the US government.

multiple: a number used to multiply against revenues, profits, or EBITDA of a company to find its valuation.

MWBE: minority and women-owned business enterprise.

NAICS: (pronounced "nakes") North American Industry Classification Systems; the US government's categorization of businesses by the goods or services they produce or activity they engage in.

NDA: see **non-disclosure agreement**.

net-net: final after-tax money that a seller receives from the sale of company after all costs are paid.

non-compete agreement or non-compete clause: a seller's contractual promise not to compete against his/her old firm for a stipulated time after the sale of the company, usually three to five years; a similar agreement between an employee and employer, usually for a shorter period, such as one year; also called non-compete clause or, simply, non-compete.

non-disclosure agreement: a contract stipulating confidentiality of shared information.

no-show job: after the sale of a company, a position for the seller that pays but has no requirement to work or be in the office.

note: a loan from a bank or private individual.

out of covenant: for a company with a loan, breaking the terms of the operating guidelines of the loan.

PEG: see **private equity group**.

private equity: ownership in a company that is private, not publicly traded.

private equity group: also PEG and private equity firm; an investment manager that oversees a fund used to buy private equities of companies.

phantom stock: stock not actually owned by selected employees but that follows the price fluctuations and pays any resulting profits to the selected employees.

platform deal: a company bought to become the centerpiece of investment to which other companies can be added.

reps and warranties: guarantees and representations a seller makes to the buyer about his or her company.

re-trade: after a company is under agreement to be sold, a renegotiation of the sales price initiated by the buyer in his or her favor.

reviewed financials: outside review by a CPA of a company's financials; a step down from audit. (See also **audited financials** and **compiled financials**.)

revolving line of credit: bank loan with a credit limit that, like a credit card, can be repeatedly borrowed and paid back.

rollover: a minority ownership position where a seller buys into his or her former company.

roll-up: the purchase by an investment group or large company to buy smaller competitors in the same business locally as well as nationally.

SB: see **sponsorless buyer.**

SBA: Small Business Administration.

S corp: see **S corporation.**

S corporation: also S corp, subchapter S corporation, sub S corporation, sub S corp; corporate structure popular with small businesses because it provides the liability protection of a corporation with the tax benefits of a partnership. (See also **C corporation** and **limited liability company.**)

SDB: Small Disadvantaged Business; a US government designation for a business at least 51 percent owned or controlled by one or more socially and economically disadvantaged persons.

senior debt: borrowed money that has first priority among a company's debts in being paid in the case of bankruptcy or liquidation; a traditional bank loan is usually in the first position. (See also **subordinated debt.**)

SG&A: selling, general, and administrative costs; a line item on a company's income statement for the expenses of running a business.

SKU: stock-keeping unit; a code identifying one specific product in one location (for example, one size of one manufacturer's brand of one type of soup.)

sponsorless buyer: also SB; an individual who has little or no money to buy a company and recruits cash partners that pay him or her and possibly provide employment when he or she finds a company that they buy.

stock purchase: buying the stock of a company that includes liabilities as well as assets.

stock sale: sale of a company with all liabilities and assets.

strategic buyer: a company that is usually a large player in an industry seeking to buy smaller companies.

subchapter S corporation: see **S corporation**.

sub debt: see **subordinated debt**.

subordinated debt: also sub debt; borrowed money that ranks below others for payment if a company files bankruptcy or must be liquidated. (See also **senior debt**.)

sub S corporation: see **S corporation**.

sweat equity: work and effort by an owner that results in an increase in value of his or her company; also the work by an employee that eventually gets stock in firm.

teaser: communication to the public describing a company for sale but not disclosing the name and other identifying information.

thought leader: an individual who creates new products or strategies for a business.

variable cost: an expense that fluctuates according to the level of output in a business, such as labor or materials. (See **fixed cost**.)

vertical: short for "vertical market"; a specific industry or sector.

WIP: work in process; materials and products not yet finished; excludes raw materials not yet in the production process and products already finished.

working capital: money available to run a business on a daily basis.

work out: a troubled company working through its issues.

YTD: year to date.